TerraNova CTBS™

A Test Prep Program

Columbus, Ohio
Chicago, Illinois

The McGraw·Hill Companies

www.sra4kids.com

Send all inquiries to:
SRA/McGraw-Hill
8787 Orion Place
Columbus, OH 43240

Printed in the United States of America.

ISBN 0-07-584078-2

2 3 4 5 6 7 8 9 QPD 07 06 05 04

The McGraw-Hill Companies

Book 1

On Your Way to Scoring High *TerraNova* CTBS™

Name ______________________________

Family Letter

Greetings!

Your child, like many students across the country, will take standardized tests throughout his or her educational experience. Standardized tests are administered for several reasons.

- It gives us a snapshot of what your child has learned (achieved). It is one of many ways we assess the skills and knowledge of students because no one test or assessment tool can give an accurate, ongoing picture of your child's development.

- We use these tests to help us determine where to strengthen our curriculum to better meet the needs of the students. It also helps us see if we are meeting the learning goals set previously.

In order to give students the best opportunity to prepare for standardized achievement tests, we will be using SRA/McGraw-Hill's test preparation program, *Scoring High TerraNova* CTBS™. Why will we be spending time using this program?

- Test-taking skills can be learned. When preparing, we focus on such skills as reading and listening carefully to directions; budgeting time; answering the easy questions first so you can spend more time on the harder ones; eliminating answer choices that are obviously wrong, and more. These are life skills that students will take with them and use again and again.

- Preparing for standardized tests assures that students won't be surprised by the format of the test. They won't be worried about the type of questions they will see, or how hard the questions will be. They'll know how to fill in answers appropriately. These, and other skills learned ahead of time, will free students to focus on the content of the test and thus give a much more accurate picture of what they know.

How can you help?

- Talk to us here at school if you have any questions. Remember, we are a team with the **same** goals in mind—the improvement of your child's educational experience.

- Encourage reading at home, and spend time together talking about what you read.

Please feel free to contact me if you have any questions.

Sincerely,

____

Your child's teacher

Scoring High on the *TerraNova* CTBS™

A program that teaches achievement test behaviors

Scoring High on the TerraNova *CTBS™* is designed to prepare students for these tests. The program provides instruction and practice in reading, language arts, word analysis, vocabulary, computation, and mathematics skills. *Scoring High* also familiarizes students with the kinds of test formats and directions that appear on the tests and teaches test-taking strategies that promote success.

Students who are used to a comfortable learning environment are often unaccustomed to the structured setting in which achievement tests are given. Even students who are used to working independently may have difficulty maintaining a silent, sustained effort or following directions that are read to a large group. *Scoring High*, with its emphasis on group instruction, teaches these test-taking skills systematically.

Using *Scoring High* to help prepare students for the *TerraNova* CTBS™ will increase the probability of your students doing their best on the tests. Students' self-confidence will be at a maximum, and their proficiency in the skills tested will be higher as a result of the newly learned test-taking strategies and increased familiarity with test formats.

Scoring High can be used effectively along with your regular reading, language arts, and mathematics curriculums. By applying subject-area skills in the context of the test-taking situation, students will not only strengthen their skills, but also accumulate a reserve of test-taking strategies.

Eight Student Books for Grades 1–8

To choose the most appropriate book for each student, match the level of the *TerraNova* CTBS™ that the student will take to the corresponding *Scoring High* book.

Grade Levels	Test Levels
Book 1	Level 11
Book 2	Level 12
Book 3	Level 13
Book 4	Level 14
Book 5	Level 15
Book 6	Level 16
Book 7	Level 17
Book 8	Level 18

Sequential Skill Development

Each student book is organized into units reflecting the subject areas covered in the corresponding levels of the *TerraNova* CTBS™. This book covers reading, language arts, word analysis, vocabulary, computation, and mathematics skills. Each lesson within a unit focuses on several subject-area skills and the test-taking strategies that complement the skills. The last lesson in each unit is designed to give students experience in taking an achievement test in that subject area.

The Test Practice section at the end of each book also provides practice in taking achievement tests and will increase students' confidence in their test-taking skills.

Note: The lessons in this book are arranged in the order in which comparable items appear on the *TerraNova*. You may find it helpful to review the lessons and administer them in the order that is most appropriate for the reading level of your students.

Features of the Student Lessons

Each student lesson in subject-area skills contains:

- A Sample section including directions and one or more teacher-directed sample questions
- A Tips section providing test-taking strategies
- A Practice section

Each Test Yourself lesson at the end of a unit is designed like an achievement test in the unit's subject areas.

How the Teacher's Edition Works

Because a program that teaches test-taking skills as well as subject-area skills may be new to your students, the Teacher's Edition makes a special effort to provide detailed lesson plans. Each lesson lists subject-area and test-taking skills. In addition, teaching suggestions are provided for handling each part of the lesson—Sample(s), Tips, and the Practice items. The text for the subject-area and Test Yourself lessons is designed to help students become familiar with following oral directions and with the terminology used on the tests.

Before you begin Lesson 1, you should use the Orientation Lesson on pages xv–xvii to acquaint students with the program organization and the procedure for using the student book.

Test-taking Skills

Choosing a picture to answer a question

Computing carefully

Considering every answer choice

Converting problems to a workable format

Following oral directions

Identifying and using key words, figures, or numbers to find the answer

Listening carefully

Managing time effectively

Marking the right answer as soon as it is found

Recalling familiar words

Recalling word meanings

Referring to a graphic

Referring to a selection to answer questions

Skipping difficult items and returning to them later

Staying with the first answer

Subvocalizing answer choices

Taking the best guess when unsure of the answer

Transferring numbers accurately to scratch paper

Trying out answer choices

Understanding unusual item formats

Using context to find the answer

Working methodically

Reading and Language Arts Skills

Changing a declarative sentence to a question

Choosing the best phrase to complete a sentence

Choosing the best sentence to complete a paragraph

Choosing the best title for a story

Choosing the best word to complete a sentence

Choosing correctly formed sentences

Deriving word meanings

Drawing conclusions

Identifying correct capitalization

Identifying correct punctuation

Identifying pronouns

Making comparisons

Making inferences

Making predictions

Matching beginning sounds

Matching vowel sounds

Predicting outcomes

Recognizing details

Recognizing sight words

Understanding feelings

Understanding figurative language

Understanding the main idea

Understanding reasons

Understanding sequence

Basic Skills

Adding whole numbers

Identifying sight words

Identifying synonyms

Identifying words from oral definitions

Identifying words in sentence context

Matching beginning sounds

Matching ending sounds

Matching vowel sounds

Subtracting whole numbers

Mathematics Skills

Adding whole numbers

Comparing height

Counting

Counting by fours

Counting by twos

Following geometric directions

Matching digital and analog times

Matching shape patterns

Naming numerals

Recognizing basic shapes

Recognizing lines of symmetry

Solving word problems

Subtracting whole numbers

Understanding the base-ten system

Understanding congruence

Understanding mathematical language

Understanding number sentences

Understanding ordinal numbers

Understanding place value

Understanding time

Understanding the value of coins

Understanding volume

Using a calendar

Using charts and graphs

Using nonstandard units of measurement

Scope and Sequence: Test-taking Skills

	UNIT			
	1	2	3	4
Choosing a picture to answer a question	✓			✓
Computing carefully		✓		✓
Considering every answer choice	✓	✓	✓	✓
Converting problems to a workable format		✓		✓
Following oral directions	✓	✓	✓	✓
Identifying and using key words, figures, or numbers to find the answer	✓		✓	✓
Listening carefully	✓	✓	✓	✓
Managing time effectively	✓			✓
Marking the right answer as soon as it is found	✓		✓	✓
Recalling familiar words	✓			✓
Recalling word meanings		✓		✓
Referring to a graphic			✓	✓
Referring to a selection to answer questions	✓			✓
Skipping difficult items and returning to them later		✓		✓
Staying with the first answer	✓			✓
Subvocalizing answer choices		✓		✓
Taking the best guess when unsure of the answer	✓	✓	✓	✓
Transferring numbers accurately to scratch paper		✓		✓
Trying out answer choices		✓		✓
Understanding unusual item formats	✓			✓
Using context to find the answer	✓	✓		✓
Working methodically	✓	✓		✓

Scope and Sequence: Reading and Language Arts Skills

	UNIT			
	1	2	3	4
Changing a declarative sentence to a question	✓			✓
Choosing the best phrase to complete a sentence	✓			✓
Choosing the best sentence to complete a paragraph	✓			✓
Choosing the best title for a story	✓			✓
Choosing the best word to complete a sentence	✓			✓
Choosing correctly formed sentences	✓			✓
Deriving word meanings	✓			✓
Drawing conclusions	✓			✓
Identifying correct capitalization	✓			✓
Identifying correct punctuation	✓			✓
Identifying pronouns	✓			✓
Making comparisons	✓			
Making inferences	✓			✓
Making predictions	✓			
Matching beginning sounds	✓			✓
Matching vowel sounds	✓			✓
Predicting outcomes	✓			
Recognizing details	✓			✓
Recognizing sight words	✓			✓
Understanding feelings	✓			
Understanding figurative language	✓			✓
Understanding the main idea	✓			✓
Understanding reasons	✓			✓
Understanding sequence	✓			✓

Scope and Sequence: Basic Skills

	UNIT 1	2	3	4
Adding whole numbers		✓		✓
Identifying sight words		✓		✓
Identifying synonyms		✓		✓
Identifying words from oral definitions		✓		✓
Identifying words in sentence context		✓		✓
Matching beginning sounds		✓		✓
Matching ending sounds		✓		✓
Matching vowel sounds		✓		✓
Subtracting whole numbers		✓		✓

Scope and Sequence: Mathematics Skills

	UNIT			
	1	2	3	4
Adding whole numbers			✓	✓
Comparing height				✓
Counting			✓	✓
Counting by fours			✓	
Counting by twos				✓
Following geometric directions			✓	✓
Matching digital and analog times			✓	✓
Matching shape patterns			✓	✓
Naming numerals			✓	
Recognizing basic shapes			✓	✓
Recognizing lines of symmetry			✓	
Solving word problems			✓	✓
Subtracting whole numbers			✓	✓
Understanding the base-ten system			✓	✓
Understanding congruence				✓
Understanding mathematical language				✓
Understanding number sentences			✓	✓
Understanding ordinal numbers				✓
Understanding place value			✓	
Understanding time			✓	✓
Understanding the value of coins			✓	✓
Understanding volume			✓	
Using a calendar				✓
Using charts and graphs			✓	✓
Using nonstandard units of measurement			✓	✓

Orientation Lesson

Focus
Understanding the purpose and structure of *Scoring High on the* TerraNova *CTBS*

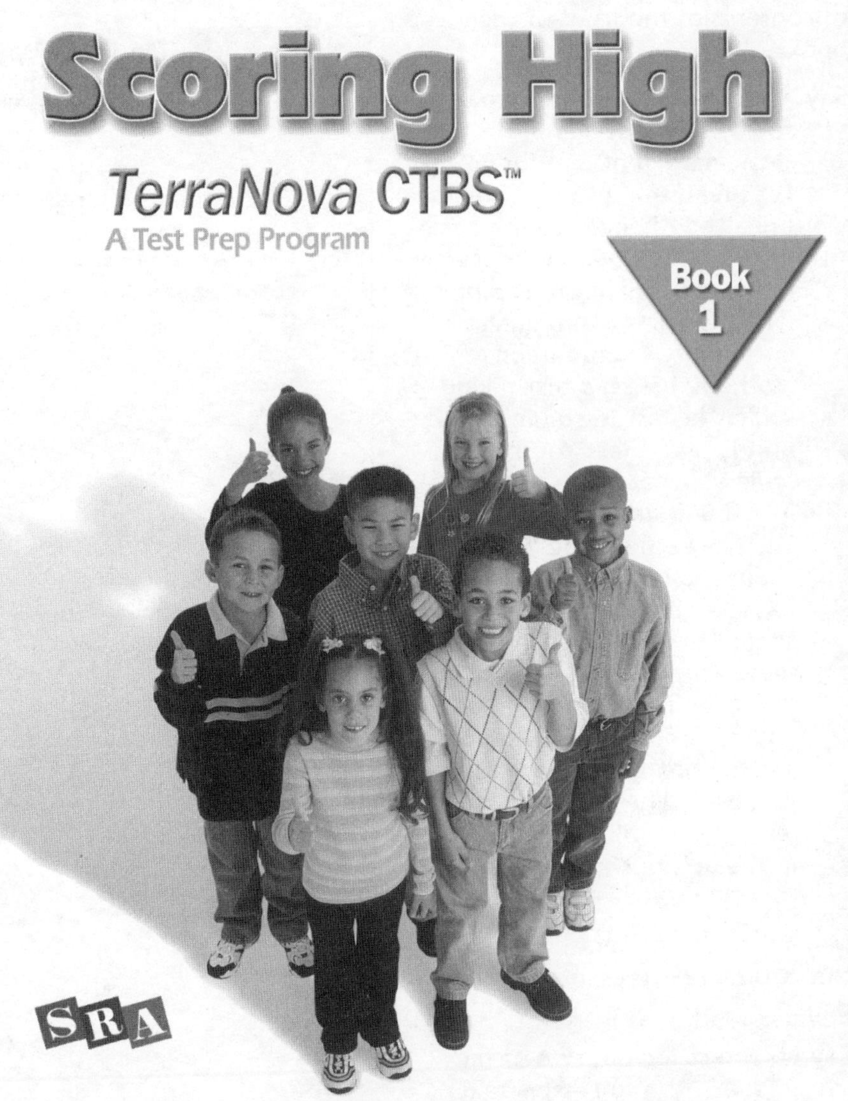

Note: Before you begin Lesson 1, use this introductory lesson to acquaint the students with the program orientation and procedures for using this book.

Say **Taking a test is something you do many times during each school year. What kind of tests have you taken?** *(math tests, reading tests, spelling tests, daily quizzes, etc.)* **Have you ever taken an achievement test that covers many subjects? An achievement test shows how well you are doing in these subjects compared to other students in your grade. Do you know how achievement tests are different from the regular tests you take in class?** *(Many students take them on the same day; special pencils, books, and answer sheets are used; etc.)* **Some students get nervous when they take achievement tests. Has this ever happened to you?**

Encourage the students to discuss their feelings about test taking. Point out that almost everyone feels anxious or worried when facing a test-taking situation.

Display the cover of *Scoring High on the* TerraNova *CTBS.*

Say **Here is a new book you'll be using for the next several weeks. The book is called *Scoring High on the* TerraNova *CTBS.***

Distribute the books to the students.

Say **This book will help you improve your reading, language arts, word analysis, vocabulary, computation, and mathematics skills. It will also help you gain the confidence and skills you need to do well on achievement tests. What does the title say you will be doing when you finish this book?** *(scoring high)* **Scoring high on achievement tests is what this program is all about. If you learn the skills taught in this book, you will be ready to do your best on the *TerraNova* CTBS.**

Inform the students about the testing date if you know when they will be taking the *TerraNova* CTBS. Then make sure the students understand that the goal of their *Scoring High* books is to improve their reading, language arts, word analysis, vocabulary, computation, mathematics, and other skills.

Tell the students to turn to the table of contents at the front of their books.

Say **This page is a progress chart. It shows the contents of the book. How many units are there?** *(4)* **Let's read the names of the units together.** *(Read the names of the units aloud.)* **In these units, you will learn reading, language arts, word analysis, vocabulary, computation, mathematics, and test-taking skills. The last lesson in each unit is called Test Yourself. It reviews what you have learned in the unit. In Unit 4, the Test Practice section, you will have a chance to use all the skills you have learned on tests that are similar to real achievement tests. This page will also help you keep track of the lessons you have completed. Do you see the box beside each lesson number? When you finish a lesson, you will write your score in the box to show your progress.**

Make sure the students understand the information presented on this page.

Say **Now let's look at two of the lessons. Turn to Lesson 1a on page 1.**

Book 1

On Your Way to **Scoring High** *TerraNova* CTBS™

Name ____________________

Check to be sure the students have found page 1.

Say **The lesson number and title are at the top of the page. The page number is at the bottom of the page. This lesson is about reading skills. When you start a lesson, you will find the lesson by its page number. The page number is always at the bottom of the page.**

Familiarize the students with the lesson layout and sequence of instruction. Have them locate the Sample items. Explain that you will work through the Samples section together. Then have the students find the STOP sign in the lower right-hand corner of the page.

Say **On some pages there is a STOP sign. When you see the STOP sign on a page, it means you should stop working. Then we will either do different items or go over the answers to the items you have already completed. I will also explain anything you did not understand.**

On some other pages is a GO sign. When you see the GO sign on a page, it means you should turn the page and continue working.

Have the students locate the Tips sign below the Samples section.

Say **What does the sign point out to you?** *(the tips)* **Each lesson has tips that suggest new ways to work through the items. Tests can be tricky. The tips will tell you what to watch out for. They will help you find the best answer quickly.**

Explain to the students that the questions in this book and on an achievement test are also called items. Tell the students that each lesson has several Practice items that they will answer by themselves.

Say **Now I'll show you how to fill in the spaces for your answers.**

Draw several circles on the chalkboard and demonstrate how to fill them in. Explain to the students that they should make dark, heavy marks and fill in the circles completely. Allow volunteers to demonstrate filling in answer circles that you have drawn on the chalkboard.

Ask the students to turn to the Test Yourself lesson on page 21 of their books. Tell the students the Test Yourself lessons may seem like real tests, but they are not. The Test Yourself lessons are designed to give them opportunities to apply the skills and tips they have learned in timed, trial-run situations. Explain that you will go over the answers together after the students complete each lesson. Then they will figure out their scores and record the number of correct answers in the boxes on the progress chart. Be sure to point out that the students' scores are only for them to see how well they are doing.

Say **Each lesson will teach you new skills and tips. What will you have learned when you finish this book?** *(reading, language arts, word analysis, vocabulary, computation, mathematics, and test-taking skills; how to do my best on an achievement test)* **When you know you can do your best, how do you think you will feel on test day? You may be a little nervous, but you should also feel confident that you are ready to do your best.**

Unit 1 **Reading and Language Arts**

Lesson 1a **Reading Skills**

Neighborhood Stories

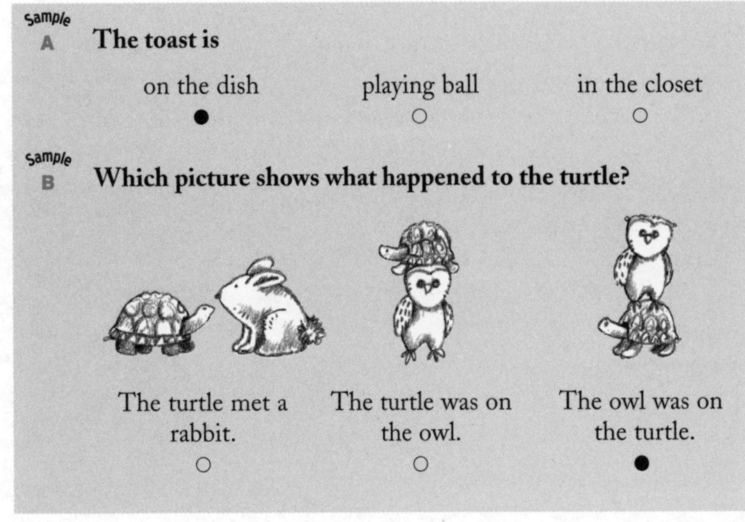

Sample A **The toast is**

● on the dish ○ playing ball ○ in the closet

Sample B **Which picture shows what happened to the turtle?**

○ The turtle met a rabbit. ○ The turtle was on the owl. ● The owl was on the turtle.

- **Listen carefully to the directions.**
- **Think about what you are supposed to do.**
- **Look at each answer before marking the one you think is right.**

Unit 1 Lesson 1a **Reading Skills** 1

Background

This unit contains five lessons that deal with reading and language arts skills. Students answer a variety of questions covering a broad range of reading and language arts skills.

• **In Lessons 1a and 1b,** students answer questions about a story or poem. Students are encouraged to follow oral directions, consider every answer choice, and take the best guess when unsure of the answer. They refer to a selection to answer questions, choose a picture to answer a question, and use key words to find the answer. Students use context to find the answer, listen carefully, and mark the right answer as soon as it is found. They stay with the first answer and recall familiar words.

• **In Lesson 2a,** students answer questions about language mechanics and usage. They review the test-taking skills introduced in previous lessons and gain familiarity with unusual item formats.

Instructional Objectives

Lesson 1a	**Reading Skills**	Given a story or poem, students answer reading and language arts questions about the story or poem.
Lesson 1b	**Reading Skills**	
Lesson 2a	**Language Arts Skills**	Given an incomplete sentence and three answers, students identify which answer best completes the sentence. Given a paragraph and three sentences, students identify which sentence best completes the paragraph. Given a declarative sentence and three answers, students identify which answer is the interrogative form of the sentence.

• **In Lesson 2b,** students answer questions about language mechanics and usage. They review the test-taking skills introduced in previous lessons.

• **In the Test Yourself lesson,** the reading, language arts, and test-taking skills introduced and used in Lessons 1a through 2b are reinforced and presented in a format that gives students the experience of taking an achievement test.

Instructional Objectives

Lesson 2b Language Arts Skills	Given a sentence with an underlined part and three pronouns, students identify which pronoun represents the underlined part. Given three answers, students identify which answer is a correctly formed sentence. Given part of a letter, students identify which punctuation mark it requires. Given text divided into three parts, students identify which part needs a capital letter.
Test Yourself	Given questions similar to those in Lessons 1a through 2b, students utilize reading and language arts skills and test-taking strategies on achievement test formats.

Lesson 1a
Reading Skills

Focus

Reading Skills
- choosing the best phrase to complete a sentence
- making inferences
- drawing conclusions
- recognizing details
- understanding feelings
- understanding the main idea
- matching beginning sounds
- matching vowel sounds
- choosing the best title for a story
- changing a declarative sentence to a question
- identifying pronouns
- choosing the best sentence to complete a paragraph

Test-taking Skills
- following oral directions
- considering every answer choice
- taking the best guess when unsure of the answer
- referring to a selection to answer questions
- choosing a picture to answer a question
- identifying and using key words to find the answer
- using context to find the answer

Unit 1 Reading and Language Arts

Lesson 1a **Reading Skills**

Neighborhood Stories

Sample A **The toast is**

on the dish	playing ball	in the closet
●	○	○

Sample B **Which picture shows what happened to the turtle?**

The turtle met a rabbit.	The turtle was on the owl.	The owl was on the turtle.
○	○	●

- **Listen carefully to the directions.**
- **Think about what you are supposed to do.**
- **Look at each answer before marking the one you think is right.**

Unit 1 Lesson 1a **Reading Skills** 1

Samples A and B

Say Turn to Lesson 1a on page 1. The page number is at the bottom of the page on the right.

Check to see that the students have found the right page.

Say In this lesson, you will read a story and answer questions about it. You will also answer some other questions about reading and writing. When you answer a question, mark the circle for the answer you think is right. Be sure your answer circle is completely filled in with a dark mark and that you have marked the correct circle for the answer you think is right. Find Sample A at the top of the page. We will do this Sample item together.

Check to see that the students have found Sample A.

Say Read the sentence. Some words are missing. Find the words that fit best with the rest of the sentence. *(pause)* Yes, *on the dish* is the correct answer. Mark the first answer circle and make sure it is completely filled in. Press your pencil firmly so your mark comes out dark.

Check to see that the students have marked the correct circle.

Say Now move down to Sample B. Look at me and listen to this story about a turtle.

Jonathan Harrison Turtle was in quite a fix. He had been taking his daily walk, when suddenly an owl flew down and landed on his shell.

Now look at the pictures and the sentences for Sample B. Which picture shows what happened to the turtle? *(pause)* The third answer is correct. The owl was on the turtle. Mark the circle for the third answer. Be sure your answer circle is completely filled in with a dark mark.

Check to see that the students have marked the correct circle.

Say Now let's look at the tips.

Read the tips aloud to the students.

Say In this book and when you take an achievement test, it is important that you listen carefully to the directions. You should think about what you are supposed to do and look at all the answer choices before picking the one you think is right. If you are not sure which answer choice is right, take your best guess. It is better to guess than to leave an answer blank.

Read the following text in an encouraging voice.

Say The place where you live is called your neighborhood. Turn the page and you'll have a chance to hear and read some stories about a neighborhood—maybe one just like yours.

Check to be sure the students have found the right page.

Lesson 1a **Reading Skills**

Neighborhood Stories

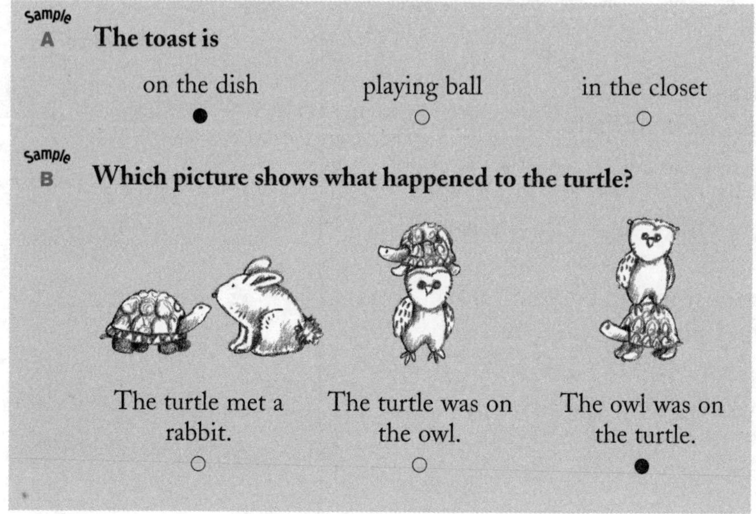

Sample A **The toast is**

on the dish ● playing ball ○ in the closet ○

Sample B **Which picture shows what happened to the turtle?**

The turtle met a rabbit. ○ The turtle was on the owl. ○ The owl was on the turtle. ●

- **Listen carefully to the directions.**
- **Think about what you are supposed to do.**
- **Look at each answer before marking the one you think is right.**

Unit 1 Lesson 1a **Reading Skills** 1

Practice

Say This story is about a girl who wants to go for a ride with a friend. Look at me and listen carefully while I read the first part of the story.

Carol wanted to ride her bike with her friend, Ramon. They would ride up the street to the playground. When she went to get her bike, Carol saw it had a flat tire.

Allow time between items for the students to fill in their answers.

Say Put your finger on Number 1 at the top of the page. Look at the pictures. What was wrong with Carol's bike? Find the picture that shows what was wrong with Carol's bike. Mark your answer.

Number 2. Look at the pictures. Where did Ramon and Carol want to go? Find the picture that shows where Ramon and Carol wanted to go. Mark your answer.

Number 3. Look at the sentences. How did Carol probably feel when she saw her bike? Find the sentence that tells how Carol probably felt when she saw her bike. Mark your answer.

Unit 1 Lesson 1a **Reading Skills**

1

2

3 She was happy. / She was sad. / She didn't care.

4 going for a ride / fixing a bike / going to the playground

2 Unit 1 Lesson 1a **Reading Skills**

Pause for a moment.

Say Look at me and listen to more of the story.

Carol told her big brother about the tire. He smiled and said, "I can fix it right now." In a few minutes, the tire was fixed, and Carol could ride with her friend.

Put your finger on Number 4. What is this story mostly about? Look at the words. Find the words that answer the question "What is this story mostly about?" Mark your answer.

Look at the next page, page 3.

Check to be sure the students are working on the right page.

Say **Now I will ask you some questions about beginning sounds. Listen carefully to what I say.**

Allow time between items for the students to fill in their answers.

Say **Put your finger on Number 5 at the top of the page. The playground was up the street. Find the word that has the same beginning sound as "street ... street." Mark your answer.**

Number 6. The tire was flat. Find the word that has the same beginning sound as "flat ... flat." Mark your answer.

Now we will do some items about middle sounds. Listen.

Number 7. The children wanted to go for a ride. Find the word that has the same vowel, or middle, sound as "ride ... ride." Mark your answer.

Number 8. Carol went to get her bike. Find the word that has the same vowel, or middle, sound as "get ... get." Mark your answer.

Pause for a moment.

Say **Look at the next page, page 4.**

Check to be sure the students are working on the right page.

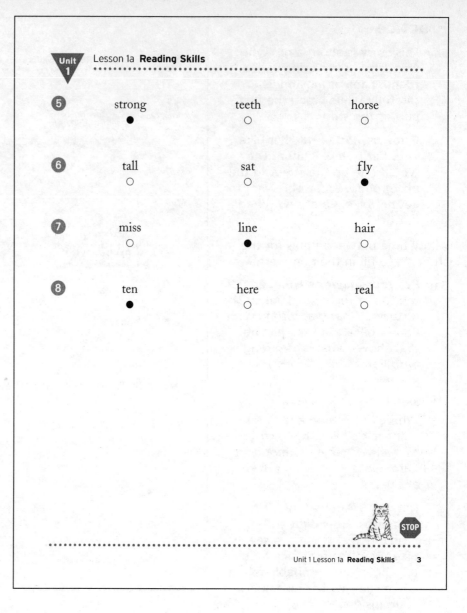

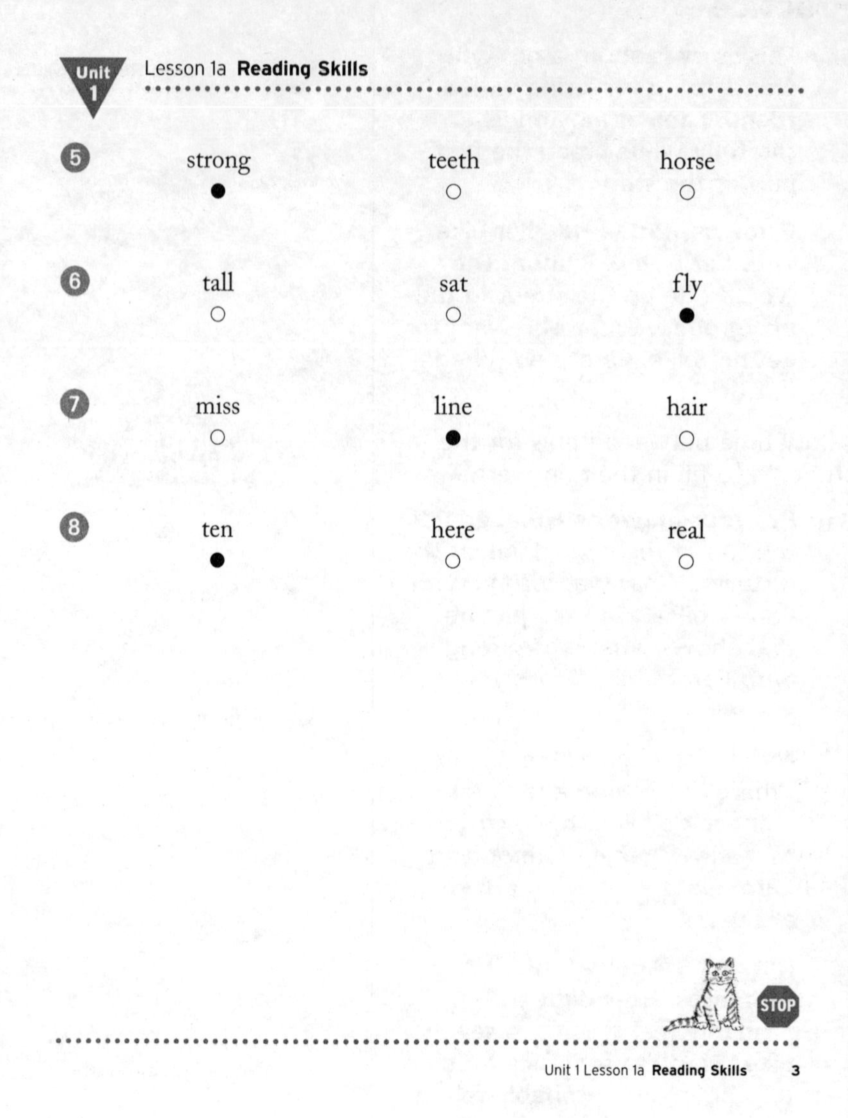

Unit 1 Lesson 1a **Reading Skills**

5	strong ●	teeth ○	horse ○
6	tall ○	sat ○	fly ●
7	miss ○	line ●	hair ○
8	ten ●	here ○	real ○

STOP

Unit 1 Lesson 1a **Reading Skills** 3

Say **Here is a story written by a boy named Francisco. You will read the story and answer questions about it. First, let's read the directions. Read them to yourself while I read the directions out loud.**

Many people in every neighborhood have pets. This story is about a boy and his pet. Read the story, then do Numbers 9 through 12.

Remember, you can look back at the story to answer the questions. Mark the circles for the answers you think are right. After you do Numbers 9 through 11, you will have to turn the page to do Number 12. Work until you come to the STOP sign after Number 12. You may begin.

Allow time for the students to fill in their answers. Check to be sure the students turn the page after Number 11 and answer only Number 12 on page 6.

Unit 1 Lesson 1a **Reading Skills**

Directions: Many people in every neighborhood have pets. This story is about a boy and his pet. Read the story, then do Numbers 9 through 12.

My dog's name is Nick. He is big and has long, brown hair. He likes to chase a ball. If I throw a ball, he catches it in his mouth. Brings it back to me. When I'm at school, Nick waits for me. He is standing near the door when I get home. He jumps up and licks my face. Then we go outside for a walk.

Francisco

4 Unit 1 Lesson 1a **Reading Skills**

9 **What does Nick look like?**

He has long, brown hair.

●

He is white with with spots.

○

He is small with curly hair.

○

10 **Where is Nick when Francisco gets home?**

- ○ in the kitchen.
- ○ on the bed
- ● by the door

11 **If Francisco throws a stick, Nick will probably**

- ○ catch a ball
- ● bring it back
- ○ lick his face

Say **It's time to stop. Now we will do different kinds of items. We will do them together. Put your finger on Number 13.**

Check to be sure the students have found Number 13. Allow time between items for the students to fill in their answers.

Say **Number 13. Francisco wrote this sentence. Read the sentence to yourself. Then read the answer choices. Find the answer that changes the sentence into a question. Mark your answer.**

Number 14. "Brings it back to me" is not a complete sentence. What should Francisco add to make it a complete sentence? Mark your answer.

Pause for a moment.

Say **Look at the next page, page 7.**

Check to be sure the students are working on the right page.

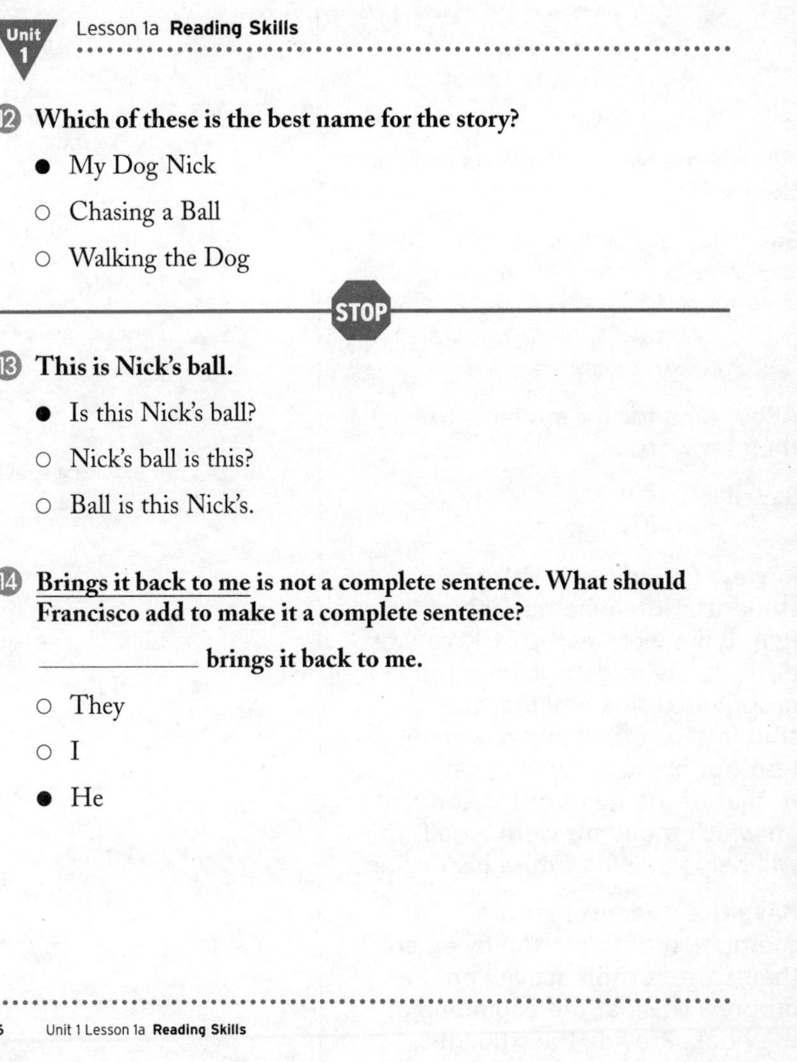

Unit 1 Lesson 1a **Reading Skills**

⑫ **Which of these is the best name for the story?**

- ● My Dog Nick
- ○ Chasing a Ball
- ○ Walking the Dog

STOP

⑬ **This is Nick's ball.**

- ● Is this Nick's ball?
- ○ Nick's ball is this?
- ○ Ball is this Nick's.

⑭ **Brings it back to me is not a complete sentence. What should Francisco add to make it a complete sentence?**

__________ brings it back to me.

- ○ They
- ○ I
- ● He

6 Unit 1 Lesson 1a **Reading Skills**

Say Put your finger on Number 15 at the top of the page. Read the story with the blank. Find the sentence that fits best in the blank to complete the story. Mark your answer.

Allow time for the students to fill in their answers.

Say Look at Number 16. Read the story with the blank. Find the sentence that fits best in the blank to complete the story. Mark your answer.

Allow time for the students to fill in their answers.

Say It's time to stop. You have finished Lesson 1a.

Review the answers with the students. Note whether any of the item types were particularly easy or difficult. Try to determine through a group discussion whether the students' incorrect answers were the result of being unfamiliar with the format of the items or the content on which the items were based. This will help you plan future instruction.

Have the students indicate completion of the lesson by entering their score for this activity on the progress chart at the beginning of the book. Provide the students whatever help is necessary to record their scores.

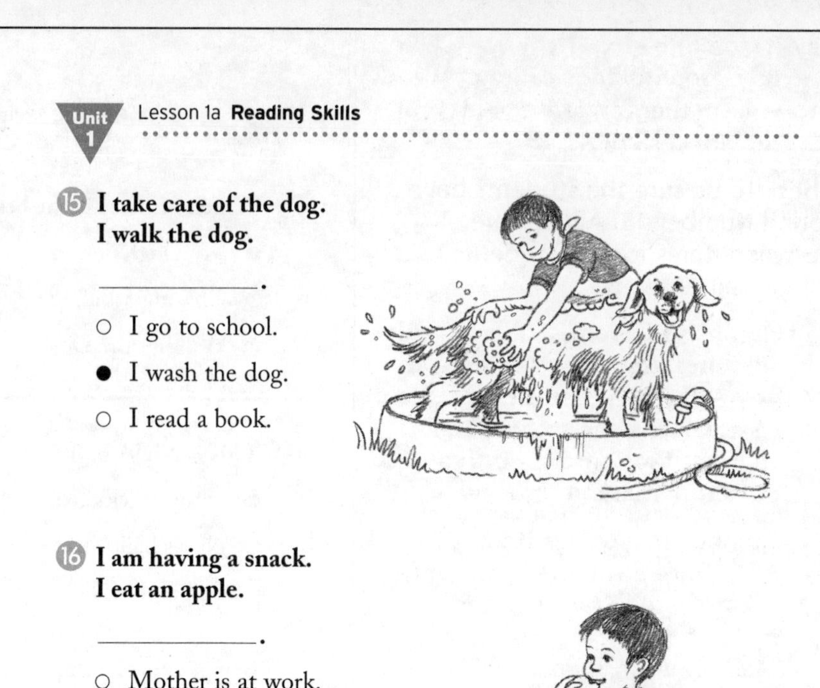

15 **I take care of the dog.**
I walk the dog.

_____________.

- ○ I go to school.
- ● I wash the dog.
- ○ I read a book.

16 **I am having a snack.**
I eat an apple.

_____________.

- ○ Mother is at work.
- ○ I like to go swimming.
- ● Then I drink some milk.

Unit 1

Lesson 1b
Reading Skills

Focus

Reading Skills
- recognizing details
- matching beginning sounds
- making inferences
- drawing conclusions
- predicting outcomes
- recognizing sight words

Test-taking Skills
- listening carefully
- marking the right answer as soon as it is found
- staying with the first answer
- using context to find the answer
- recalling familiar words

Samples A and B

Say Open your book to Lesson 1b on page 8. There are pictures of a girl, a cat, and a boy on the page.

Check to see that the students have found the right page.

Say In this lesson, you will listen to a poem and answer questions about it. You will also answer other questions about reading and writing. When you answer a question, mark the circle for the answer you think is right. Be sure your answer circle is completely filled in with a dark mark. Put your finger under Sample A at the top of the page.

Check to see that the students have found Sample A.

Say Look at me and listen to this poem.

The kitten curled up on my lap.

Pretty soon, it took a nap.

Look at the pictures for Sample A. Which picture shows who took a nap? *(pause)* The second answer is correct because the poem says that the kitten took a nap. Mark the circle under the picture of the kitten. Be sure your answer circle is completely filled in with a dark mark.

Check to see that the students have marked the correct circle.

Reading and Language Arts

Lesson 1b **Reading Skills**

Reading a Poem

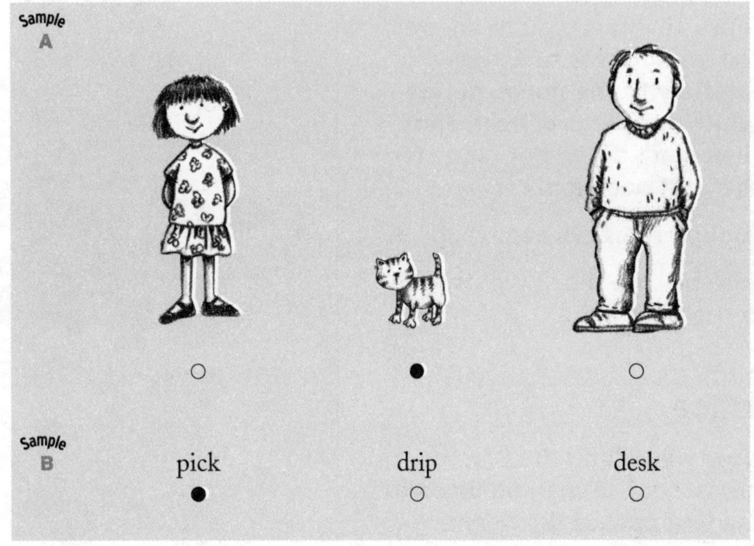

- **Think about the poem while you listen to it.**
- **Mark your answer as soon as you know which one is right.**
- **Change your answer only if you are sure it is wrong.**

8 Unit 1 Lesson 1b **Reading Skills**

Say Put your finger under Sample B. Look at the words and listen carefully. Which word has the same beginning sound as "pull ... pull"? *(pause)* The first answer, *pick*, has the same beginning sound as *pull*. Mark the circle under the first word. Be sure your answer circle is completely filled in with a dark mark.

Check to see that the students have marked the correct circle.

TIPS

Say Now let's look at the tips.

Read the tips aloud to the students.

Say Think about the poem while I read it. Try to remember what I am saying. As soon as you know which answer is right, mark your answer. And once you have marked your answer, change it only if you are sure it is wrong and another one is right. The best way to answer the questions is to listen carefully to the poem, decide which answer is correct, and then mark it and get ready for the next question.

Look at the next page, page 9.

Check to be sure the students have found the right page.

Practice

Say Now we will do the Practice items. Look at me and listen to the first part of the poem.

In a small house whose color is blue

Are lots of toy animals in Marilyn's zoo.

Allow time between items for the students to fill in their answers.

Say Put your finger on Number 1 at the top of the page. Look at the pictures. Where is the zoo? Find the picture that shows where the zoo is. Mark your answer.

Number 2. Look at the pictures. Which of these might be in the zoo? Find the picture that shows which might be in the zoo. Mark your answer.

Here is the next part of the poem. Look at me and listen while I read it.

Some are small, like Reggie Raccoon,

But others are huge, like Betty Baboon.

Number 3. Look at the pictures. Which stuffed animal is named Reggie? Find the picture that shows what Reggie is. Mark your answer.

Look at the next page, page 10.

Check to be sure the students have found the right page.

Say Put your finger on Number 4 at the top of the page. Look at the pictures. Which of these shows Marilyn with Betty Baboon? Find the picture that shows Marilyn with Betty Baboon. Mark your answer.

Pause for a moment.

Say Here is the last part of the poem. Look at me and listen to what I say.

Marilyn's bedroom is home to the zoo.

If you ever visit, she'll show it to you.

Put your finger on Number 5. Look at the pictures. Where does Marilyn keep her animals? Find the picture that shows where Marilyn keeps her animals. Mark your answer.

Number 6. Look at the pictures. If someone visited Marilyn, what would Marilyn want to do first? Find the picture that shows what Marilyn would want to do first if someone visited her. Mark your answer.

Look at the next page, page 11.

Check to be sure the students have found the right page.

Allow time between items for the students to fill in their answers.

Say **Put your finger on Number 7 at the top of the page. You will do some items about beginning sounds.**

Some of Marilyn's toy animals are large. Find the word that has the same beginning sound as "large ... large." Mark your answer.

Number 8. Marilyn's older brother, Dean, likes to play golf. Find the word that has the same beginning sound as "golf ... golf." Mark your answer.

Now you will do some items about words. Listen carefully to the sentence I read. Think about the meaning of the sentence. I will ask you to find a word in the sentence.

Number 9. Listen to this sentence: Mr. Palmer will buy a new car. Find the word "buy ... buy." Mark your answer.

Number 10. Listen to this sentence: Marilyn keeps her room very neat. Find the word "room ... room." Mark your answer.

Number 11. Listen to this sentence: Mrs. Palmer drove to work. Find the word "work ... work." Mark your answer.

It's time to stop. You have finished Lesson 1b.

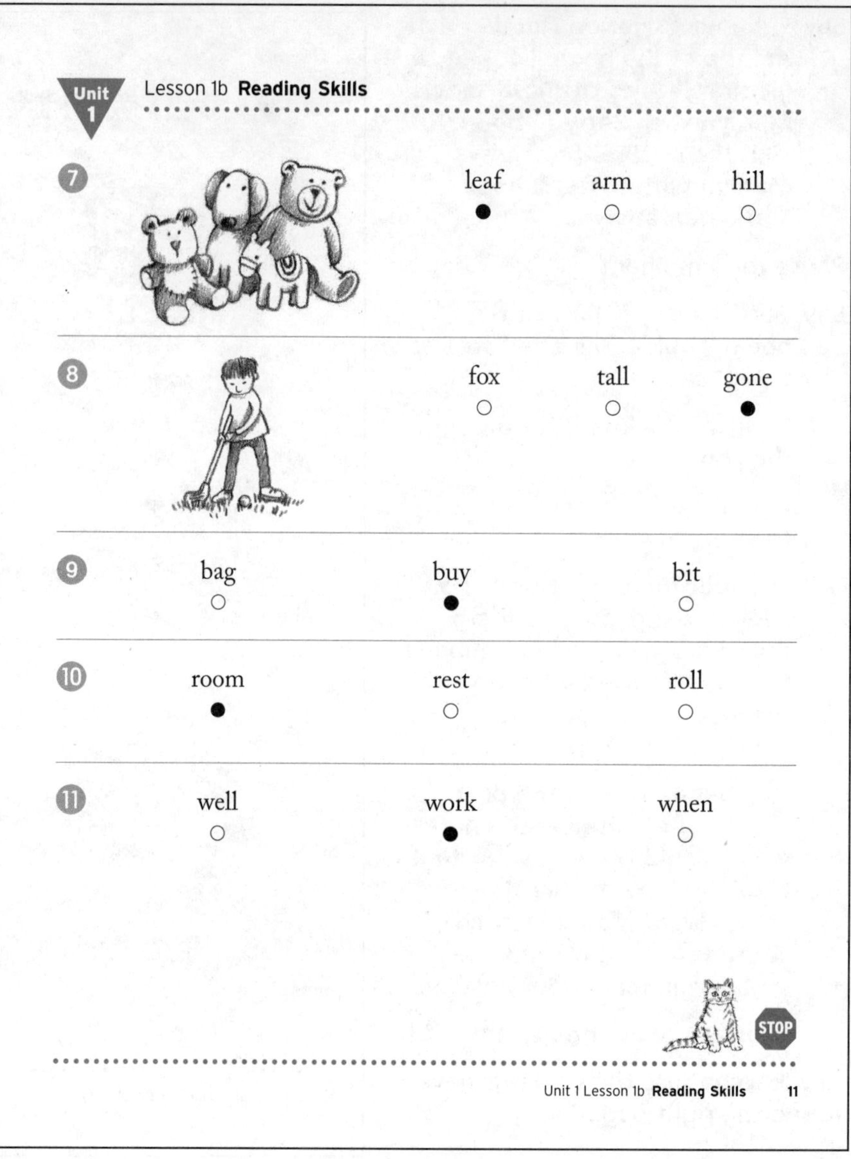

Review the answers with the students. Begin by reading the poem aloud and then answering the comprehension questions one by one. Urge the students to listen carefully to the poem and try to remember the important details. Many young students have poor listening skills because they don't attempt to remember what they hear. If you can encourage them to listen and remember, they will be more likely to do well on an achievement test. For the beginning sound and sight vocabulary items, encourage the students to listen carefully to the beginning of the word or to all the sounds in a word. Even if students can't recall the word, they can choose the right answer by matching the sounds in the words.

Have the students indicate completion of the lesson by entering their score for this activity on the progress chart at the beginning of the book. Provide the students whatever help is necessary to record their scores.

Lesson 2a Language Arts Skills

Focus

Language Arts Skills
- choosing the best phrase to complete a sentence
- choosing the best sentence to complete a paragraph
- changing a declarative sentence to a question

Test-taking Skills
- listening carefully
- using context to find the answer
- understanding unusual item formats

Sample A

Say Open your book to Lesson 2a on page 12.

Check to see that the students have found the right page.

Say In this lesson, you will answer questions about correct English. When you answer a question, mark the circle for the answer you think is right. Be sure your answer circle is completely filled in with a dark mark. Put your finger under Sample A at the top of the page.

Check to see that the students have found Sample A.

Say "Went home" is not a complete sentence. What should be added to make it a complete sentence? *(pause)* The last answer is correct because the word *I* will make the sentence complete. Mark the circle beside the last answer. Be sure your answer circle is completely filled in with a dark mark.

Check to see that the students have marked the correct circle.

Reading and Language Arts

Lesson 2a **Language Arts Skills**

Sample A

Went home is not a complete sentence. What should be added to make it a complete sentence?

_________ went home.

○ To

○ The

● I

Pay attention to the directions for each kind of question.

1 **Ate her lunch is not a complete sentence. What should be added to make it a complete sentence?**

_________ ate her lunch.

○ Them

● Beth

○ Soon

TIPS

Say Now let's look at the tip.

Read the tip aloud to the students.

Say Listen carefully to what I say. There are different kinds of questions in this lesson, and the best way to get them right is to listen to what I say while you look at the question.

Practice

Say Now we will do the Practice items. Look at me and listen carefully.

Allow time between items for the students to fill in their answers.

Say Put your finger on Number 1 below the tip. "Ate her lunch" is not a complete sentence. What should be added to make it a complete sentence? Mark your answer.

Look at the next page, page 13.

Check to be sure the students have found the right page.

Say Put your finger on Number 2 at the top of the page. "Is playing ball" is not a complete sentence. What should be added to make it a complete sentence? Mark your answer.

Move down to Number 3. "The brown dog" is not a complete sentence. What should be added to make it a complete sentence? Mark your answer.

Look at the next page, page 14.

Check to be sure the students have found the right page.

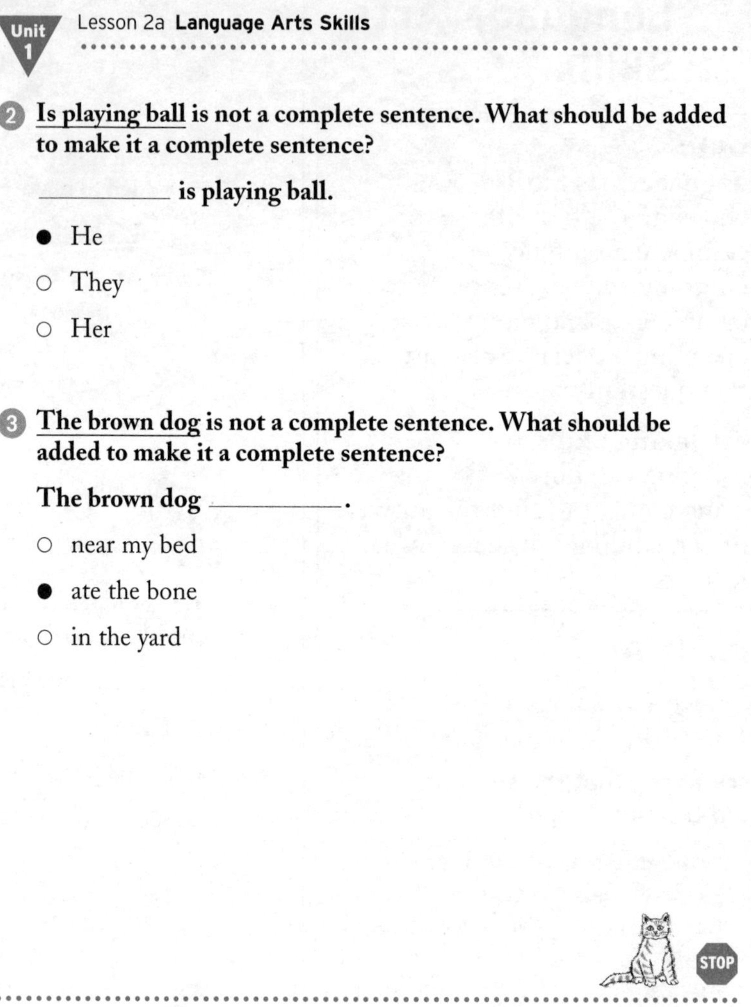

Unit 1 Lesson 2a **Language Arts Skills**

2 **Is playing ball is not a complete sentence. What should be added to make it a complete sentence?**

__________ is playing ball.

● He

○ They

○ Her

3 **The brown dog is not a complete sentence. What should be added to make it a complete sentence?**

The brown dog __________.

○ near my bed

● ate the bone

○ in the yard

STOP

Unit 1 Lesson 2a **Language Arts Skills** 13

Sample B

Say **Now you will answer different kinds of questions. Put your finger under Sample B at the top of the page.**

Check to see that the students have found Sample B.

Say **Read the story. Part of the story is missing. Find the sentence that best completes the story.** *(pause)* **The last answer is correct because *The bird lays eggs* is the best choice to complete the story. Mark the circle beside the last answer. Be sure your answer circle is completely filled in with a dark mark.**

Check to see that the students have marked the correct circle.

Say **Put your finger on Number 4 below the sample. Read the story. Part of the story is missing. Find the sentence that best completes the story. Mark your answer.**

Pause for a moment.

Say **Look at the next page, page 15.**

Check to be sure the students have found the right page.

Lesson 2a **Language Arts Skills**

Sample **B** **The bird is blue.**
It builds a nest.

__________.

○ My pet is a bird.

○ Trees are pretty.

● The bird lays eggs.

4 **Ann likes to swim.**
She goes to the pool.

__________.

● Ann enjoys the water.

○ She read a book.

○ Her mother is cooking.

14 Unit 1 Lesson 2a **Language Arts Skills**

Allow time between items for the students to fill in their answers.

Say Put your finger on Number 5 at the top of the page. Read the story. Part of the story is missing. Find the sentence that best completes the story. Mark your answer.

Number 6. Read the story. Part of the story is missing. Find the sentence that best completes the story. Mark your answer.

Pause for a moment.

Say Look at the next page, page 16.

Check to be sure the students have found the right page.

5 **It is raining.**
The wind is blowing.

______.

- ○ The sun is shining
- ● The children are wet
- ○ The sky is blue

6 **My mom has a job.**
She is a doctor.

______.

- ● She helps sick people
- ○ Mom likes sports
- ○ A job is a good thing

Sample C

Say Now you will answer different kinds of questions. Put your finger under Sample C at the top of the page.

Check to see that the students have found Sample C.

Say Read the sentence. Then read the answer choices below it. Find the answer choice that correctly changes the sentence into a question. *(pause)* The third answer is correct because *Is Bill here* is the best way to change the first sentence into a question. Mark the circle beside the third answer. Be sure your answer circle is completely filled in with a dark mark.

Check to see that the students have marked the correct circle. Spend whatever time is necessary to ensure that the students understand this item type.

Say Move down to Number 7 below the sample. Read the sentence. Then read the answer choices below it. Find the answer choice that correctly changes the sentence into a question. Mark your answer.

Number 8. Read the sentence. Then read the answer choices below it. Find the answer choice that correctly changes the sentence into a question. Mark your answer.

It's time to stop. You have finished Lesson 2a.

Review the answers with the students. Be sure they understood what they were supposed to do for each of the item types. Explain thoroughly why the correct answer is better than the other choices.

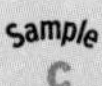

Bill is here.

○ Here Bill is?

○ Bill here is?

● Is Bill here?

7 **The door was open.**

● Was the door open?

○ Open was the door?

○ The door open was?

8 **The cat is Nan's.**

○ Cat is the Nan's?

● Is the cat Nan's?

○ Nan's is cat the?

16 Unit 1 Lesson 2a **Language Arts Skills**

Have the students indicate completion of the lesson by entering their score for this activity on the progress chart at the beginning of the book. Provide the students whatever help is necessary to record their scores.

Lesson 2b Language Arts Skills

Focus

Language Arts Skills
- identifying pronouns
- choosing correctly formed sentences
- identifying correct punctuation
- identifying correct capitalization

Test-taking Skills
- working methodically
- considering every answer choice
- understanding unusual item formats

Reading and Language Arts

Lesson 2b **Language Arts Skills**

Sample A **Carol is reading a book.**

- ● She
- ○ We
- ○ Her

Read each answer choice carefully.

1. **Meg and Jim sang a song.**
   - ○ She
   - ○ We
   - ● They

2. **My friend and I will walk home.**
   - ○ She
   - ● We
   - ○ Us

Sample A

Say Open your book to Lesson 2b on page 17.

Check to see that the students have found the right page.

Say In this lesson, you will answer more questions about correct English. When you answer a question, mark the circle for the answer you think is right. Be sure your answer circle is completely filled in with a dark mark. Put your finger under Sample A at the top of the page.

Check to see that the students have found Sample A.

Say Read the sentence for Sample A. Look at the underlined word. Which word can take the place of "Carol" in the sentence? *(pause)* The first answer is correct because *She* is the pronoun that can take the place of the word "Carol." Mark the circle beside the first answer. Be sure your answer circle is completely filled in with a dark mark.

Check to see that the students have marked the correct circle.

TIPS

Say Now let's look at the tip.

Read the tip aloud to the students.

Say Be sure to read the answer choices carefully. Think about the question, look at all the answer choices, and then decide which one is right. Remember, you are looking for the answer that shows correct English.

Practice

Say Now we will do the Practice items. Look at me and listen carefully.

Allow time between items for the students to fill in their answers.

Say Put your finger on Number 1 below the tip. Find the word that can take the place of "Meg and Jim" in the sentence. Mark your answer.

Move down to Number 2. Find the word that can take the place of "My friend and I" in the sentence. Mark your answer.

Look at the next page, page 18.

Check to be sure the students have found the right page.

Reading and Language Arts

Lesson 2b **Language Arts Skills**

Sample A Carol is reading a book.

- ● She
- ○ We
- ○ Her

Read each answer choice carefully.

1 Meg and Jim sang a song.

- ○ She
- ○ We
- ● They

2 My friend and I will walk home.

- ○ She
- ● We
- ○ Us

Unit 1 Lesson 2b **Language Arts Skills** 17

Sample B

Say Now you will answer different kinds of questions. Put your finger under Sample B at the top of the page.

Check to see that the students have found Sample B.

Say Read the three sentences. Find the sentence that is written correctly. *(pause)* The last answer is correct because it is written correctly. Mark the circle beside the last answer. Be sure your answer circle is completely filled in with a dark mark.

Check to see that the students have marked the correct circle.

Say Put your finger on Number 3 below the sample. Look at the three sentences. Find the sentence that is written correctly. Mark your answer.

Number 4. Look at the three sentences. Find the sentence that is written correctly. Mark your answer.

Pause for a moment.

Say Look at the next page, page 19.

Check to be sure the students have found the right page.

Lesson 2b **Language Arts Skills**

Sample B
- ○ Nancy going to the store.
- ○ She need some milk.
- ● Her mother will go, too.

3
- ● The cows went into the barn.
- ○ They was hungry.
- ○ The farmer to feed them.

4
- ○ My parents buyed a new car.
- ● It is a red van.
- ○ We has a big family.

18 Unit 1 Lesson 2b **Language Arts Skills**

Say Carla's aunt gave her a gift, and Carla wrote a letter thanking her aunt. Look at Carla's letter to her aunt as you answer Numbers 5 through 8.

Allow time between items for the students to fill in their answers.

Say Put your finger on Number 5 at the top of the page. Read the words. Which punctuation mark comes at the end? Mark your answer.

Do Number 6 just as you did Number 5. Read the words. Which punctuation mark comes at the end? Mark your answer.

Number 7. Read the sentence that is divided into parts. Find the part of the sentence that needs a capital letter. Mark your answer.

Number 8. Read the sentence that is divided into parts. Find the part of the sentence that needs a capital letter. Mark your answer.

Pause for a moment.

Say Look at the next page, page 20.

Check to be sure the students have found the right page.

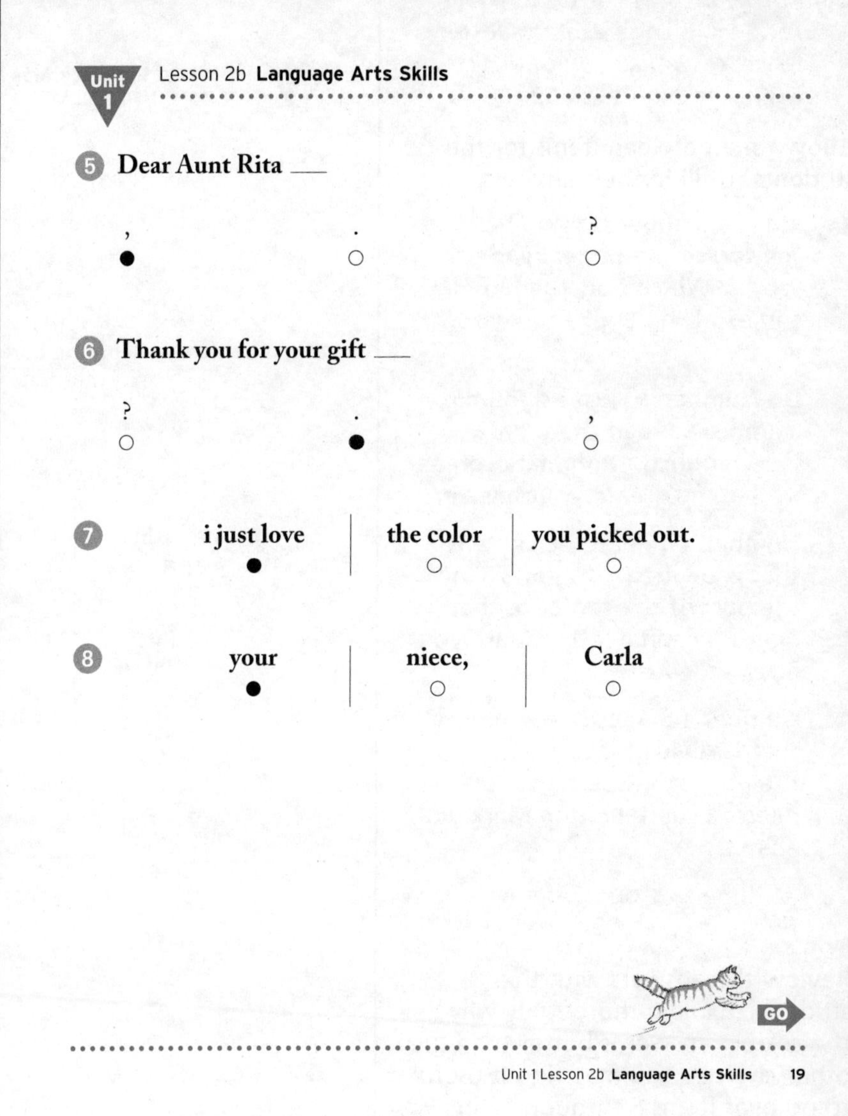

Unit 1 Lesson 2b **Language Arts Skills**

5 **Dear Aunt Rita __**

,	.	?
●	○	○

6 **Thank you for your gift __**

?	.	,
○	●	○

7

i just love	the color	you picked out.
●	○	○

8

your	niece,	Carla
●	○	○

Unit 1 Lesson 2b **Language Arts Skills** 19

Say Rob wants his cousin to come for a visit. Look at Rob's letter to his cousin as you answer Numbers 9 through 12.

Allow time between items for the students to fill in their answers.

Say Put your finger on Number 9 at the top of the page. Read the words. Which punctuation mark comes at the end? Mark your answer.

Do Number 10 just as you did Number 9. Read the words. Which punctuation mark comes at the end? Mark your answer.

Number 11. Read the sentence that is divided into parts. Find the part of the sentence that needs a capital letter. Mark your answer.

Number 12. Read the sentence that is divided into parts. Find the part of the sentence that needs a capital letter. Mark your answer.

It's time to stop. You have finished Lesson 2b.

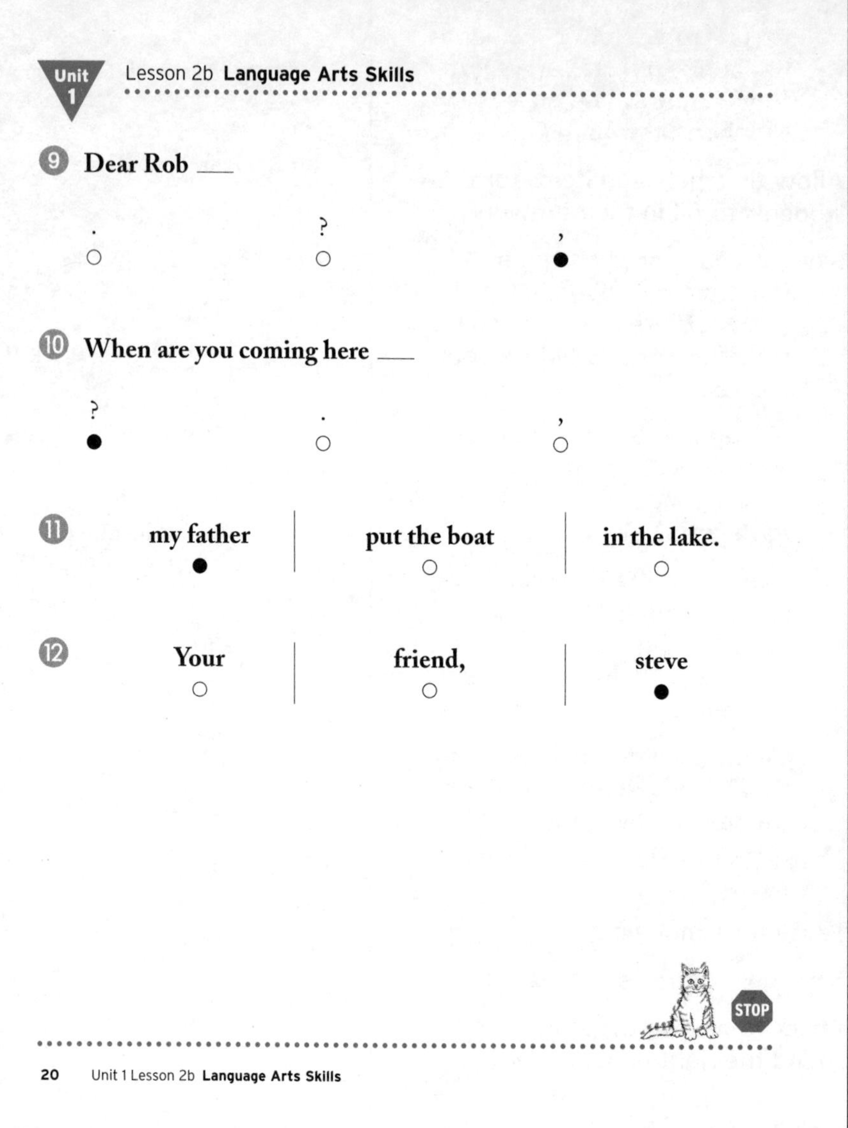

Review the answers with the students. Explain thoroughly why the correct answer is better than the other choices. You may find it useful to go over items 5 through 12 in detail. These items are in an unusual format, and students may be unfamiliar with both the content and the format of the items. It may be helpful to write the letter in standard form on the chalkboard when you review the items.

Have the students indicate completion of the lesson by entering their score for this activity on the progress chart at the beginning of the book. Provide the students whatever help is necessary to record their scores.

Test Yourself: **Reading and Language Arts**

Focus

Reading and Language Arts Skills

- recognizing details
- understanding figurative language
- deriving word meanings
- understanding reasons
- making comparisons
- choosing the best word to complete a sentence
- identifying pronouns
- choosing correctly formed sentences
- drawing conclusions
- understanding sequence
- making predictions
- choosing the best title for a story
- choosing the best phrase to complete a sentence
- changing a declarative sentence to a question
- choosing the best sentence to complete a paragraph
- making inferences
- identifying correct punctuation
- identifying correct capitalization

Test-taking Skills

- managing time effectively
- following oral directions
- considering every answer choice
- taking the best guess when unsure of the answer
- referring to a selection to answer questions
- choosing a picture to answer a question
- identifying and using key words to find the answer
- using context to find the answer
- listening carefully
- marking the right answer as soon as it is found
- staying with the first answer
- recalling familiar words
- understanding unusual item formats
- working methodically

Test Yourself: Reading and Language Arts

Sample

Flowers are pretty. They are also food for some animals like bees, other insects, and birds.

Who gets food from a flower?

a bee	a snake	a fish
●	○	○

Directions: **Brenda is a butterfly who has a problem. Winter is coming and she is getting cold. Read the story about Brenda, then do Numbers 1 through 5.**

Brenda was cold. She had never been cold before. She lived in a sunny place that was usually warm. Brenda did not like being cold.

Brenda's friend, Ralph, saw that she was sad. "Why the long face?" asked Ralph.

"I'm cold," answered Brenda, "and I don't know what to do."

This lesson simulates an actual test-taking experience. Therefore, it is recommended that the directions be read verbatim and the suggested procedures be followed.

Directions

Administration Time: approximately 50 minutes in two sessions

Say Turn to the Test Yourself lesson on page 21.

Check to be sure the students have found the right page. Point out to the students that this is not a real test and that they will score it themselves to see how well they are doing.

Say This lesson will check how well you remember some things you practiced in other lessons. Put your finger under the sample at the top of the page. Find the story for the sample. Read the story to yourself while I read it out loud.

Flowers are pretty. They are also food for some animals like bees, other insects, and birds.

Now look at the question and answer choices. Read them to yourself. Which answer do you think is correct? Mark the circle for your answer. *(pause)* The first answer, *a bee*, is correct because bees get their food from a flower. Fill in the circle under the first answer. Be sure the circle is completely filled in with a dark mark.

Check to see that the students have marked the correct circle.

Say Now you will do more items. You will read a story and answer questions about it. Let's begin by reading the directions. Read them to yourself while I read them out loud.

Brenda is a butterfly who has a problem. Winter is coming and she is getting cold. Read the story about Brenda. Then do Numbers 1 through 5.

When you come to the GO sign at the bottom of the page, go to the next page and continue working. Work until you come to the STOP sign after Number 5 on page 23. You should look back at the story to answer the questions. If you are not sure which answer is correct, take your best guess. Mark the circles for your answers and make sure you fill in your answer circles completely with dark marks. Completely erase any marks for answers you change. Do you have any questions about what to do?

Answer any questions the students have.

Say You may begin. Remember, you can look back at the story to find the answers. You have ten minutes.

Test Yourself: Reading and Language Arts

Ralph grinned at Brenda. He answered, "My mother told me what to do. She said we should follow the other butterflies and fly south. It's warm there all the time."

Brenda and Ralph saw some other butterflies. They followed them south, and soon Brenda was happy again.

1 **Ralph says that Brenda has a "long face." He is saying that __________.**

- ○ Brenda's face is long
- ● Brenda looks sad
- ○ Brenda is a very tall butterfly

22 Unit 1 **Test Yourself: Reading and Language Arts**

Allow ten minutes. Check the students as they work to be sure they are answering all the questions. Make sure they stop after Number 5 on page 23.

Say It's time to stop. You should be on page 23. Now you are going to do different items. Look at the next page, page 24.

Check to be sure the students are on the right page and have found the directions.

2 In the story,

Ralph grinned at Brenda.

What does this mean?

- ○ He was cold, too.
- ○ He didn't know what to do.
- ● He smiled at her.

3 Why was Brenda happy at the end of the story?

- ○ She knows winter is coming.
- ● She was warm again.
- ○ Ralph showed her how to fly.

4 In which direction do Ralph and Brenda fly?

- ○ north
- ○ west
- ● south

5 Birds sometimes go south for the winter. How else are they like butterflies?

- ● Both fly.
- ○ Both swim.
- ○ Both have six legs.

Say Read along to yourself as I read the directions out loud for Numbers 6 and 7.

For Numbers 6 and 7, find the word that fits in each blank in the story.

Read the whole story before you try to answer the questions. Mark the circles for the answers you think are correct. You may begin.

Allow time between items for the students to fill in their answers. Be sure they stop after Number 7.

Say Put your finger on Number 8. Read the sentence. Find the answer that can take the place of "Brenda and Ralph" in the sentence. Mark your answer.

Pause for a moment.

Say Move down to Number 9. Look at the three sentences. Find the sentence that is written correctly. Mark your answer.

Allow time for the students to fill in their answers.

Say Look at the next page, page 25.

Check to be sure the students have found the right page.

Directions: For Numbers 6 and 7, find the word that fits in each blank in the story.

> While they were going south, Brenda and Ralph flew over a (6). They saw some (7) in it and people swimming.

6
- ○ field
- ● lake
- ○ farm

7
- ○ cars
- ○ trucks
- ● boats

8 **Some children saw Brenda and Ralph.**
- ● them
- ○ they
- ○ it

9
- ○ Many miles with their friends.
- ● They flew to a warm place.
- ○ Tasty flowers all around.

Say The students in Miss Terry's class wrote some stories. You will get to read some of the stories. Here is a story written by Darren Vega. I will read the directions out loud. You may read along silently with me.

Moving to a new home can be hard. Finding a special place of your own helps. Read Darren Vega's story about when he found a special place of his own. Then answer Numbers 10 through 13.

When you come to the GO sign at the bottom of the page, go on to the next page and continue working. You may look back at the story to answer the questions. Be sure to answer Numbers 10 through 13. When you come to the STOP sign after Number 13, wait for me to tell you what to do next. You may begin.

Allow ten minutes. Check the students as they work to be sure they are answering all the questions. Make sure they stop after Number 13 on page 27.

Directions: Moving to a new home can be hard. Finding a special place of your own helps. Read Darren Vega's story about when he found a special place of his own. Then answer Numbers 10 through 13.

I pull myself up to the first branch. Up, up I go, away from the new house. The bark is like sandpaper. The leaves are a green umbrella. I miss my old house. I sit and cry. Wipe away my tears. I feel better. I am happy in this special place. I will come here again.

by Darren

10 **What is Darren most likely doing in the story?**

- ○ He is walking in the rain.
- ● He is climbing a tree.
- ○ He is using sandpaper.

11 **What does Darren do just after he sits?**

- ● He cries.
- ○ He goes higher.
- ○ He wipes his hands.

12 **The next time Darren feels sad he will probably ________.**

- ○ write a story about it
- ○ find a new house
- ● go to his special place

Say It's time to stop. You should be on page 27. Now we are going to do different items. For Numbers 14 through 17, we will read the questions together. For each question, fill in the circle that goes with the answer you choose.

Allow time between items for the students to fill in their answers.

Say Number 14. "Wipe away tears" is not a complete sentence. What could Darren add if he wanted to make it a complete sentence? Mark your answer.

Number 15. Here is a sentence that Sam wrote. Read the first sentence. Then read the answer choices below it. Find the answer choice that correctly changes the sentence into a question. Mark your answer.

Look at the next page, page 28.

Check to be sure the students have found the right page.

13 **Which of these is the best name for the story?**

- ● A New Place
- ○ The Sky that Cried
- ○ Building a Tree Fort

STOP

14 **Wipe away my tears is not a complete sentence. What could Darren add if he wanted to make it a complete sentence?**

__________ wipe away my tears.

- ○ Darren
- ○ He
- ● I

15 **Sam is six years old.**

- ○ Six years old Sam is?
- ● Is Sam six years old?
- ○ Sam is old six years?

Say Put your finger under Number 16. Read the story. Part of the story is missing. Find the sentence that best completes the story. Mark your answer.

Number 17. Read the story. Find the sentence that best completes the story. Mark your answer.

Give the students some time to rest before continuing. You may choose to administer the rest of the Test Yourself lesson later in the day or on another day.

Say Look at the next page, page 29.

Check to be sure the students have found the right page.

16 **I like playing outside.**

I go for long walks.

______.

- ○ I help cook dinner.
- ○ I take naps.
- ● I ride my bike.

17 **Dad and I bake bread.**

We mix the batter together.

______.

- ○ We like sandwiches.
- ● Then we bake it.
- ○ My mom is a doctor.

Say Here is one of Miss Terry's favorite stories to read in class. You will read it on your own. I will read the directions out loud.

Apple and Banana are two fruits who do not get along. Here is a story about them. Read the whole story. Then answer Numbers 18 through 22.

You may look back at the story to answer the questions. When you come to a GO sign at the bottom of a page, go on to the next page and continue working. When you come to the STOP sign after Number 22, wait for me to tell you what to do next. You may begin.

Allow fifteen minutes. Check the students as they work to be sure they are answering all the questions. Make sure they stop after Number 22 on page 34.

Directions: Apple and Banana are two fruits who do not get along. Here is a story about them. Read the whole story. Then answer Numbers 18 through 22.

Apple sat in a bowl in the kitchen. One day, Banana joined her. Apple was unhappy. She thought the bowl was hers. She did not like sharing it with Banana.

"You do not belong here," she said. "Besides, apples are better than bananas."

"Says who?" asked Banana. He would not back down.

"Says me," replied Apple. Then she explained why. She talked about apple pie, applesauce, and candy apples.

"Hmpf," said Banana. He had his own list. "What about banana bread, banana splits, and banana cream pie?" He smiled proudly.

Apple was silent. She thought about what Banana said. Maybe he was right. Maybe bananas were just as good as apples.

"I have an idea," Apple said finally. "Let's let someone else decide." Banana nodded. That seemed fair.

Just then, two children came into the kitchen. They were looking for snacks. One child grabbed Apple and ran outside. The other child reached for Banana and followed.

Now, which was better, Apple or Banana?

18 Why was Apple angry?

- ○ Banana teased her.
- ○ The children wanted to eat her.
- ● Banana sat in her bowl.

19 How does Apple try to show that she is better?

- ● She names some apple dishes.
- ○ She says she can bake a pie.
- ○ She tells Banana to leave.

20 The story says this about Banana

He would not back down.

What does this mean?

- ○ He did not sit down.
- ● He did not agree.
- ○ He did not listen.

21 <u>Hmpf</u> is a strange word that Banana uses.

<u>Hmpf</u> means about the same as

- ● So what?
- ○ Oh dear...
- ○ Hooray!

Say It's time to stop. You should be on page 34. Now you are going to do different items. For Numbers 23 and 24, find the word for each blank that best completes the story. Read the whole story in the box. Be sure to answer Numbers 23 and 24. Mark your answers.

Allow time for the students to fill in their answers.

Say Look at the next page, page 35.

Check to be sure the students have found the right page.

22 What happens at the end of the story?

- ○ Apple proves she is better than Banana.
- ● Both Apple and Banana are eaten as snacks.
- ○ Banana and Apple are turned into fruit salad.

Directions: **For Numbers 23 and 24, find the word for each blank that best completes the story. Read the whole story in the box. Be sure to answer Numbers 23 and 24. Mark your answers.**

> Anna's father worked
> at a (23).
> He (24) their pens and
> cared for the animals.

23
- ○ store
- ○ factory
- ● zoo

24
- ● cleaned
- ○ found
- ○ made

Say Now you will do some different items. Read along to yourself as I read the directions out loud for Numbers 25 and 26.

For Numbers 25 and 26, find the word for each blank that best completes the story. Read the whole story in the box. Be sure to answer Numbers 25 and 26. Mark your answers.

Allow time for the students to fill in their answers. Be sure they stop after Number 26.

Say Put your finger on Number 27. Read the sentence. Find the answer that can take the place of "Anna and her father" in the sentence. Mark your answer.

Pause for a moment.

Say Move over to Number 28. Look at the three sentences. Find the sentence that is written correctly. Mark your answer.

Allow time for the students to fill in their answers.

Say Look at the next page, page 36.

Check to be sure the students have found the right page.

Directions: For Numbers 25 and 26, find the word for each blank that best completes the story. Read the whole story in the box. Be sure to answer Numbers 25 and 26. Mark your answers.

> Anna's father sometimes saw animals being __(25)__. He __(26)__ pictures of the tiny babies to show Anna.

25
- ○ moved
- ● born
- ○ named

26
- ● took
- ○ saw
- ○ read

STOP

27 **Anna and her father both love animals.**
- ○ We
- ○ She
- ● They

28
- ● Now Anna wants a pet.
- ○ Her father wants a dog last year.
- ○ At first, Anna want a kitten.

Say Miss Terry asked the class to write thank-you letters. The students wrote letters to a visitor who came to class. Look at one of Ben's letters as you answer Numbers 29 through 32.

Allow time between items for the students to fill in their answers.

Say Put your finger on Number 29 at the top of the page. Read the words. Which punctuation mark comes at the end? Mark your answer.

Do Number 30 just as you did Number 29. Read the words. Which punctuation mark comes at the end? Mark your answer.

Number 31. Read the sentence that is divided into parts. Find the part of the sentence that needs a capital letter. Mark your answer.

Number 32. Read the sentence that is divided into parts. Find the part of the sentence that needs a capital letter. Mark your answer.

It's time to stop. You have completed the Test Yourself lesson.

Review the answers with the students. Have the students indicate completion of the lesson by entering their score for this activity on the progress chart at the beginning of the book. Provide the students whatever help is necessary to record their scores.

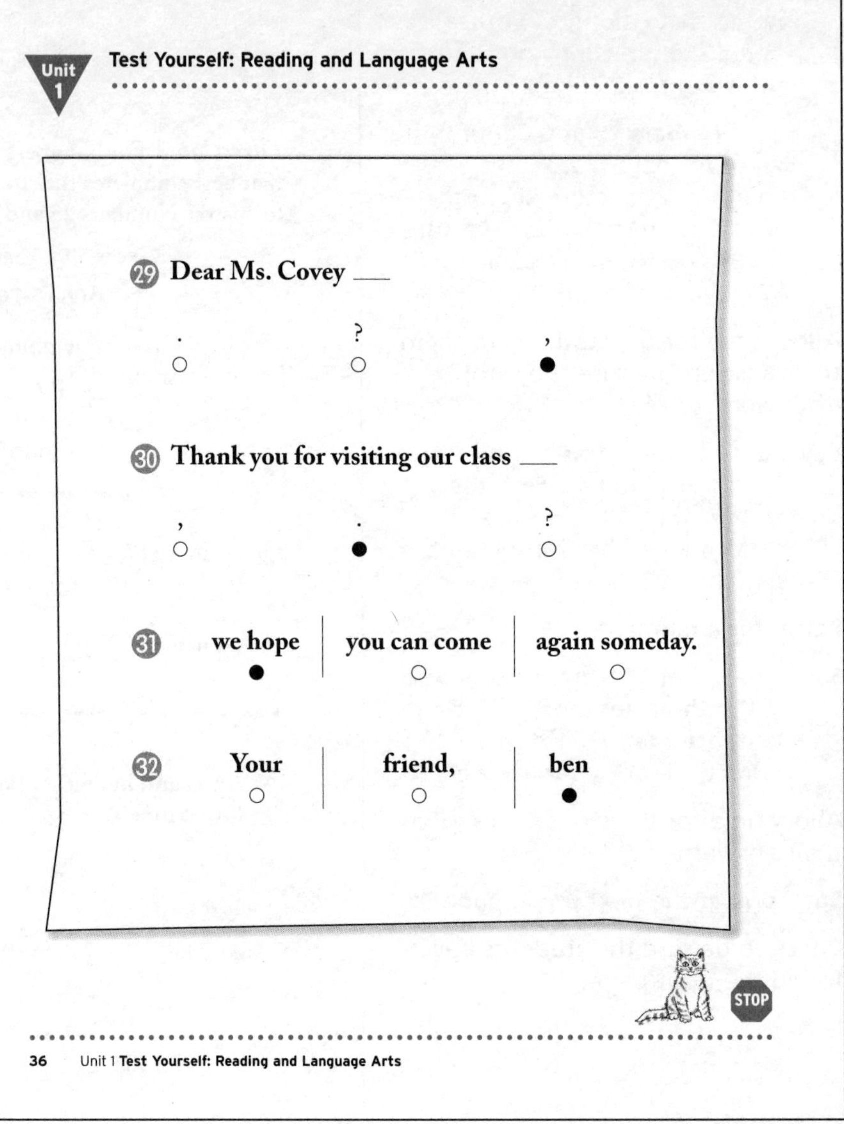

Unit 1 **Test Yourself: Reading and Language Arts**

29 Dear Ms. Covey ___

.	?	,
○	○	●

30 Thank you for visiting our class ___

,	.	?
○	●	○

31

we hope	you can come	again someday.
●	○	○

32

Your	friend,	ben
○	○	●

36 Unit 1 **Test Yourself: Reading and Language Arts**

Background

This unit contains seven lessons that deal with basic skills. Students answer a variety of questions about word analysis, vocabulary, and computation skills.

• **In Lessons 3a and 3b,** students answer questions about word sounds and sight words. Students are encouraged to follow oral directions, listen carefully, consider every answer choice, and subvocalize answer choices.

Instructional Objectives

Lesson 3a **Word Analysis** Lesson 3b **Word Analysis**	Given an oral prompt, students identify the answer choice that begins with the same consonant sound. Given an oral prompt, students identify the answer choice that ends with the same consonant sound. Given an oral prompt and a picture, students identify which of four answer choices has the same medial vowel sound. Given an oral prompt, students identify which of four answer choices has the same medial vowel sound. Given an oral prompt, students identify which of four answer choices is the targeted sight word.

• **In Lessons 4a and 4b,** students answer vocabulary questions. They review the test-taking skills introduced in previous lessons and work methodically. Students also skip difficult items and return to them later, use context to find the answer, try out answer choices, and recall word meanings.

• **In Lessons 5a and 5b,** students solve addition and subtraction computation problems. They review the test-taking skills introduced in previous lessons and work methodically. Students also convert items to a workable format, transfer numbers accurately to scratch paper, compute carefully, and take the best guess when unsure of the answer.

• **In the Test Yourself lesson,** the word analysis, vocabulary, mathematics computation, and test-taking skills introduced and used in Lessons 3a through 5b are reinforced and presented in a format that gives students the experience of taking an achievement test.

Instructional Objectives

Lesson 4a **Vocabulary** Lesson 4b **Vocabulary**	Given an oral definition, students identify which of four answer choices means the same as the definition. Given a phrase with an underlined word, students identify which of four answer choices means the same as the underlined word. Given a brief story with a blank, students identify which answer choice fits best in the blank.
Lesson 5a **Mathematics Computation** Lesson 5b **Mathematics Computation**	Given an addition or subtraction problem, students identify which of four answer choices is the solution to the problem.
Test Yourself	Given questions similar to those in Lessons 3a through 5b, students utilize basic skills and test-taking strategies on achievement test formats.

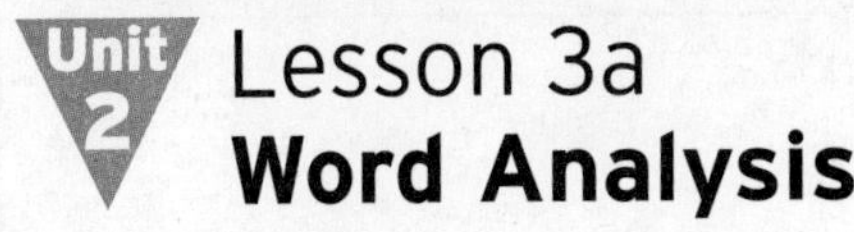

Lesson 3a
Word Analysis

Focus

Word Analysis Skills
- matching beginning sounds
- matching ending sounds
- matching vowel sounds
- identifying sight words

Test-taking Skills
- following oral directions
- listening carefully
- considering every answer choice
- subvocalizing answer choices

Sample A

Say Turn to Lesson 3a on page 37. The page number is at the bottom of the page on the right.

Check to see that the students have found the right page.

Say In this lesson, you will show how well you understand word sounds. When you answer a question, fill in the circle for the answer you think is right. Be sure your answer circle is completely filled in with a dark mark and that you have marked the correct circle for the answer you think is right. Find Sample A at the top of the page.

Check to see that the students have found Sample A.

Say Look at the words. Find the word that has the same beginning sound as "bell ... bell." *(pause)* The second answer is correct because *bell* and *boat* begin with *b*. Mark the circle under *boat*. Be sure your answer circle is completely filled in with a dark mark.

Check to see that the students have marked the correct circle.

TIPS

Say Now let's look at the tip.

Read the tip aloud to the students.

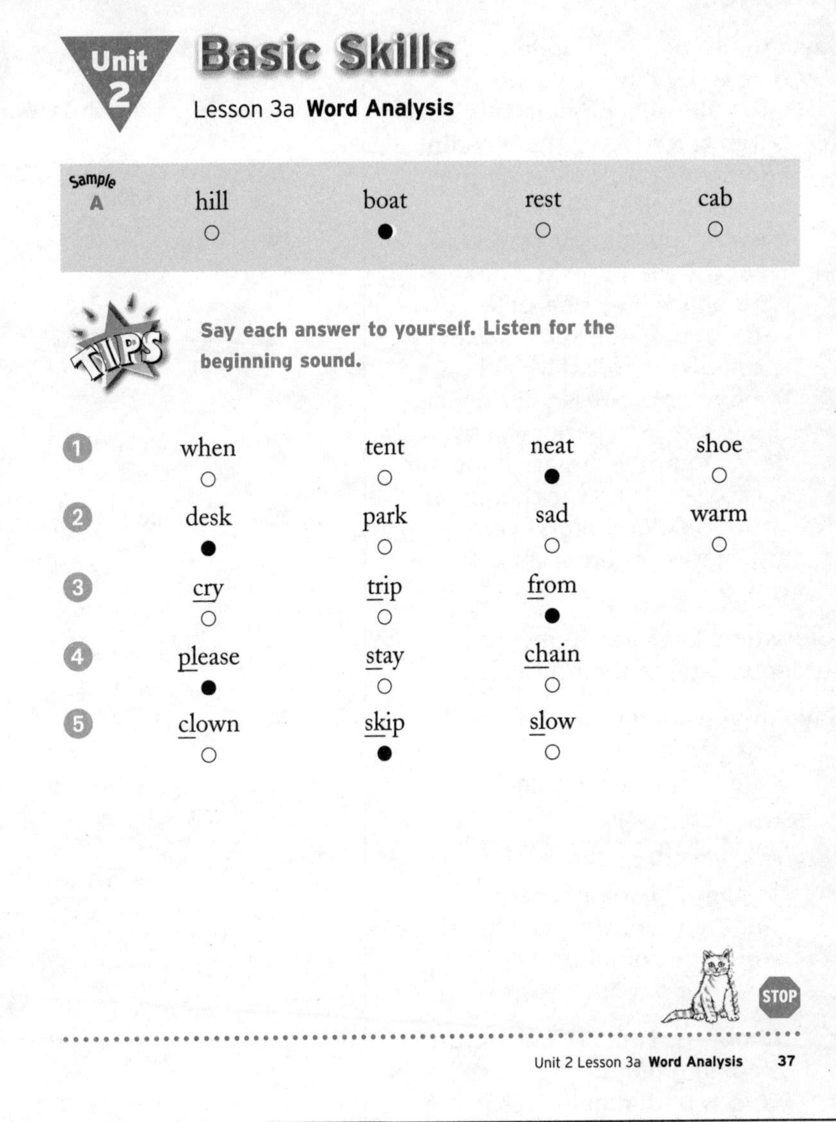

Say It is important that you listen carefully to the directions and look at the answer choices before picking the one you think is correct. Think about the beginning sound of the word I say and then look at each answer choice. Say each word to yourself and think about the beginning sound. Remember, listen only for the beginning sound.

Practice

Say You are going to do more items that show how well you understand beginning sounds. Listen carefully to the directions I give you and look at all the answer choices. Mark the answer you think is correct. Then get ready for the next item. Mark only one circle for each item. Make sure the circle is completely filled in and remember to press your pencil firmly so your mark comes out dark. Do not write anything except your answer choices in your book. Completely erase any marks for answers you change.

Allow time between items for the students to fill in their answers.

Say Put your finger on Number 1. Look at the words. Find the word that has the same beginning sound as "new ... new." Mark your answer.

Number 2. Look at the words. Find the word that has the same beginning sound as "dark ... dark." Mark your answer.

Number 3. Look at the words. The beginning part of each word is underlined. This is the part of the word I want you to listen to. Find the word that has the same beginning sound as "friend ... friend." Mark your answer.

Number 4. Look at the words. Find the word that has the same beginning sound as "play ... play." Mark your answer.

Number 5. Look at the words. Find the word that has the same beginning sound as "skin ... skin." Mark your answer.

Look at the next page, page 38.

Check to be sure the students have found the right page.

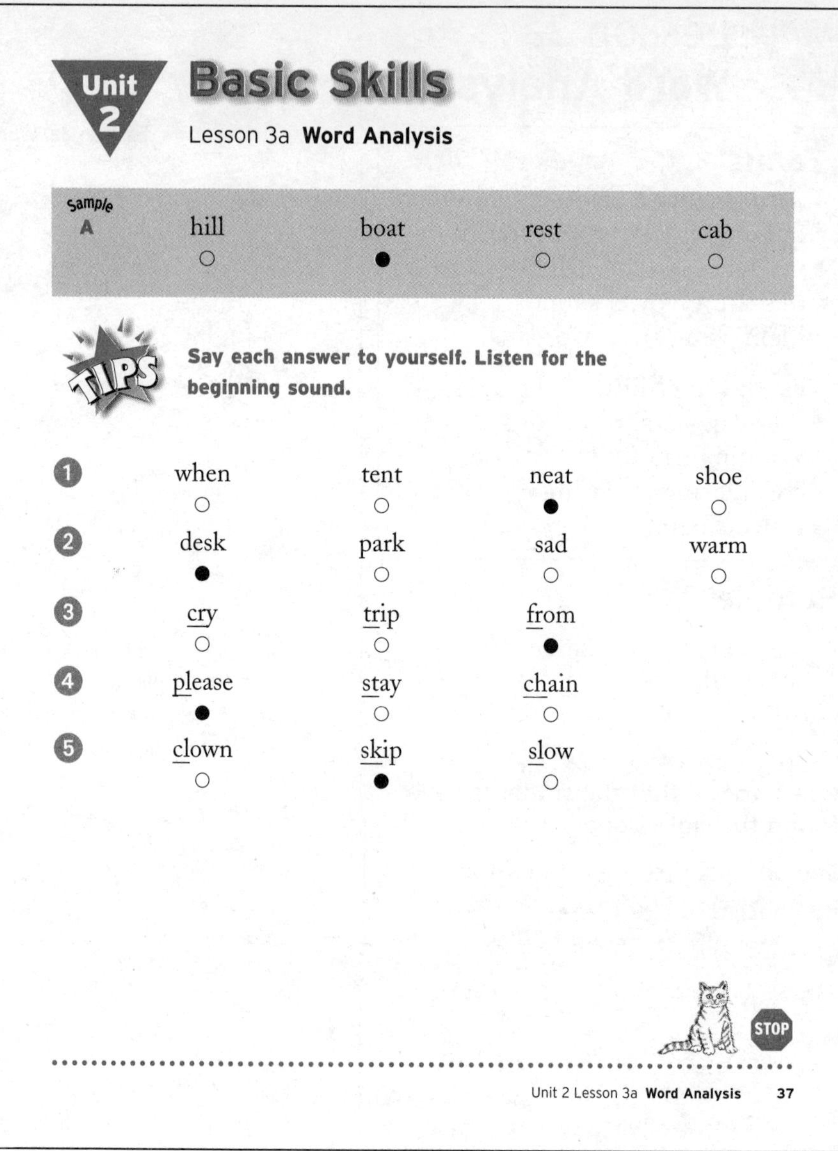

Unit 2 **Basic Skills**

Lesson 3a **Word Analysis**

Sample A	hill ○	boat ●	rest ○	cab ○

TIPS **Say each answer to yourself. Listen for the beginning sound.**

1	when ○	tent ○	neat ●	shoe ○
2	desk ●	park ○	sad ○	warm ○
3	cry ○	trip ○	from ●	
4	please ●	stay ○	chain ○	
5	clown ○	skip ●	slow ○	

STOP

Unit 2 Lesson 3a **Word Analysis** 37

Sample B

Say Now you will do a different kind of item. Put your finger on Sample B. Look at the words. Which word has the same <u>ending</u> sound as "far ... far"? *(pause)* The last answer is correct because *far* and *her* end with *r*. Mark the last answer circle. Make sure your answer circle is completely filled in with a dark mark.

Check to see that the students have marked the correct circle.

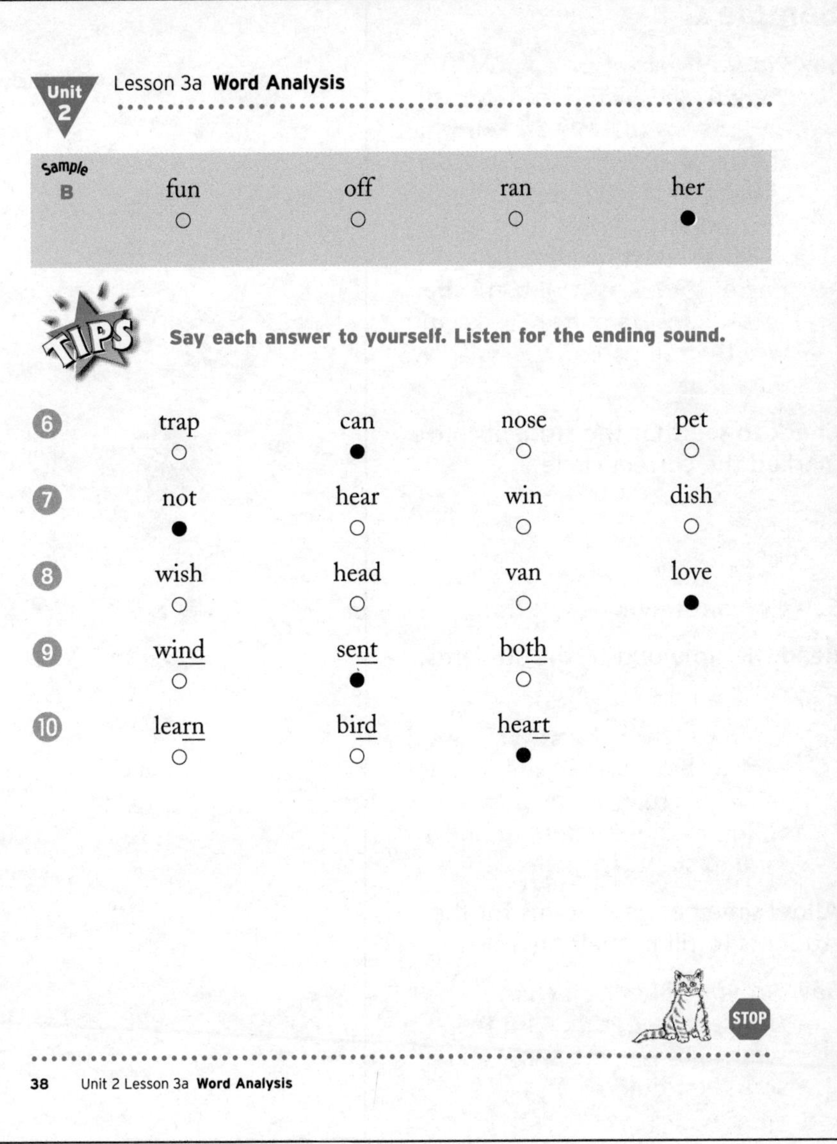

Sample B	fun	off	ran	her
	○	○	○	●

TIPS Say each answer to yourself. Listen for the ending sound.

6	trap ○	can ●	nose ○	pet ○
7	not ●	hear ○	win ○	dish ○
8	wish ○	head ○	van ○	love ●
9	wi<u>nd</u> ○	se<u>nt</u> ●	bo<u>th</u> ○	
10	lea<u>rn</u> ○	bi<u>rd</u> ○	hea<u>rt</u> ●	

STOP

★TIPS

Say Now let's look at the tip.

Read the tip aloud to the students.

Say Think about the ending sound of the word I say and then look at each answer choice. Say each word to yourself and think about the ending sound. Remember, listen only for the ending sound.

Allow time between items for the students to fill in their answers.

Say Put your finger on Number 6. Look at the words. Find the word that has the same <u>ending</u> sound as "pin ... pin." Mark your answer.

Number 7. Look at the words. Find the word that has the same <u>ending</u> sound as "hit ... hit." Mark your answer.

Number 8. Look at the words. Find the word that has the same <u>ending</u> sound as "have ... have." Mark your answer.

Number 9. Now you are going to find a different kind of ending sound. Look at the words. The ending part of each word is underlined. This is the part of the word I want you to listen to. Find the word that has the same <u>ending</u> sound as "want ... want." Mark your answer.

Number 10. Look at the words. Find the word that has the same <u>ending</u> sound as "dirt ... dirt." Mark your answer.

Look at the next page, page 39.

Check to be sure the students are working on the right page.

Sample C

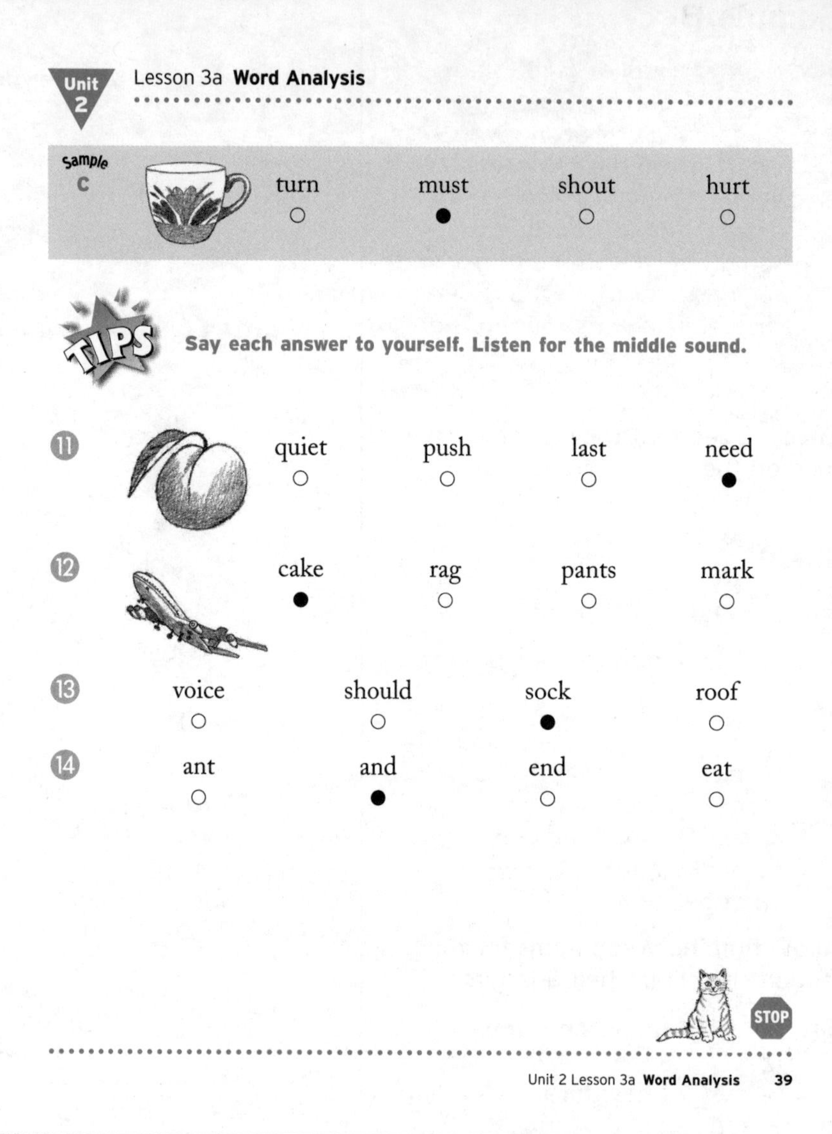
Unit 2 Lesson 3a **Word Analysis**

Sample C

turn	must	shout	hurt
○	●	○	○

TIPS **Say each answer to yourself. Listen for the middle sound.**

	quiet	push	last	need
11	○	○	○	●

	cake	rag	pants	mark
12	●	○	○	○

	voice	should	sock	roof
13	○	○	●	○

	ant	and	end	eat
14	○	●	○	○

STOP

Unit 2 Lesson 3a **Word Analysis** 39

Say Put your finger on Sample C. Look at the picture of the cup and the words. Which word has the same vowel sound (middle sound) as "cup ... cup"? *(pause)* The second answer is correct because *must* has the same vowel sound as *cup*. Mark the second answer circle. Make sure you fill it in completely with a dark mark.

Check to see that the students have marked the correct circle.

★TIPS

Say Now let's look at the tip.

Read the tip aloud to the students.

Say Remember, for these items, listen only for the vowel sound. This is the sound in the middle of the word. You must be sure to ignore the beginning and ending sounds.

Allow time between items for the students to fill in their answers.

Say Put your finger on Number 11. Look at the peach. Find the word that has the same vowel sound (middle sound) as "peach ... peach." Mark your answer.

Number 12. Look at the plane. Find the word that has the same vowel sound (middle sound) as "plane ... plane." Mark your answer.

Number 13. This is a different kind of item. Listen to this sentence: "I lost my sock." Look at the words. Find the word "sock ... sock." Mark your answer.

Number 14. This item is also different. Listen to this sentence: "Kim and Martin are here." Look at the words. Find the word "and ... and." Mark your answer.

It's time to stop. You have finished Lesson 3a.

Review the answers with the students. If any items caused particular difficulty, work through each of the answer choices. The item types in this lesson are relatively simple, so if any students are having difficulty, they should receive additional practice in listening for beginning, vowel, and ending sounds and identifying the corresponding sound of printed words. Keep in mind that the purpose of the practice is not to teach students to read, but to help them do their best on an achievement test.

Have the students indicate completion of the lesson by entering their score for this activity on the progress chart at the beginning of the book. Provide the students whatever help is necessary to record their scores.

Lesson 3b
Word Analysis

Focus
Word Analysis Skills
- matching beginning sounds
- matching ending sounds
- matching vowel sounds
- identifying sight words

Test-taking Skills
- following oral directions
- listening carefully
- considering every answer choice
- subvocalizing answer choices

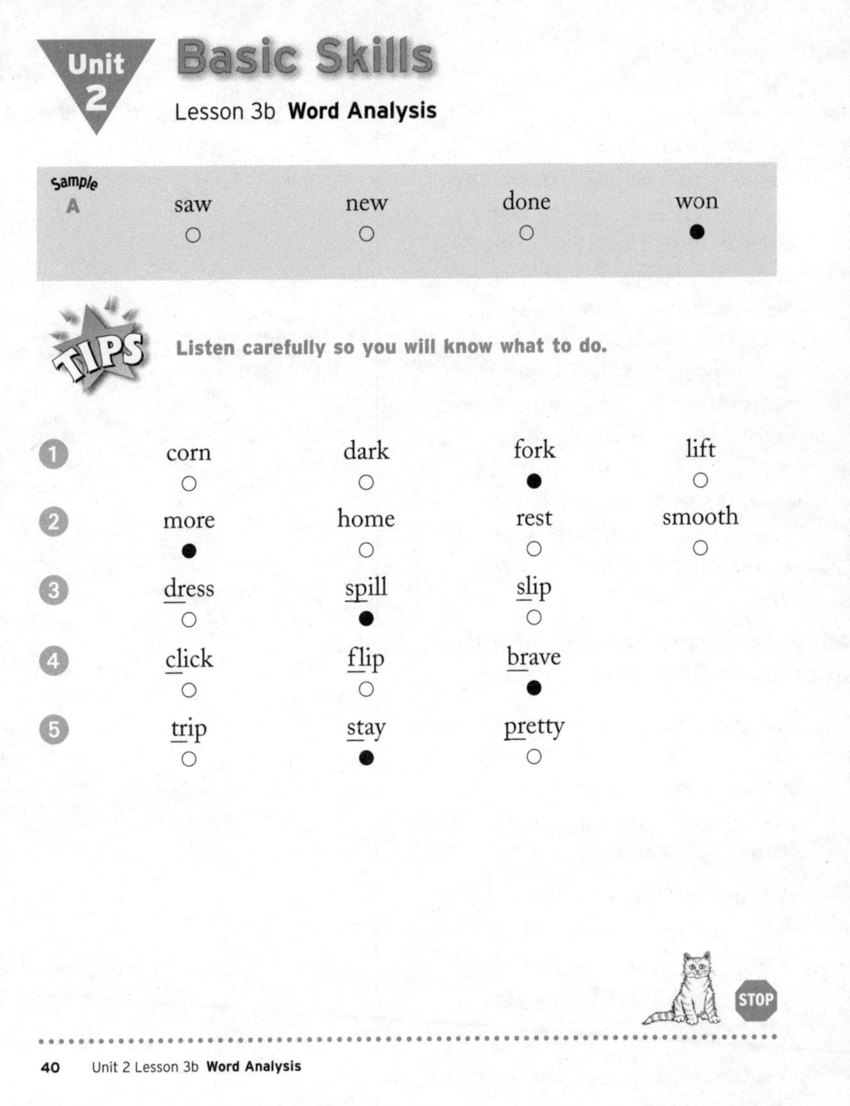

Basic Skills
Lesson 3b **Word Analysis**

Sample A	saw	new	done	won
	○	○	○	●

TIPS Listen carefully so you will know what to do.

1	corn ○	dark ○	fork ●	lift ○
2	more ●	home ○	rest ○	smooth ○
3	dress ○	spill ●	slip ○	
4	click ○	flip ○	brave ●	
5	trip ○	stay ●	pretty ○	

STOP

40 Unit 2 Lesson 3b **Word Analysis**

Sample A

Say Turn to Lesson 3b on page 40. The page number is at the bottom of the page on the right.

Check to see that the students have found the right page.

Say In this lesson, you will practice more word sounds. When you answer a question, fill in the circle for the answer you think is right. Be sure your answer circle is completely filled in with a dark mark and that you have marked the correct circle for the answer you think is right. Find Sample A at the top of the page.

Check to see that the students have found Sample A.

Say Look at the words. Find the word that has the same <u>beginning</u> sound as "will ... will." *(pause)* The last answer is correct because *will* and *won* begin with *w*. Mark the circle under *won*. Be sure your answer circle is completely filled in with a dark mark.

Check to see that the students have marked the correct circle.

★TIPS

Say Now let's look at the tip.

Read the tip aloud to the students.

Say It is important that you listen carefully to the directions and look at the answer choices before picking the one you think is correct. There are different kinds of questions in this lesson, so be sure to pay attention to what you are supposed to do.

Practice

Say You are going to do more items that show how well you understand beginning sounds. Listen carefully to the directions I give you and look at all the answer choices. Mark the answer you think is correct. Then get ready for the next item. Mark only one circle for each item. Make sure the circle is completely filled in and remember to press your pencil firmly so your mark comes out dark. Do not write anything except your answer choices in your book. Completely erase any marks for answers you change.

Allow time between items for the students to fill in their answers.

Say Put your finger on Number 1. Look at the words. Find the word that has the same beginning sound as "four ... four." Mark your answer.

Number 2. Look at the words. Find the word that has the same beginning sound as "map ... map." Mark your answer.

Number 3. Look at the words. The beginning part of each word is underlined. This is the part of the word I want you to listen to. Find the word that has the same beginning sound as "speak ... speak." Mark your answer.

Number 4. Look at the words. Find the word that has the same beginning sound as "bread ... bread." Mark your answer.

Number 5. Look at the words. Find the word that has the same beginning sound as "stop ... stop." Mark your answer.

Look at the next page, page 41.

Check to be sure the students have found the right page.

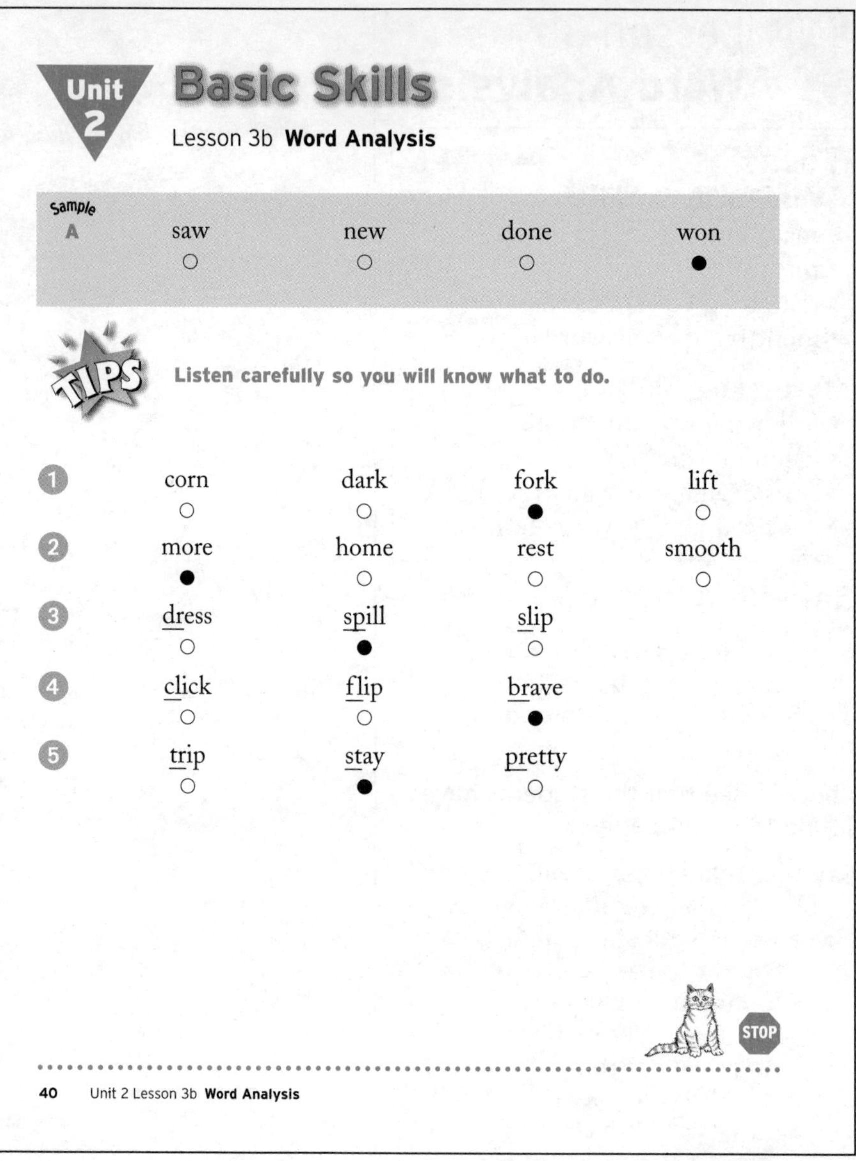

Unit 2 **Basic Skills**

Lesson 3b **Word Analysis**

Sample A	saw ○	new ○	done ○	won ●

TIPS **Listen carefully so you will know what to do.**

1	corn ○	dark ○	fork ●	lift ○
2	more ●	home ○	rest ○	smooth ○
3	dress ○	spill ●	slip ○	
4	click ○	flip ○	brave ●	
5	trip ○	stay ●	pretty ○	

STOP

40 Unit 2 Lesson 3b **Word Analysis**

Sample B

Say Now you will do a different kind of item. Put your finger on Sample B. Look at the words. Which word has the same ending sound as "fog ... fog"? *(pause)* The first answer is correct because *fog* and *rug* end with *g*. Mark the first answer circle. Make sure your answer circle is completely filled in with a dark mark.

Check to see that the students have marked the correct circle. For the following items, allow time between items for students to fill in their answers.

Say Put your finger on Number 6. Look at the words. Find the word that has the same ending sound as "test ... test." Mark your answer.

Number 7. Look at the words. Find the word that has the same ending sound as "make ... make." Mark your answer.

Number 8. Look at the words. Find the word that has the same ending sound as "boat ... boat." Mark your answer.

Number 9. Now you are going to find a different kind of ending sound. Look at the words. The ending part of each word is underlined. This is the part of the word I want you to listen to. Find the word that has the same ending sound as "mild ... mild." Mark your answer.

Number 10. Look at the words. Find the word that has the same ending sound as "fork ... fork." Mark your answer.

Look at the next page, page 42.

Check to be sure the students are working on the right page.

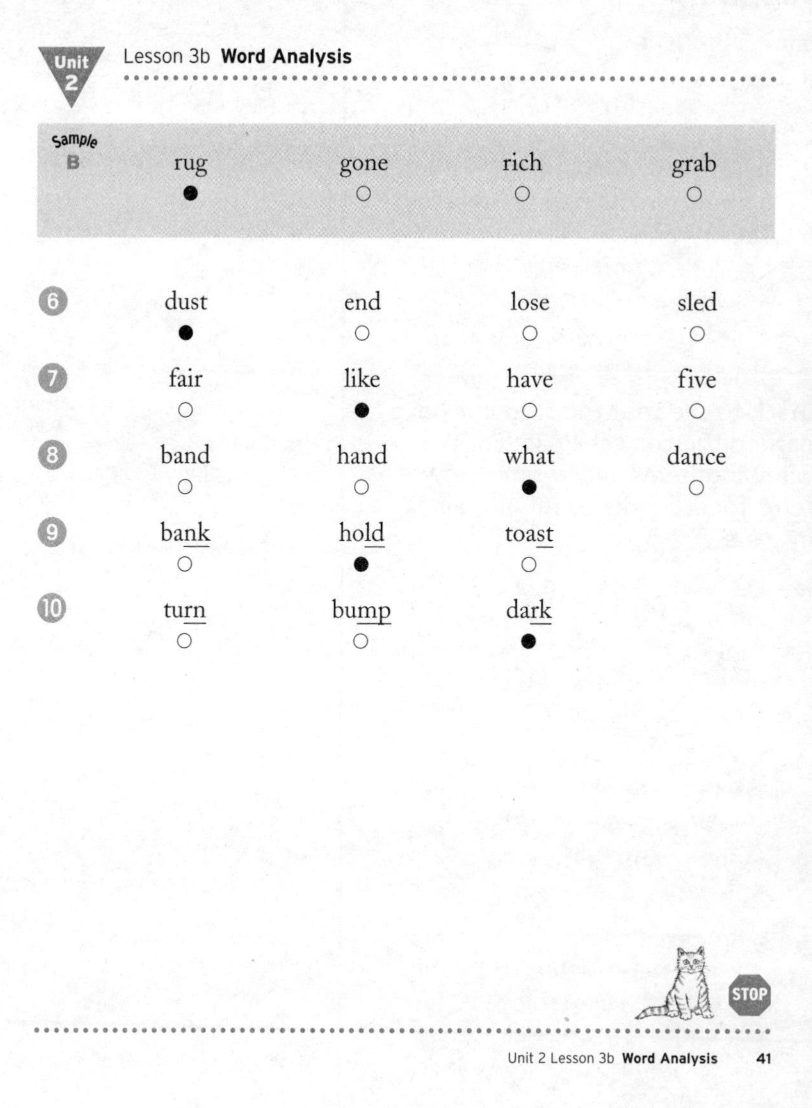
Unit 2 Lesson 3b **Word Analysis**

Sample B	rug ●	gone ○	rich ○	grab ○
6	dust ●	end ○	lose ○	sled ○
7	fair ○	like ●	have ○	five ○
8	band ○	hand ○	what ●	dance ○
9	bank ○	hold ●	toast ○	
10	turn ○	bump ○	dark ●	

Unit 2 Lesson 3b **Word Analysis** 41

Sample C

Say Put your finger on Sample C. Look at the picture of the bird and the words. Which word has the same vowel sound (middle sound) as "bird ... bird"? *(pause)* The second answer is correct because *heard* has the same vowel sound as *bird*. Mark the second answer circle. Make sure you fill it in completely with a dark mark.

Check to see that the students have marked the correct circle. For the following items, allow time between items for students to fill in their answers.

Say Put your finger on Number 11. Look at the cow. Find the word that has the same vowel sound (middle sound) as "cow ... cow." Mark your answer.

Number 12. Look at the tent. Find the word that has the same vowel sound (middle sound) as "tent ... tent." Mark your answer.

Number 13. This is a different kind of item. Listen to this sentence: "The game was fun." Look at the words. Find the word "game ... game." Mark your answer.

Number 14. This item is also different. Listen to this sentence: "A carrot is the root of a plant." Look at the words. Find the word "root ... root." Mark your answer.

It's time to stop. You have finished Lesson 3b.

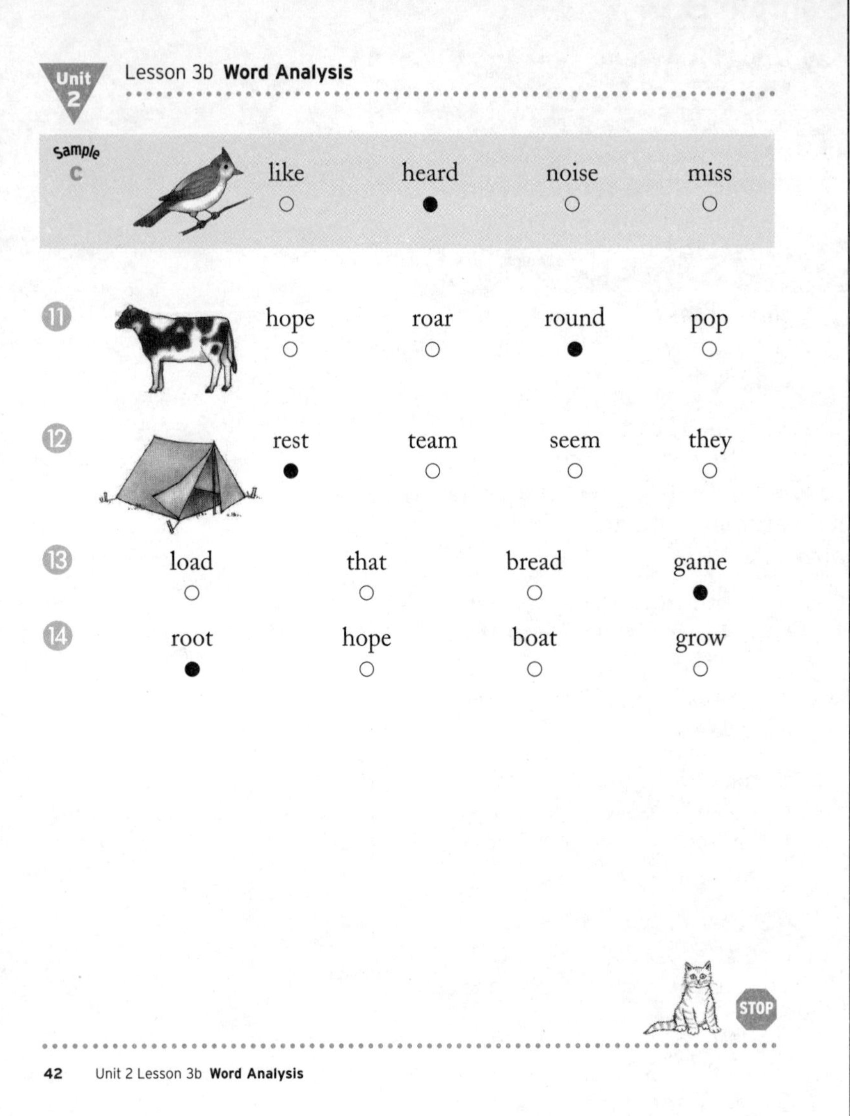

Unit 2
Lesson 3b Word Analysis
Sample C
like
heard
noise
miss
11
hope
roar
round
pop
12
rest
team
seem
they
13
load
that
bread
game
14
root
hope
boat
grow
STOP
42 Unit 2 Lesson 3b Word Analysis

Review the answers with the students. If any items caused particular difficulty, work through each of the answer choices.

Have the students indicate completion of the lesson by entering their score for this activity on the progress chart at the beginning of the book. Provide the students whatever help is necessary to record their scores.

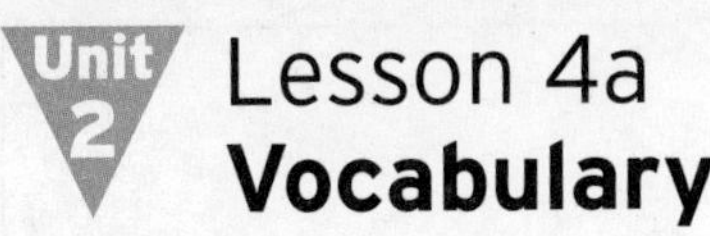

Lesson 4a Vocabulary

Focus

Vocabulary Skills

- identifying words from oral definitions
- identifying synonyms
- identifying words in sentence context

Test-taking Skills

- working methodically
- skipping difficult items and returning to them later
- using context to find the answer
- trying out answer choices

Sample A

Say Open your book to Lesson 4a on page 43.

Check to see that the students have found the right page.

Say In this lesson, you will show how well you understand what words mean. Find Sample A at the top of the page.

Check to see that the students have found Sample A.

Say Look at the words for Sample A. Find the word that means "big ... big." *(pause)* The answer is *large*. Mark the circle under *large*. Be sure your answer circle is completely filled in with a dark mark.

Check to see that the students have marked the correct circle.

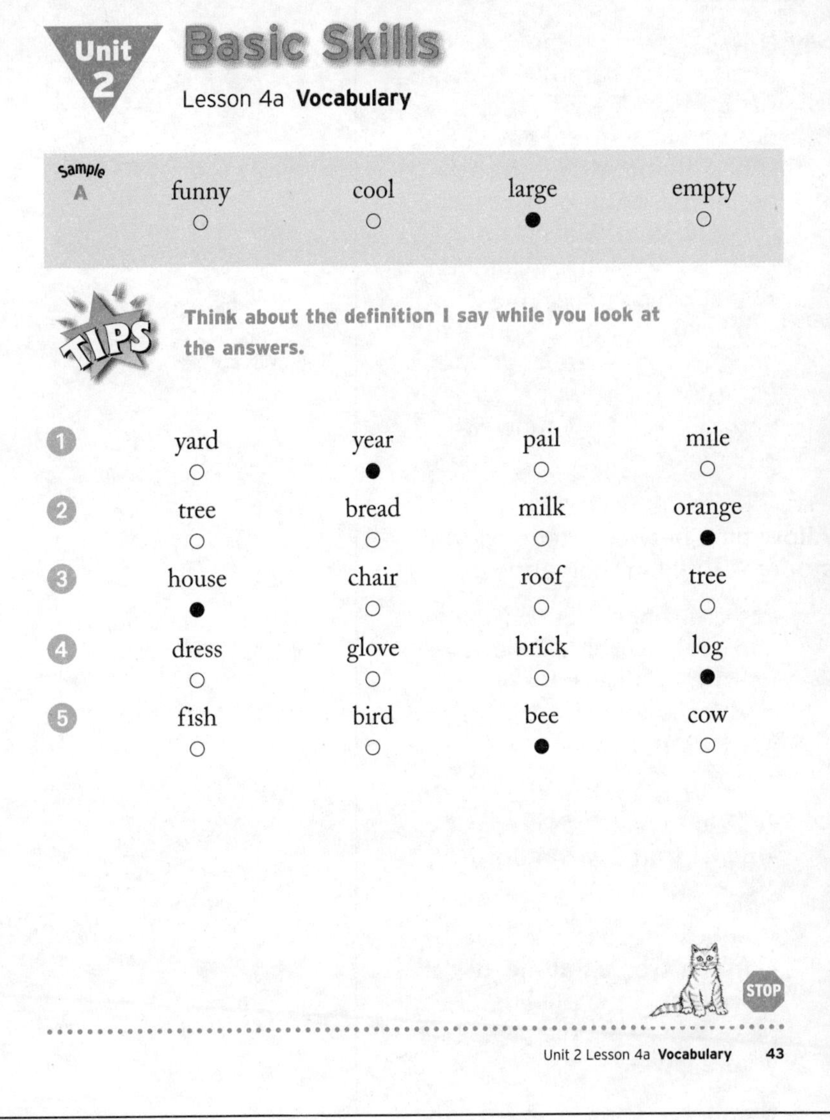

★TIPS

Say Now let's look at the tip.

Read the tip aloud to the students.

Say In this part of the lesson, you should listen carefully to what I say while you look at the answer choices. Think about the definition I say and try to match it to one of the answer choices. Look only at the answer choices for the item on which you are working and think only about the definition I said.

Practice

Say Now you will do the Practice items. Listen carefully to what I say and think about the definition. Find the answer choice that matches the definition. Mark only one circle for each item. Make sure the circle is completely filled in and remember to press your pencil firmly so your mark comes out dark. Do not write anything except your answer choices in your book. Completely erase any marks for answers you change.

Allow time between items for the students to fill in their answers.

Say Put your finger beside Number 1. Look at the words. Find the word that means "twelve months ... twelve months." Mark your answer.

Number 2. Look at the words. Find the word that means "a kind of fruit ... a kind of fruit." Mark your answer.

Number 3. Look at the words. Find the word that means "a place where people live ... a place where people live." Mark your answer.

Number 4. Look at the words. Find the word that means "something made of wood ... something made of wood." Mark your answer.

Number 5. Look at the words. Find the word that means "something that makes honey ... something that makes honey." Mark your answer.

Allow the students a moment to rest.

Say Look at the next page, page 44.

Check to be sure the students have found the right page.

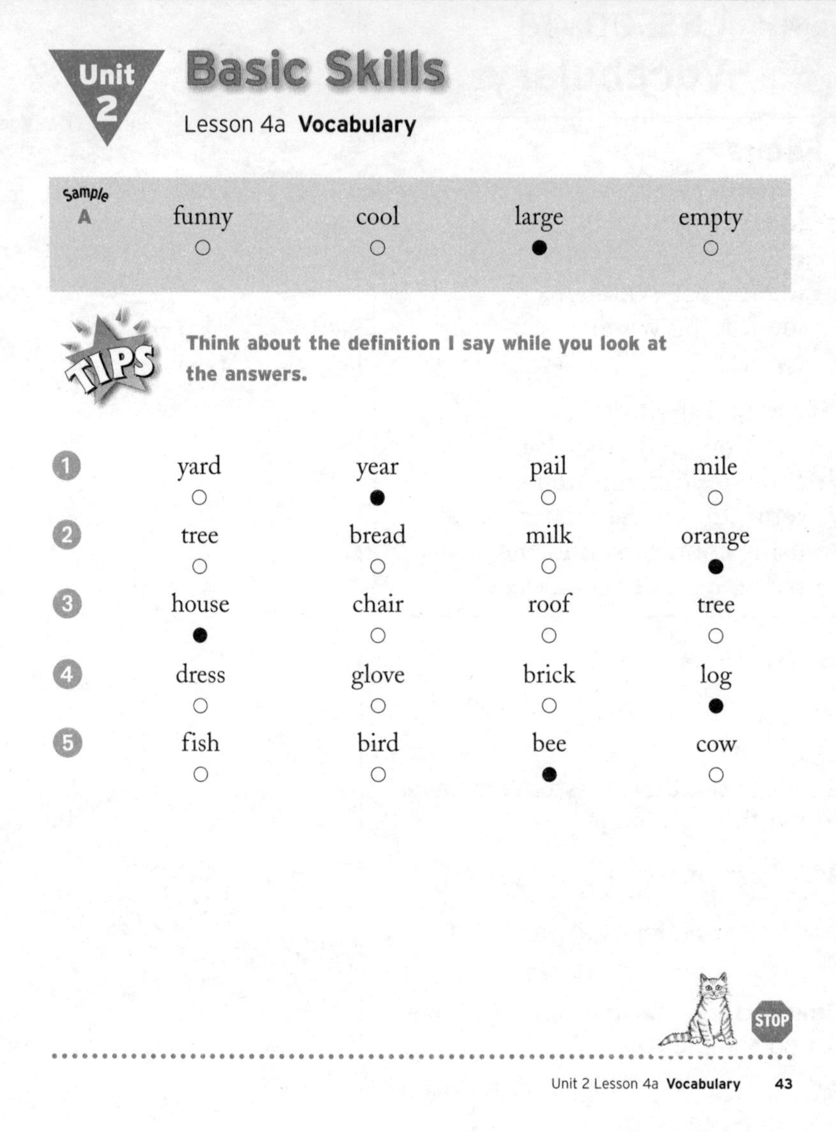

Unit 2 **Basic Skills**

Lesson 4a **Vocabulary**

Sample A	funny ○	cool ○	large ●	empty ○

TIPS **Think about the definition I say while you look at the answers.**

1	yard ○	year ●	pail ○	mile ○
2	tree ○	bread ○	milk ○	orange ●
3	house ●	chair ○	roof ○	tree ○
4	dress ○	glove ○	brick ○	log ●
5	fish ○	bird ○	bee ●	cow ○

STOP

Unit 2 Lesson 4a **Vocabulary** 43

Samples B and C

Say Find Sample B. Read the phrase with the underlined word and think about what the word means. Now look at the answers. Which answer means about the same as the underlined word? *(pause)* The right answer is *pick*. *Choose* and *pick* mean about the same thing. Mark the circle beside the word *pick*. Be sure your answer circle is completely filled in with a dark mark.

Check to see that the students have marked the correct circle.

Say Put your finger on Sample C. Read the phrase with the underlined word. Find the answer that means about the same as the underlined word. *(pause)* The correct answer is *bad*. *Awful* and *bad* mean about the same thing. Mark the circle beside the word *bad*. Be sure your answer circle is completely filled in with a dark mark.

Check to see that the students have marked the correct circle.

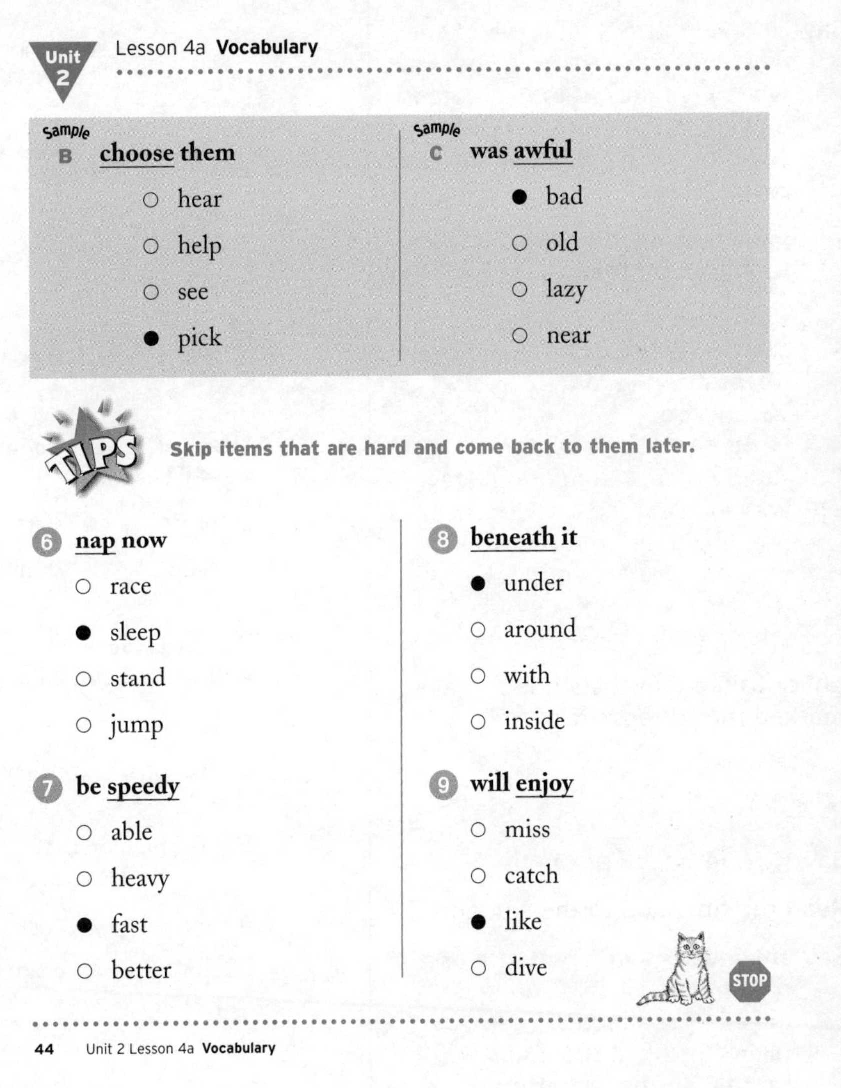

Unit 2 Lesson 4a **Vocabulary**

Sample B **choose them**
- ○ hear
- ○ help
- ○ see
- ● pick

Sample C **was awful**
- ● bad
- ○ old
- ○ lazy
- ○ near

TIPS **Skip items that are hard and come back to them later.**

6 **nap now**
- ○ race
- ● sleep
- ○ stand
- ○ jump

7 **be speedy**
- ○ able
- ○ heavy
- ● fast
- ○ better

8 **beneath it**
- ● under
- ○ around
- ○ with
- ○ inside

9 **will enjoy**
- ○ miss
- ○ catch
- ● like
- ○ dive

STOP

44 Unit 2 Lesson 4a **Vocabulary**

TIPS

Say Now let's look at the tip.

Read the tip aloud to the students.

Say Sometimes you might find that an item is hard and that you can't find the answer right away. When this happens, skip the item and come back to it later. Don't get stuck on one item, or you won't be able to do the others.

Elaborate the discussion of skipping an item to be sure the students understand what it means.

Say Put your finger on Number 6. For Numbers 6 through 9, mark the circle for the answer that means about the same as the underlined word in the phrase. Work until you come to the STOP sign after Number 9. Start working now.

Allow time for the students to complete the items.

Say Look at the next page, page 45.

Check to be sure the students have found the right page.

Sample D

Say Find Sample D at the top of the page. Read the story to yourself while I read it out loud. There is a blank in the story. When I come to the blank, I will say the word "blank."

The blank deer was shy. It stood beside its mother.

Now look at the answer choices. Which answer choice fits best in the blank? *(pause)* The answer is *young*. It fits best in the blank. The sentence should read, "The *young* deer was shy. It stood beside its mother." Mark the circle beside the first answer, *young*. Be sure the circle is completely filled in with a dark mark.

Check to see that the students have marked the correct circle.

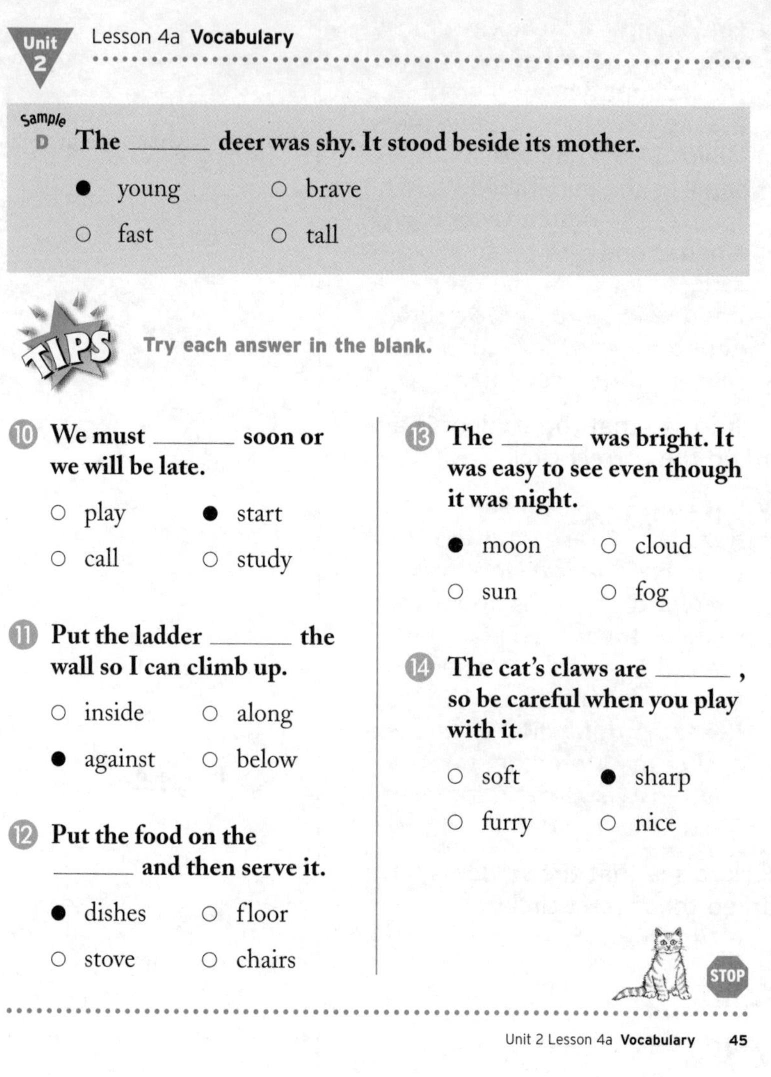

Unit 2 Lesson 4a **Vocabulary**

Sample D The ______ deer was shy. It stood beside its mother.

- ● young ○ brave
- ○ fast ○ tall

TIPS Try each answer in the blank.

10 We must ______ soon or we will be late.

- ○ play ● start
- ○ call ○ study

11 Put the ladder ______ the wall so I can climb up.

- ○ inside ○ along
- ● against ○ below

12 Put the food on the ______ and then serve it.

- ● dishes ○ floor
- ○ stove ○ chairs

13 The ______ was bright. It was easy to see even though it was night.

- ● moon ○ cloud
- ○ sun ○ fog

14 The cat's claws are ______, so be careful when you play with it.

- ○ soft ● sharp
- ○ furry ○ nice

STOP

Unit 2 Lesson 4a **Vocabulary** 45

TIPS

Say Now let's look at the tip.

Read the tip aloud to the students.

Say The meaning of a sentence or a paragraph will help you find the meaning of a word. When you fill in a blank, it should make sense with the rest of the sentence or paragraph. One way to do this is to try each word in the blank. You don't have to try each word in the blank, but if you aren't sure which answer is correct, it is a good strategy to use.

Demonstrate for the Sample item how each answer choice can be substituted in the blank.

Say Put your finger on Number 10. For Numbers 10 through 14, I will read the story out loud while you read it to yourself. Then you will look at the answer choices and find the word that fits best in each blank. If you aren't sure which answer is correct, try each one in the blank. Mark the circle for your answer. Work until you come to the STOP sign after Number 14. Fill in each answer circle with a dark mark and completely erase any marks for answers you change. Do you have any questions? Let's begin.

Allow time between items for the students to fill in their answers.

Say Number 10. Listen carefully. "We must blank soon or we will be late." Mark your answer.

Number 11. Listen carefully. "Put the ladder blank the wall so I can climb up." Mark your answer.

Number 12. Listen carefully. "Put the food on the blank and then serve it." Mark your answer.

Number 13. Listen carefully. "The blank was bright. It was easy to see even though it was night." Mark your answer.

Number 14. Listen carefully. "The cat's claws are blank, so be careful when you play with it." Mark your answer.

It's time to stop. You have finished Lesson 4a.

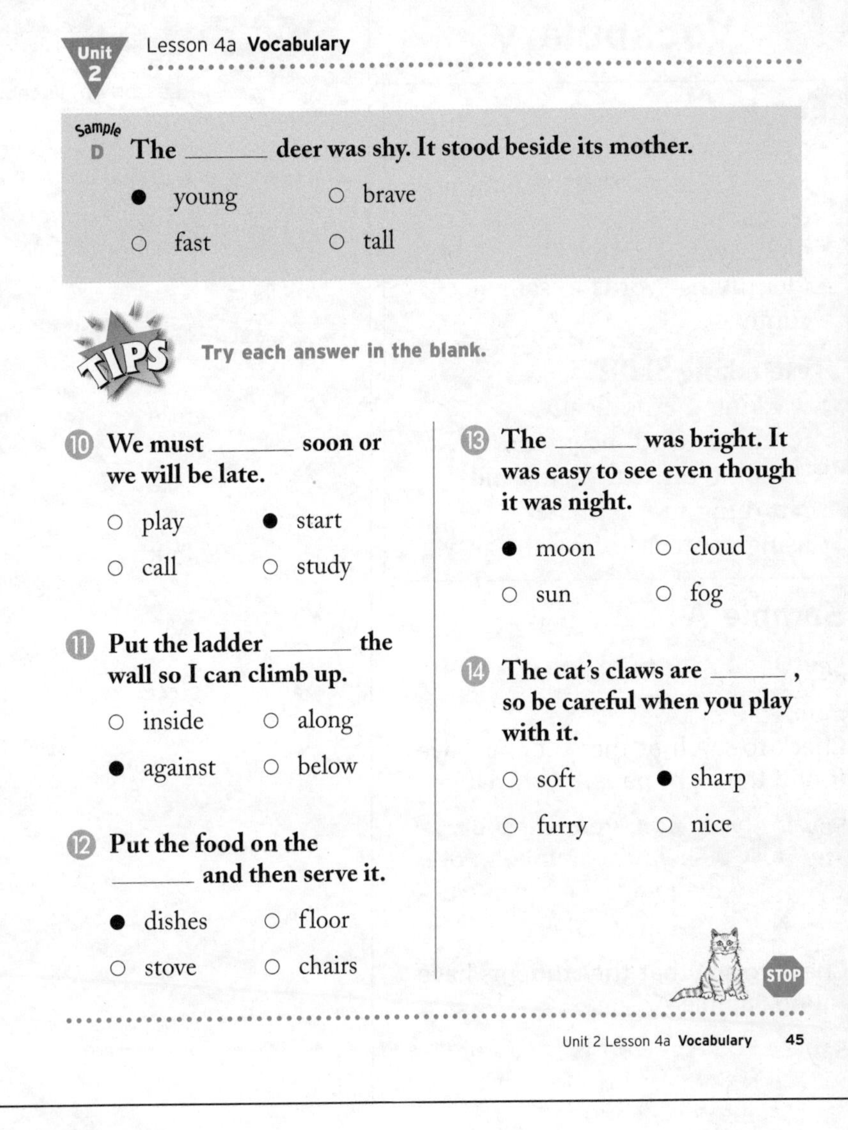

Unit 2 Lesson 4a **Vocabulary**

Sample D **The ______ deer was shy. It stood beside its mother.**

- ● young
- ○ brave
- ○ fast
- ○ tall

TIPS **Try each answer in the blank.**

10 **We must ______ soon or we will be late.**

- ○ play
- ● start
- ○ call
- ○ study

11 **Put the ladder ______ the wall so I can climb up.**

- ○ inside
- ○ along
- ● against
- ○ below

12 **Put the food on the ______ and then serve it.**

- ● dishes
- ○ floor
- ○ stove
- ○ chairs

13 **The ______ was bright. It was easy to see even though it was night.**

- ● moon
- ○ cloud
- ○ sun
- ○ fog

14 **The cat's claws are ______, so be careful when you play with it.**

- ○ soft
- ● sharp
- ○ furry
- ○ nice

STOP

Unit 2 Lesson 4a **Vocabulary** 45

Review the answers with the students. Discuss the meaning of each story and how it determines which answer is correct. For each item, try each answer in the blank and show how only one fits best with the meaning of the sentence.

Have the students indicate completion of the lesson by entering their score for this activity on the progress chart at the beginning of the book. Provide the students whatever help is necessary to record their scores.

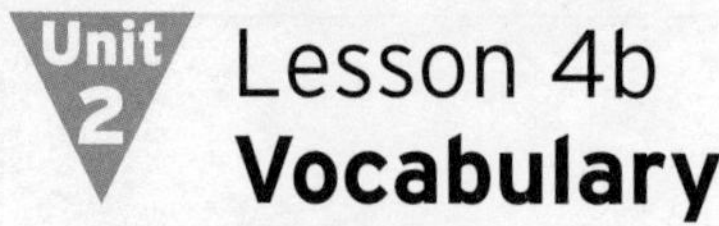

Lesson 4b Vocabulary

Focus

Vocabulary Skills
- identifying words from oral definitions
- identifying synonyms
- identifying words in sentence context

Test-taking Skills
- working methodically
- recalling word meanings
- skipping difficult items and returning to them later
- using context to find the answer

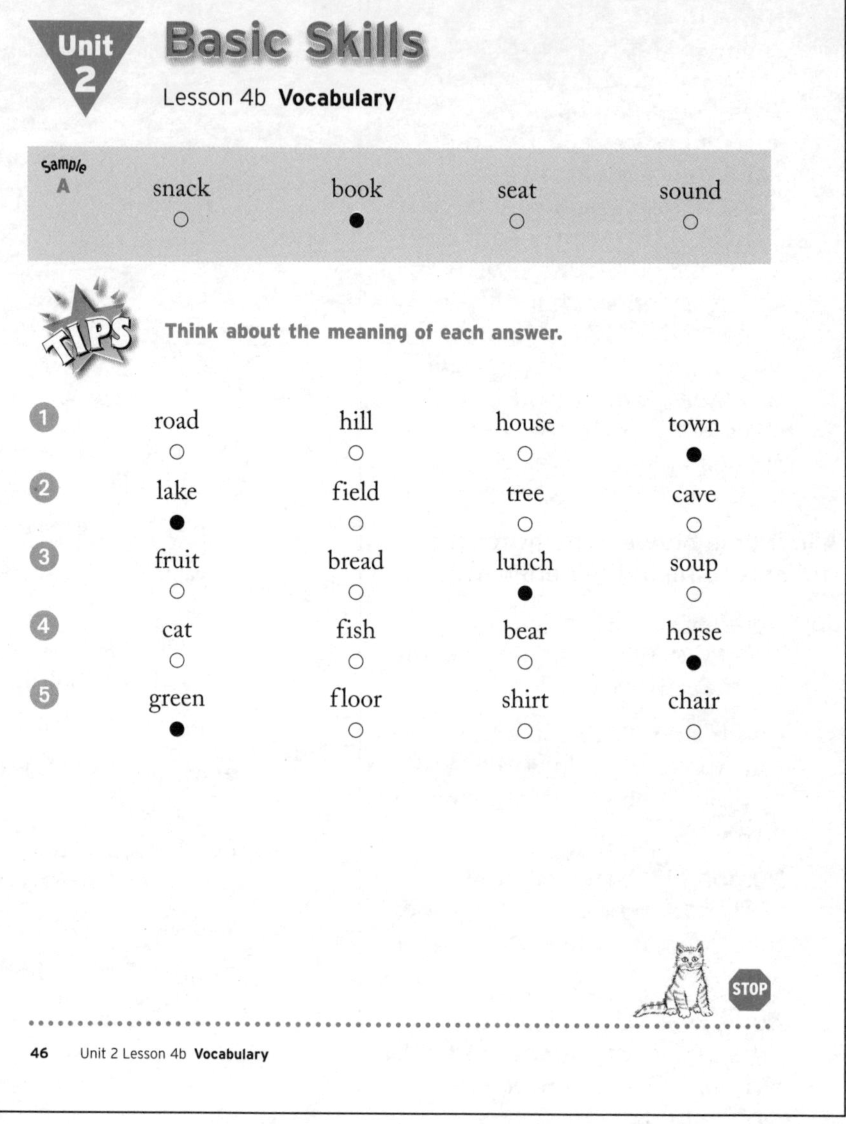

Unit 2 **Basic Skills**

Lesson 4b **Vocabulary**

Sample A	snack ○	book ●	seat ○	sound ○

TIPS Think about the meaning of each answer.

1	road ○	hill ○	house ○	town ●
2	lake ●	field ○	tree ○	cave ○
3	fruit ○	bread ○	lunch ●	soup ○
4	cat ○	fish ○	bear ○	horse ●
5	green ●	floor ○	shirt ○	chair ○

STOP

46 Unit 2 Lesson 4b **Vocabulary**

Sample A

Say Open your book to Lesson 4b on page 46.

Check to see that the students have found the right page.

Say In this lesson, you will show how well you remember more word meanings. Find Sample A at the top of the page.

Check to see that the students have found Sample A.

Say Look at the words for Sample A. Find the word that means "something you read ... something you read" *(pause)* The answer is *book*. Mark the circle under *book*. Be sure your answer circle is completely filled in with a dark mark.

Check to see that the students have marked the correct circle.

TIPS

Say Now let's look at the tip.

Read the tip aloud to the students.

Say As you listen to what I say, look at each answer and think about what the word means. Choose the answer that means about the same as what I say.

Practice

Say Now you will do the Practice items. Listen carefully to what I say and think about the definition. Find the answer choice that matches the definition. Mark only one circle for each item. Make sure the circle is completely filled in and remember to press your pencil firmly so your mark comes out dark. Do not write anything except your answer choices in your book. Completely erase any marks for answers you change.

Allow time between items for the students to fill in their answers.

Say Put your finger beside Number 1. Look at the words. Find the word that means "a small city ... a small city." Mark your answer.

Number 2. Look at the words. Find the word that means "a body of water ... a body of water." Mark your answer.

Number 3. Look at the words. Find the word that means "the name of a meal ... the name of a meal." Mark your answer.

Number 4. Look at the words. Find the word that means "an animal you ride ... an animal you ride." Mark your answer.

Number 5. Look at the words. Find the word that means "a color ... a color." Mark your answer.

Allow the students a moment to rest.

Say Look at the next page, page 47.

Check to be sure the students have found the right page.

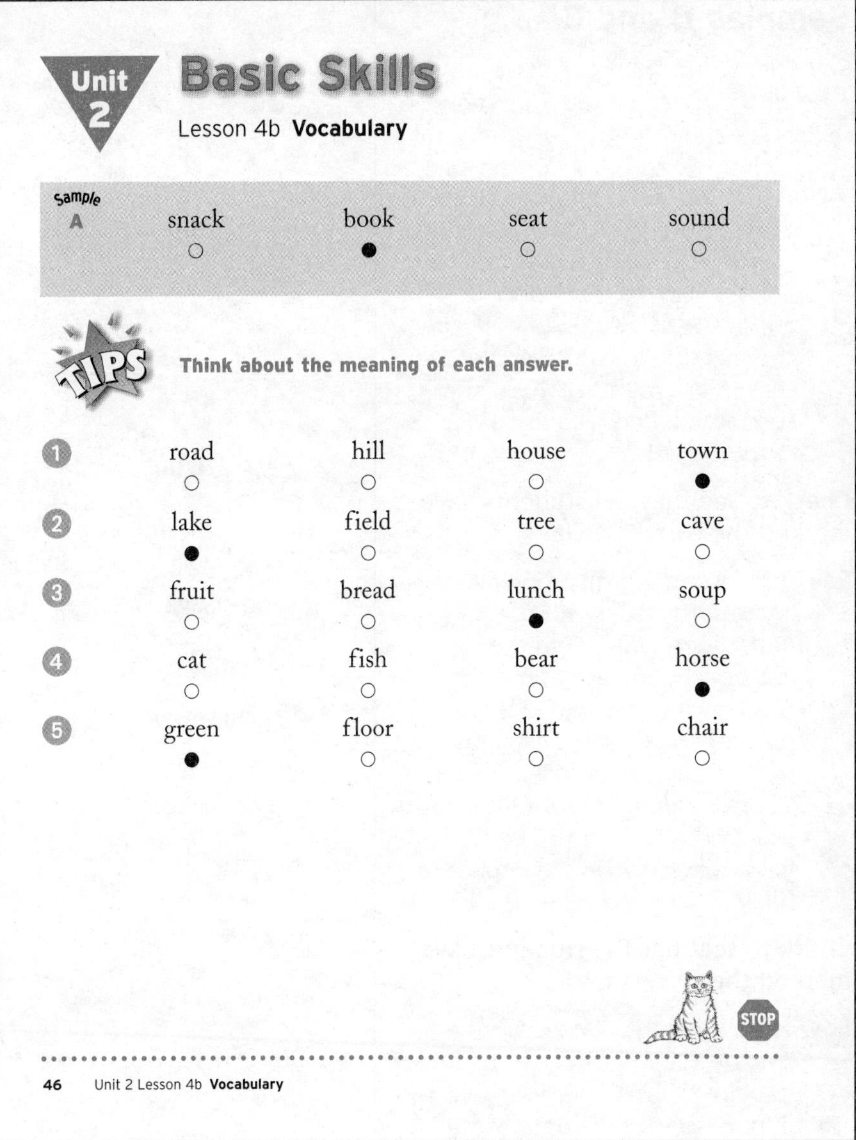

Samples B and C

Say Find Sample B. Read the phrase with the underlined word and think about what the word means. Now look at the answers. Which answer means about the same as the underlined word? *(pause)* The right answer is *father*. *Dad* and *father* mean about the same thing. Mark the circle beside the word *father*. Be sure your answer circle is completely filled in with a dark mark.

Check to see that the students have marked the correct circle.

Say Put your finger on Sample C. Read the phrase with the underlined word. Find the answer that means about the same as the underlined word. *(pause)* The correct answer is *dash*. *Dash* and *run* mean about the same thing. Mark the circle beside the word *dash*. Be sure your answer circle is completely filled in with a dark mark.

Check to see that the students have marked the correct circle.

Say Put your finger on Number 6. For Numbers 6 through 9, mark the circle for the answer that means about the same as the underlined word in the phrase. Work until you come to the STOP sign after Number 9. Start working now.

Allow time for the students to complete the items.

Say Look at the next page, page 48.

Check to be sure the students have found the right page.

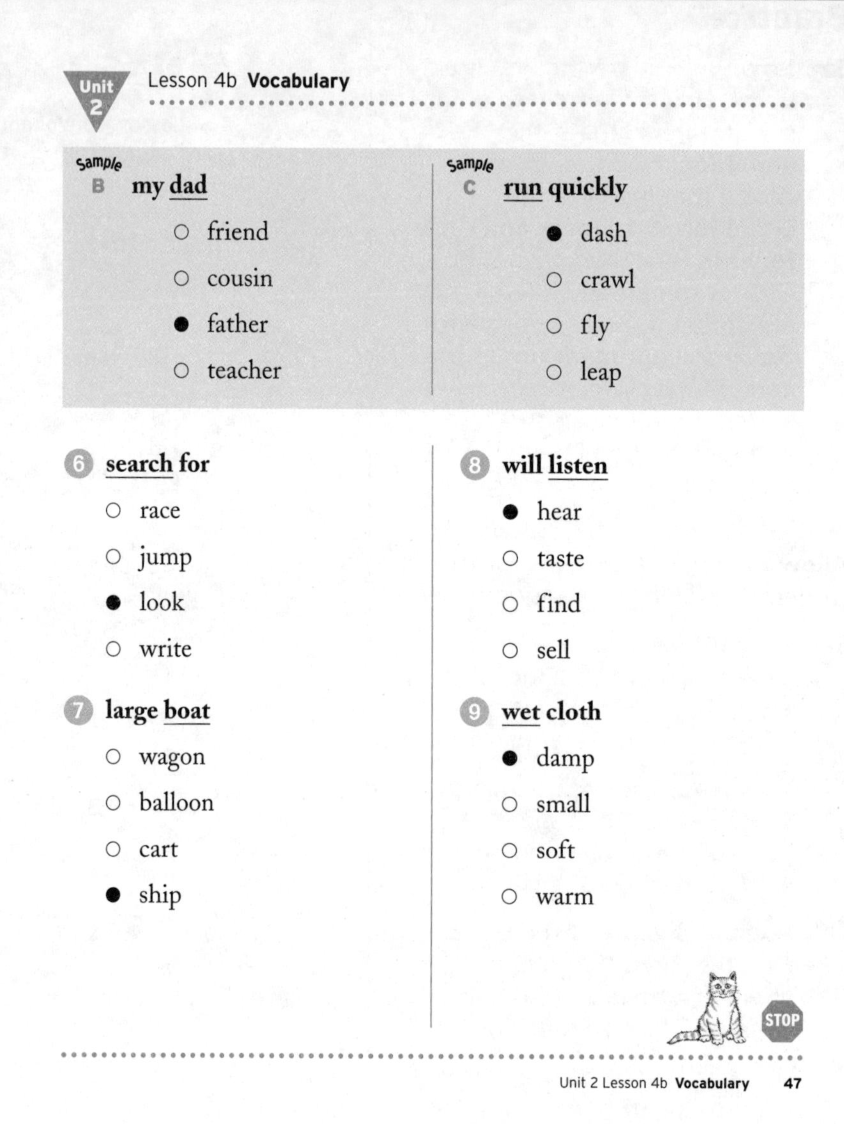

Unit 2 Lesson 4b **Vocabulary**

Sample B **my dad**

- ○ friend
- ○ cousin
- ● father
- ○ teacher

Sample C **run quickly**

- ● dash
- ○ crawl
- ○ fly
- ○ leap

6 **search for**

- ○ race
- ○ jump
- ● look
- ○ write

7 **large boat**

- ○ wagon
- ○ balloon
- ○ cart
- ● ship

8 **will listen**

- ● hear
- ○ taste
- ○ find
- ○ sell

9 **wet cloth**

- ● damp
- ○ small
- ○ soft
- ○ warm

Unit 2 Lesson 4b **Vocabulary** 47

Sample D

Say Find Sample D at the top of the page. Read the story to yourself while I read it out loud. There is a blank in the story. When I come to the blank, I will say the word "blank."

The ice was blank. We couldn't walk on it.

Now look at the answer choices. Which answer choice fits best in the blank? *(pause)* The answer is *thin*. It fits best in the blank. The sentence should read, "The ice was *thin*. We couldn't walk on it." Mark the circle beside the word *thin*. Be sure the circle is completely filled in with a dark mark.

Check to see that the students have marked the correct circle.

Say Put your finger on Number 10. For Numbers 10 through 15, I will read the story out loud while you read it to yourself. You will find the word that fits best in each blank. Mark the circle for your answer. You will work until you come to the STOP sign after Number 15. Fill in each answer circle with a dark mark and completely erase any marks for answers you change. Do you have any questions? Let's begin.

Unit 2 Lesson 4b **Vocabulary**

Sample D The ice was ______. We couldn't walk on it.

○ safe ○ thick
● thin ○ cold

10 The box was so heavy it took two of us to ______ it.

● lift ○ find
○ see ○ buy

11 The oven is hot. Now we can ______ the cookies.

○ taste ○ buy
○ eat ● bake

12 Put your coat in the ______ and then close the door.

○ garden ● closet
○ box ○ oven

13 The dog was ______. It made a lot of noise.

○ running ○ sleeping
● barking ○ eating

14 The truck was ______. It could not fit in the street.

● huge ○ loaded
○ fast ○ moving

15 Dad made a ______. It was Mom's birthday.

○ sandwich ● cake
○ garden ○ joke

STOP

48 Unit 2 Lesson 4b **Vocabulary**

Allow time between items for the students to fill in their answers.

Say Number 10. Listen carefully. "The box was so heavy it took two of us to blank it." Mark your answer.

Number 11. Listen carefully. "The oven is hot. Now we can blank the cookies." Mark your answer.

Number 12. Listen carefully. "Put your coat in the blank and then close the door." Mark your answer.

Number 13. Listen carefully. "The dog was blank. It made a lot of noise." Mark your answer.

Number 14. Listen carefully. "The truck was blank. It could not fit in the street." Mark your answer.

Number 15. Listen carefully. "Dad made a blank. It was Mom's birthday." Mark your answer.

It's time to stop. You have finished Lesson 4b.

Review the answers with the students. Discuss the meaning of each answer choice and why the correct answer is the right choice.

Have the students indicate completion of the lesson by entering their score for this activity on the progress chart at the beginning of the book. Provide the students whatever help is necessary to record their scores.

Unit 2 Lesson 5a Mathematics Computation

Focus

Computation Skills

- adding whole numbers
- subtracting whole numbers

Test-taking Skills

- working methodically
- converting problems to a workable format
- transferring numbers accurately to scratch paper
- computing carefully

Sample A

Distribute scratch paper to the students.

Say Open your book to Lesson 5a on page 49.

Check to see that the students have found the right page.

Say In this lesson, you will show how well you can solve arithmetic problems. Listen very carefully to what I say. When you answer a question, fill in the circle for the answer you think is right. Don't write anything else on the page. If you want to work a problem, use the scratch paper I gave you. Find Sample A at the top of the page.

Check to see that the students have found Sample A.

Say Look at the addition problem and the numbers beside it. Which answer is the solution to the problem? *(pause)* The second answer, 5, is correct. Mark the circle for the second answer. Be sure your answer circle is completely filled in with a dark mark.

Check to see that the students have marked the correct circle.

Say Now let's look at the tip.

Read the tip aloud to the students.

Basic Skills

Lesson 5a **Mathematics Computation**

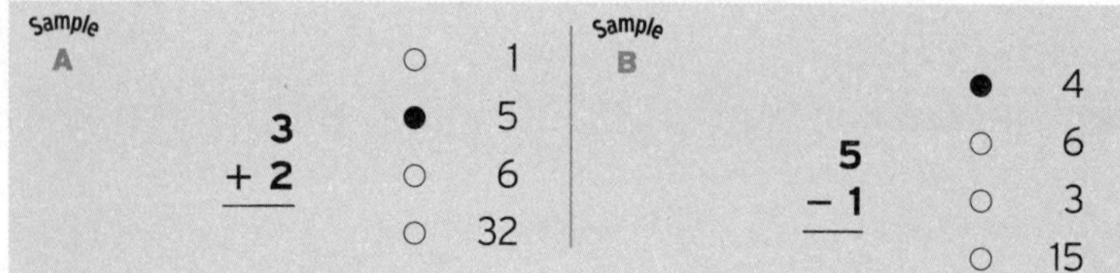

Sample A: 3 + 2 — ○ 1, ● 5, ○ 6, ○ 32

Sample B: 5 − 1 — ● 4, ○ 6, ○ 3, ○ 15

Pay attention to the operation sign so you know what to do.

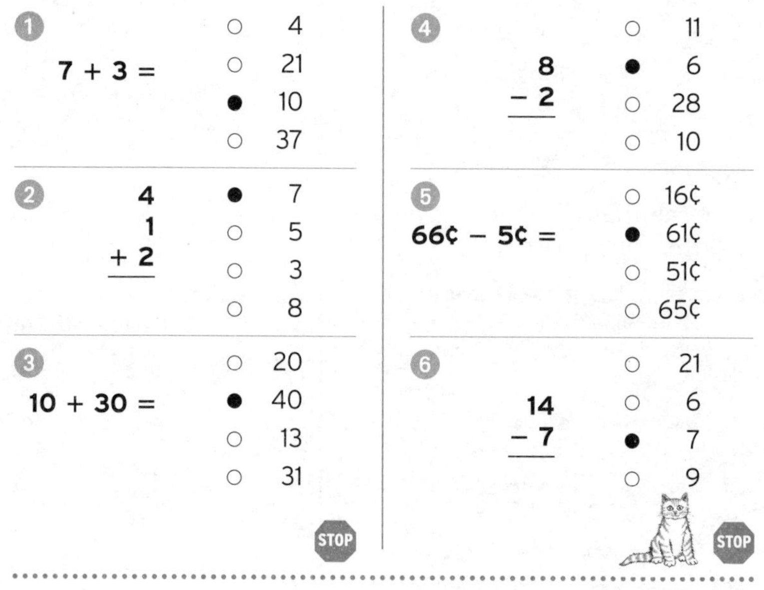

1. 7 + 3 = — ○ 4, ○ 21, ● 10, ○ 37
2. 4 + 1 + 2 — ● 7, ○ 5, ○ 3, ○ 8
3. 10 + 30 = — ○ 20, ● 40, ○ 13, ○ 31

STOP

4. 8 − 2 — ○ 11, ● 6, ○ 28, ○ 10
5. 66¢ − 5¢ = — ○ 16¢, ● 61¢, ○ 51¢, ○ 65¢
6. 14 − 7 — ○ 21, ○ 6, ● 7, ○ 9

STOP

Unit 2 Lesson 5a **Mathematics Computation** 49

Say In this lesson, you should pay attention the operation signs for each problem so you know what do do.

Practice

Say You will do Numbers 1 through 3 by yourself. You can work on scratch paper to solve the problems, if you wish. Mark only one circle for each item. Make sure the circle is completely filled in and remember to press your pencil firmly so your mark comes out dark. Do not write anything except your answer choices in your book. Completely erase any marks for answers you change. Work until you come to the STOP sign after Number 3. Are you ready? You may begin. Remember, these are addition items.

Allow time for the students to fill in their answers. Walk around the room to make sure the students stop after Number 3.

Sample B

Say Find Sample B at the top of the page.

Check to see that the students have found Sample B.

Say This is a subtraction problem. Look at the problem and the numbers beside it. Which answer is the solution to the problem "five minus one"? *(pause)* The first answer, 4, is correct. Mark the circle for the first answer. Be sure your answer circle is completely filled in with a dark mark.

Check to see that the students have marked the correct circle.

Say Now you will do Numbers 4 through 6 by yourself. You can work on scratch paper to solve the problems, if you wish. Mark only one circle for each item. Make sure the circle is completely filled in and remember to press your pencil firmly so your mark comes out dark. Do not write anything except your answer choices in your book. Completely erase any marks for answers you change. Work until you come to the STOP sign after Number 6. Are you ready? You may begin. Remember, these are subtraction items.

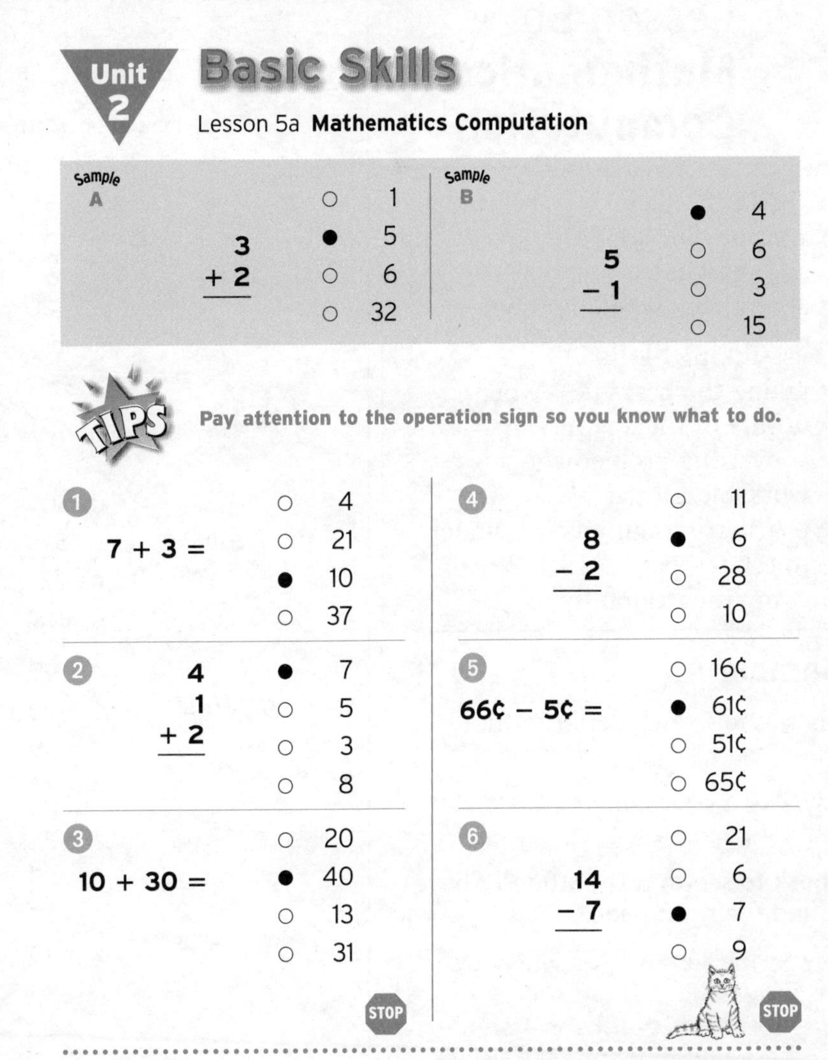

Unit 2 **Basic Skills**

Lesson 5a **Mathematics Computation**

Sample A

$3 + 2$

○ 1
● 5
○ 6
○ 32

Sample B

$5 - 1$

● 4
○ 6
○ 3
○ 15

TIPS **Pay attention to the operation sign so you know what to do.**

1. $7 + 3 =$
○ 4
○ 21
● 10
○ 37

2. $4 + 1 + 2$
● 7
○ 5
○ 3
○ 8

3. $10 + 30 =$
○ 20
● 40
○ 13
○ 31

STOP

4. $8 - 2$
○ 11
● 6
○ 28
○ 10

5. 66¢ − 5¢ =
○ 16¢
● 61¢
○ 51¢
○ 65¢

6. $14 - 7$
○ 21
○ 6
● 7
○ 9

STOP

Unit 2 Lesson 5a **Mathematics Computation** 49

Allow time for the students to fill in their answers.

Say It's time to stop. You have finished Lesson 5a. Check to see that you have filled in your answer circles completely with dark marks.

Review the answers with the students. Solve each problem on the chalkboard, emphasizing the operation sign and all the steps. Demonstrate how some of the answer choices are correct if you use the wrong operation.

Have the students indicate completion of the lesson by entering their score for this activity on the progress chart at the beginning of the book. Provide the students whatever help is necessary to record their scores.

Lesson 5b Mathematics Computation

Focus

Computation Skills

- adding whole numbers
- subtracting whole numbers

Test-taking Skills

- taking the best guess when unsure of the answer
- converting problems to a workable format
- transferring numbers accurately to scratch paper
- computing carefully

Sample A

Distribute scratch paper to the students.

Say Open your book to Lesson 5b on page 50.

Check to see that the students have found the right page.

Say In this lesson, you will show how well you can solve arithmetic problems. Listen very carefully to what I say. When you answer a question, fill in the circle for the answer you think is right. Don't write anything else on the page. If you want to work a problem, use the scratch paper I gave you. Find Sample A at the top of the page.

Check to see that the students have found Sample A.

Say Look at the addition problem and the numbers beside it. Which answer is the solution to the problem? *(pause)* The first answer, *12*, is correct. Mark the circle for the first answer. Be sure your answer circle is completely filled in with a dark mark.

Check to see that the students have marked the correct circle.

Basic Skills

Lesson 5b **Mathematics Computation**

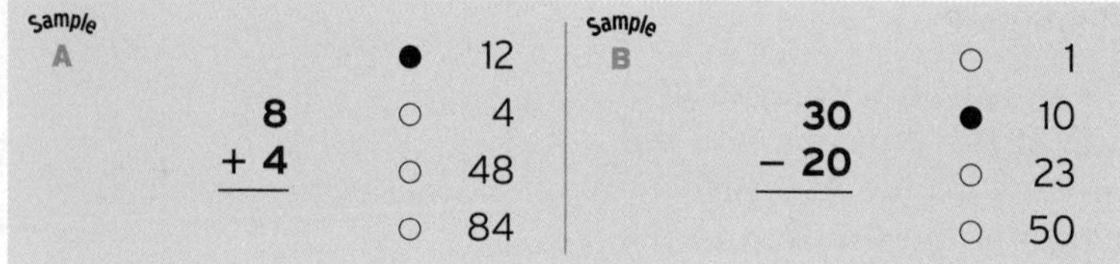

Sample A: 8 + 4 — ● 12 ○ 4 ○ 48 ○ 84

Sample B: 30 − 20 — ○ 1 ● 10 ○ 23 ○ 50

If you are not sure which answer is correct, mark the answer you think might be right.

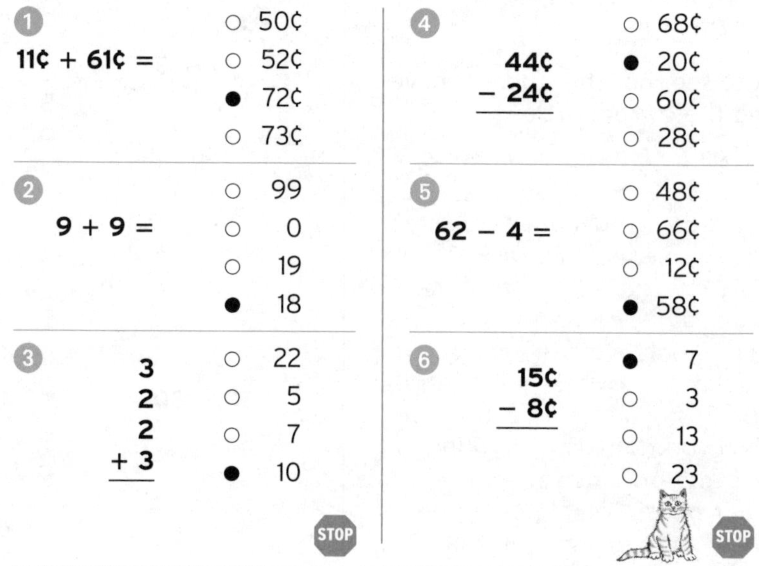

1. 11¢ + 61¢ = — ○ 50¢ ○ 52¢ ● 72¢ ○ 73¢
2. 9 + 9 = — ○ 99 ○ 0 ○ 19 ● 18
3. 3 + 2 + 2 + 3 — ○ 22 ○ 5 ○ 7 ● 10
4. 44¢ − 24¢ — ○ 68¢ ● 20¢ ○ 60¢ ○ 28¢
5. 62 − 4 = — ○ 48¢ ○ 66¢ ○ 12¢ ● 58¢
6. 15¢ − 8¢ — ● 7 ○ 3 ○ 13 ○ 23

STOP

50 Unit 2 Lesson 5b **Mathematics Computation**

TIPS

Say Now let's look at the tip.

Read the tip aloud to the students.

Say Sometimes when you take a test, you won't be sure which answer is correct. When this happens, take your best guess. This means you should choose the answer you think might be right. It is better to guess than to leave an item blank.

Practice

Say You will do Numbers 1 through 3 by yourself. You can work on scratch paper to solve the problems, if you wish. Mark only one circle for each item. Make sure the circle is completely filled in and remember to press your pencil firmly so your mark comes out dark. Do not write anything except your answer choices in your book. Completely erase any marks for answers you change. Work until you come to the STOP sign after Number 3. Are you ready? You may begin. Remember, these are addition items.

Allow time for the students to fill in their answers. Walk around the room to make sure the students stop after Number 3.

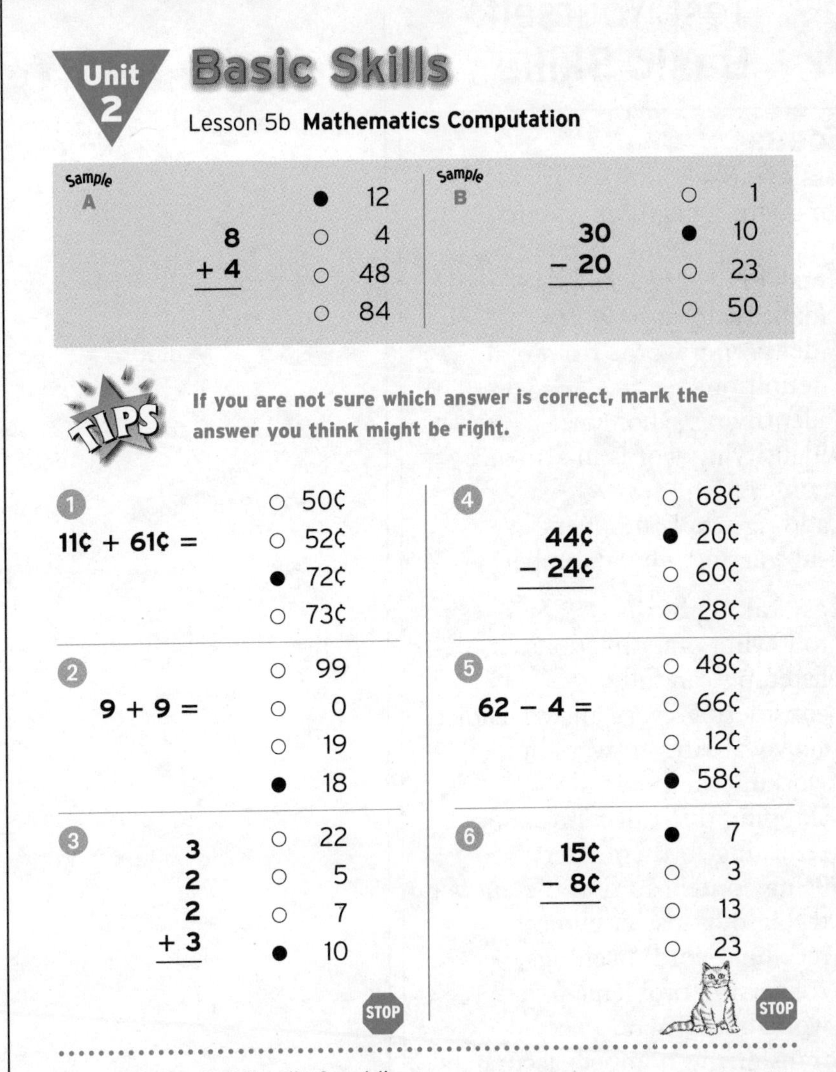

Sample B

Say Find Sample B at the top of the page.

Check to see that the students have found Sample B.

Say This is a subtraction problem. Look at the problem and the numbers beside it. Which answer is the solution to the problem "thirty minus twenty"? *(pause)* The second answer, *10*, is correct. Mark the circle for the second answer. Be sure your answer circle is completely filled in with a dark mark.

Check to see that the students have marked the correct circle.

Say Now you will do Numbers 4 through 6 by yourself. You can work on scratch paper to solve the problems, if you wish. Mark only one circle for each item. Make sure the circle is completely filled in and remember to press your pencil firmly so your mark comes out dark. Do not write anything except your answer choices in your book. Completely erase any marks for answers you change. Work until you come to the STOP sign after Number 6. Are you ready? You may begin. Remember, these are subtraction items.

Allow time for the students to fill in their answers.

Say It's time to stop. You have finished Lesson 5b. Check to see that you have filled in your answer circles completely with dark marks.

Review the answers with the students. Solve each problem on the chalkboard, emphasizing the operation sign and all the steps. Be sure students understand the meaning of the cents symbol. Review the addition of three numbers, if necessary.

Have the students indicate completion of the lesson by entering their score for this activity on the progress chart at the beginning of the book. Provide the students whatever help is necessary to record their scores.

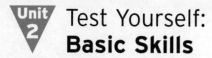

Unit 2

Test Yourself: **Basic Skills**

Focus

Basic Skills

- matching beginning sounds
- matching ending sounds
- matching vowel sounds
- identifying sight words
- identifying words from oral definitions
- identifying synonyms
- identifying words in sentence context
- adding whole numbers
- subtracting whole numbers

Test-taking Skills

- following oral directions
- listening carefully
- considering every answer choice
- subvocalizing answer choices
- working methodically
- skipping difficult items and returning to them later
- using context to find the answer
- trying out answer choices
- recalling word meanings
- converting problems to a workable format
- transferring numbers accurately to scratch paper
- computing carefully
- taking the best guess when unsure of the answer

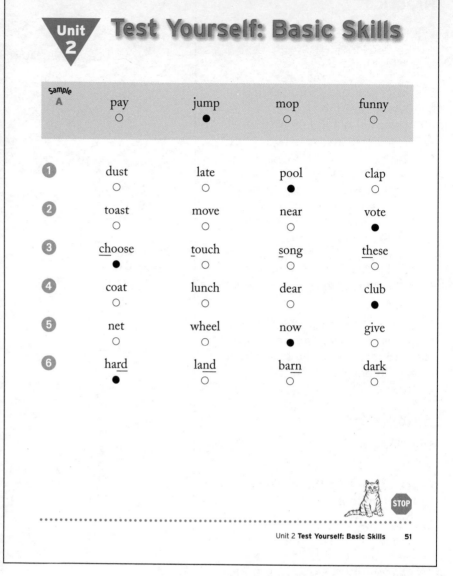

This lesson simulates an actual test-taking experience. Therefore, it is recommended that the directions be read verbatim and the suggested procedures be followed.

Directions

Administration Time: approximately 25 minutes

Distribute scratch paper to the students for the computation items.

Say **Turn to the Test Yourself lesson on page 51.**

Check to be sure the students have found the right page. Point out to the students that this is not a real test and that they will score it themselves to see how well they are doing.

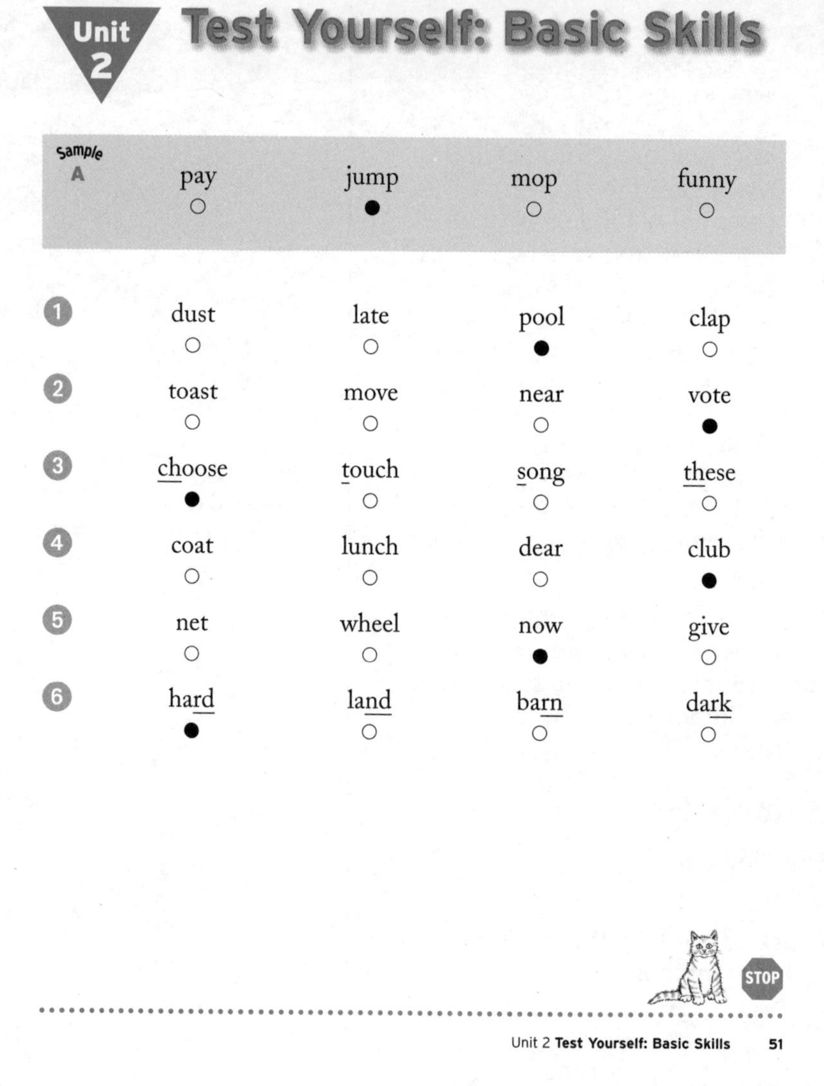

Unit 2 **Test Yourself: Basic Skills**

Sample A	pay ○	jump ●	mop ○	funny ○
1	dust ○	late ○	pool ●	clap ○
2	toast ○	move ○	near ○	vote ●
3	choose ●	touch ○	song ○	these ○
4	coat ○	lunch ○	dear ○	club ●
5	net ○	wheel ○	now ●	give ○
6	hard ●	land ○	barn ○	dark ○

Say **This lesson will check how well you remember some things you practiced in other lessons. Find Sample A at the top of the page. Look at the words. Find the word that has the same beginning sound as "joke ... joke."** *(pause)* **The second answer, *jump*, is correct. *Joke* and *jump* begin with the same sound. Mark the circle for the second answer. Be sure your answer circle is completely filled in with a dark mark.**

Check to see that the students have filled in the correct answer circle.

Say Now you will do the Test Yourself items. Listen carefully to what I say because there are many different kinds of items in this part. Are you ready? Let's begin.

Allow time between items for the students to fill in their answers.

Say Put your finger beside Number 1. Look at the four words. Find the word that has the same beginning sound as "park ... park." Mark your answer.

Number 2. Look at the words. Find the word that has the same beginning sound as "van ... van." Mark your answer.

Number 3. Look at the words. The beginning part of each word is underlined. This is the part of the word I want you to listen to. Find the word that has the same beginning sound as "chest ... chest." Mark your answer.

Put your finger beside Number 4. This item is a little different. Look at the four words. Find the word that has the same ending sound as "knob ... knob." Mark your answer.

Number 5. Look at the words. Find the word that has the same ending sound as "stew ... stew." Mark your answer.

Number 6. Look at the words. The ending part of each word is underlined. This is the part of the word I want you to listen to. Find the word that has the same ending sound as "third ... third." Mark your answer.

Look at the next page, page 52.

Check to be sure the students have found the right page.

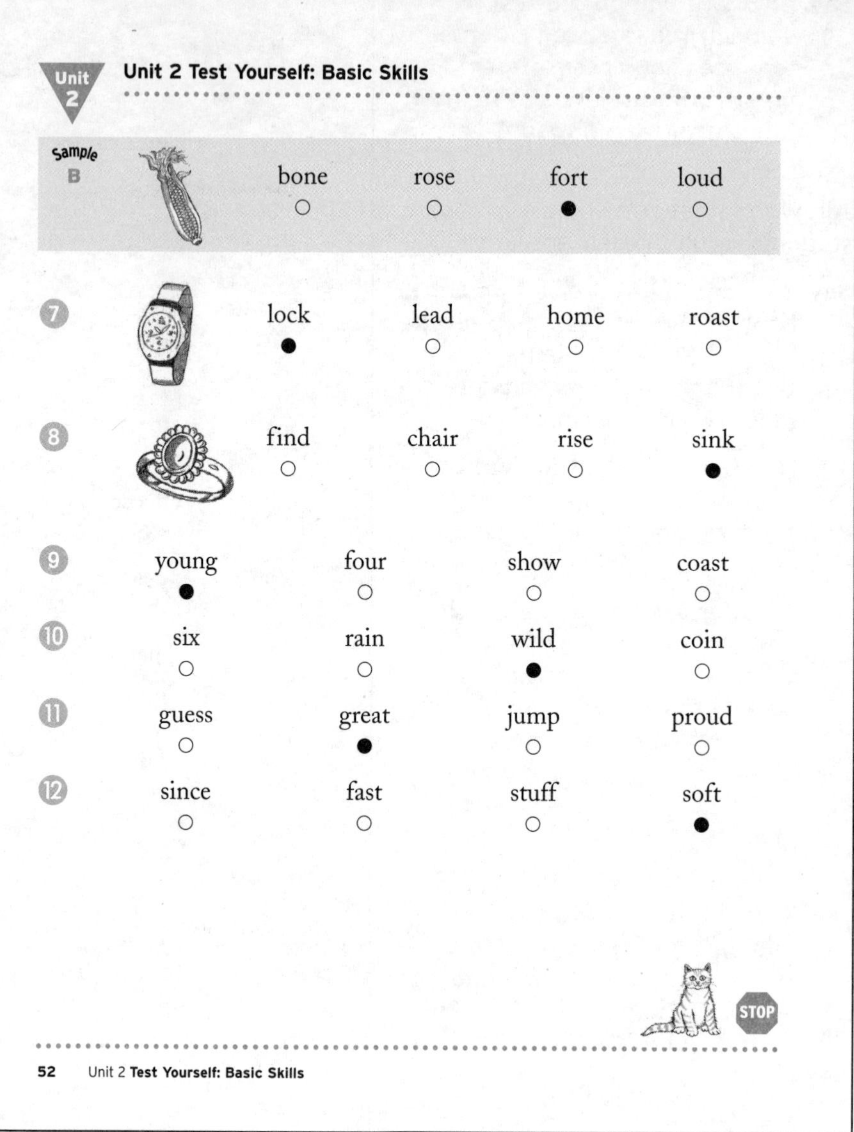
Unit 2 Test Yourself: Basic Skills

Sample B	(corn)	bone ○	rose ○	fort ●	loud ○
7	(watch)	lock ●	lead ○	home ○	roast ○
8	(ring)	find ○	chair ○	rise ○	sink ●
9		young ●	four ○	show ○	coast ○
10		six ○	rain ○	wild ●	coin ○
11		guess ○	great ●	jump ○	proud ○
12		since ○	fast ○	stuff ○	soft ●

STOP

52 Unit 2 Test Yourself: Basic Skills

Say Put your finger on Sample B at the top of the page. Look at the picture of the corn and the words beside it. Which word has the same vowel sound (middle sound) as "corn ... corn"? *(pause)* The correct answer is *fort*. Mark the circle for the third answer. Be sure your answer circle is completely filled in with a dark mark.

Check to see that the students have filled in the correct answer circle.

Say Remember, for these items, listen only for the vowel sound. This is the sound in the middle of the word. You must be sure to ignore the beginning and ending sounds.

Allow time between items for the students to fill in their answers.

Say Put your finger on Number 7. Look at the watch. Find the word that has the same vowel sound (middle sound) as "watch ... watch." Mark your answer.

Number 8. Look at the ring. Find the word that has the same vowel sound (middle sound) as "ring ... ring." Mark your answer.

Number 9. This is a different kind of item. Listen to this sentence: "My sister has a <u>bump</u> on her head." Look at the words. Find the word that has the same vowel sound (middle sound) as "bump ... bump." Mark your answer.

Number 10. Listen to this sentence: "<u>Nine</u> players are on a baseball team." Look at the words. Find the word that has the same vowel sound (middle sound) as "nine ... nine." Mark your answer.

Number 11. This item is also different. Listen to this sentence: "We saw a great big bear." Look at the words. Find the word "great ... great." Mark your answer.

Number 12. Listen to this sentence: "The new snow feels very soft." Look at the words. Find the word "soft ... soft. Mark your answer.

Look at the next page, page 53.

Check to be sure the students have found the right page.

Say Look at the words for Sample C at the top of the page. Find the word that means "a small horse ... a small horse." *(pause)* The correct answer is *pony*. Mark the circle for the last answer. Be sure your answer circle is completely filled in with a dark mark.

Check to see that the students have filled in the correct answer circle.

Say Now you will do more items like Sample C. Listen carefully to what I say and think about the definition. Find the answer choice that matches the definition. Mark the space for your answer. Are you ready? Let's begin.

Allow time between items for the students to fill in their answers.

Say Put your finger beside Number 13. Look at the words. Find the word that means "a color ... a color." Mark your answer.

Number 14. Look at the words. Find the word that means "a tool ... a tool." Mark your answer.

Pause for a moment.

Say Now you will do some different items. For Numbers 15 through 18, read the phrase with the underlined word. Find the answer that means about the same as the underlined word. Mark the space for your answer to each item. Are you ready? You may begin. Remember to stop after Number 18.

Allow time for the students to fill in their answers.

Say Look at the next page, page 54.

Check to be sure the students have found the right page.

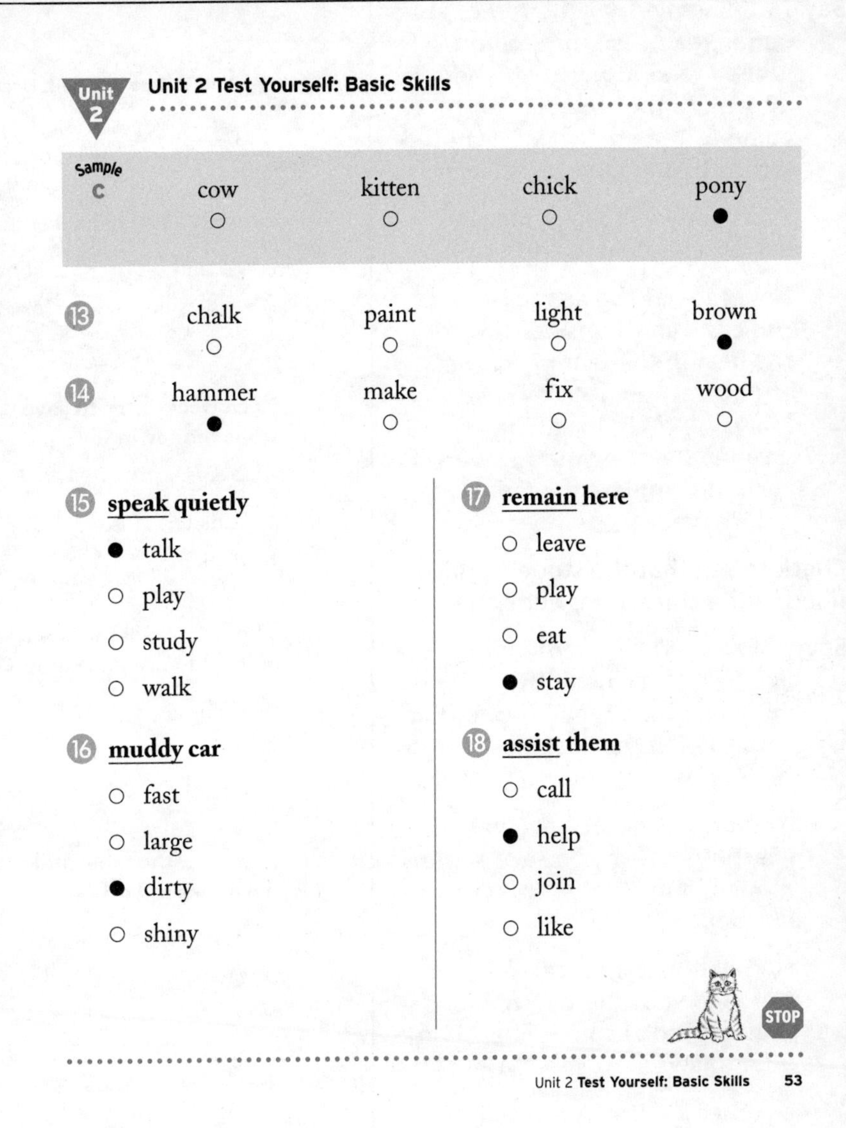
Unit 2 Test Yourself: Basic Skills

Sample C: cow ○ kitten ○ chick ○ pony ●

13. chalk ○ paint ○ light ○ brown ●

14. hammer ● make ○ fix ○ wood ○

15. speak quietly
- ● talk
- ○ play
- ○ study
- ○ walk

16. muddy car
- ○ fast
- ○ large
- ● dirty
- ○ shiny

17. remain here
- ○ leave
- ○ play
- ○ eat
- ● stay

18. assist them
- ○ call
- ● help
- ○ join
- ○ like

STOP

Unit 2 Test Yourself: Basic Skills 53

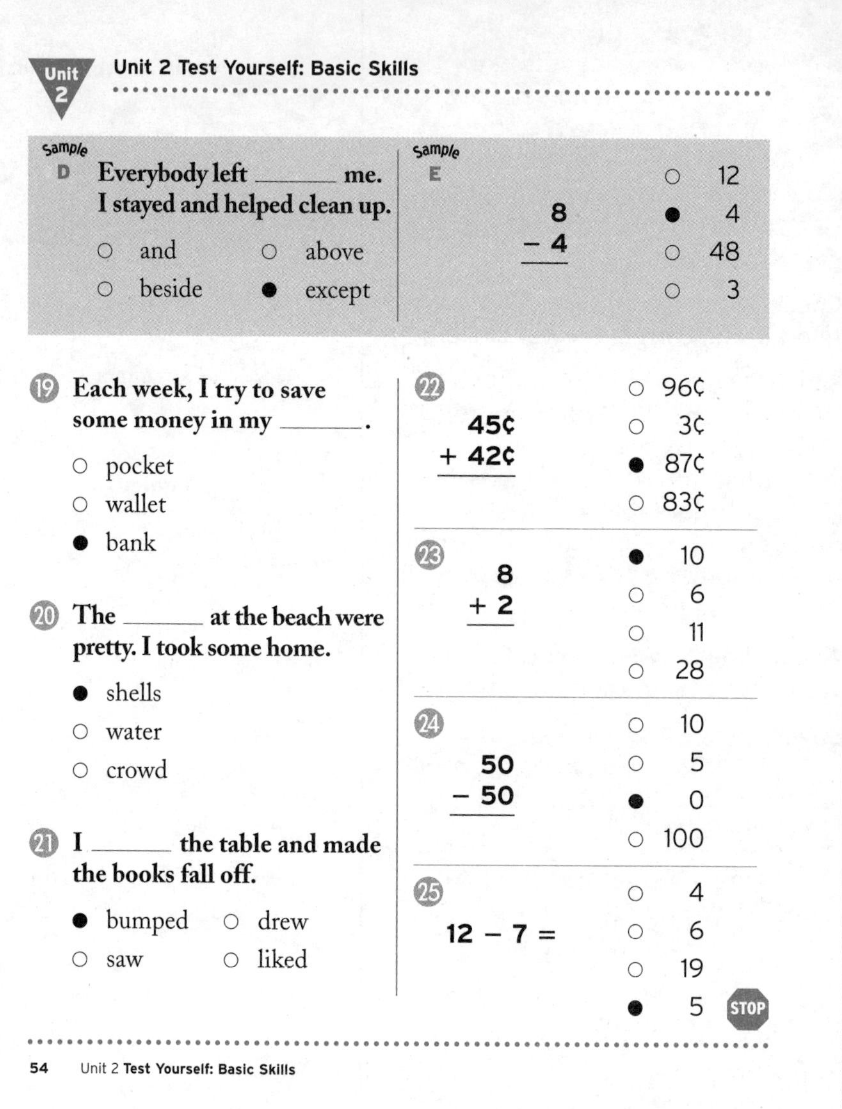
Unit 2

Unit 2 Test Yourself: Basic Skills

Sample D **Everybody left ______ me. I stayed and helped clean up.**

○ and ○ above
○ beside ● except

Sample E

$$\begin{array}{r} 8 \\ -\ 4 \\ \hline \end{array}$$

○ 12
● 4
○ 48
○ 3

19 **Each week, I try to save some money in my ______.**

○ pocket
○ wallet
● bank

20 **The ______ at the beach were pretty. I took some home.**

● shells
○ water
○ crowd

21 **I ______ the table and made the books fall off.**

● bumped ○ drew
○ saw ○ liked

22

$$\begin{array}{r} 45¢ \\ +\ 42¢ \\ \hline \end{array}$$

○ 96¢
○ 3¢
● 87¢
○ 83¢

23

$$\begin{array}{r} 8 \\ +\ 2 \\ \hline \end{array}$$

● 10
○ 6
○ 11
○ 28

24

$$\begin{array}{r} 50 \\ -\ 50 \\ \hline \end{array}$$

○ 10
○ 5
● 0
○ 100

25 $12 - 7 =$

○ 4
○ 6
○ 19
● 5

STOP

54 Unit 2 **Test Yourself: Basic Skills**

Say Find Sample D at the top of the page. Read the story to yourself while I read it out loud. There is a blank in the story. When I come to the blank, I will say the word "blank."

Everybody left blank me. I stayed and helped clean up.

Now look at the answer choices. Which answer choice fits best in the blank? *(pause)* The correct answer is *except*. Mark the circle for the last answer. Be sure your answer circle is completely filled in with a dark mark.

Check to see that the students have filled in the correct answer circle.

Say Now you will do more items like Sample D. Read the story to yourself while I read it out loud. Find the answer that fits best in the blank.

Number 19. Listen carefully. "Each week, I try to save some money in my blank." Mark your answer.

Number 20. Listen carefully. "The blank at the beach were pretty. I took some home." Mark your answer.

Number 21. Listen carefully. "I blank the table and made the books fall off." Mark your answer.

Pause for a moment.

Say Find Sample E at the top of the page. Look at the subtraction problem and the numbers beside it. Which answer is correct? You may use the scratch paper I gave you to solve the problem. *(pause)* The second answer, *4*, is correct. Mark the circle for the second answer. Be sure your answer circle is completely filled in with a dark mark.

Check to see that the students have filled in the correct answer circle.

Say Now you will do Numbers 22 through 25. Read each problem. Numbers 22 and 23 are addition problems. Numbers 24 and 25 are subtraction problems. Mark the space beside the correct answer to each problem. You can use the scratch paper I gave you to solve the problems, if you wish. Are you ready? You may begin.

Allow time for the students to fill in their answers.

Say It's time to stop. You have completed the Test Yourself lesson.

Review the answers with the students. Have the students indicate completion of the lesson by entering their score for this activity on the progress chart at the beginning of the book. Provide the students whatever help is necessary to record their scores.

Background

This unit contains three lessons that deal with mathematics skills. Students answer a variety of questions covering numeration, procedures, geometry and measurement, and graphs.

• **In Lessons 6a and 6b,** students solve mathematics problems. Students are encouraged to follow oral directions, listen carefully, and consider every answer choice. They identify and use key words, figures, or numbers; mark the right answer as soon as it is found; and refer to a graphic. They take the best guess when unsure of the answer.

• **In the Test Yourself lesson,** the mathematics and test-taking skills introduced and used in Lessons 6a and 6b are reinforced and presented in a format that gives students the experience of taking an achievement test.

Instructional Objectives

Lesson	Skill	Objective
Lesson 6a Lesson 6b	**Mathematics Skills** **Mathematics Skills**	Given a problem involving numeration, procedures, geometry and measurement, or a graph, students identify which of four answer choices is correct.
	Test Yourself	Given questions similar to those in Lessons 6a and 6b, students utilize mathematics skills and test-taking strategies on achievement test formats.

Lesson 6a Mathematics Skills

Focus

Mathematics Skills

- solving word problems
- using charts and graphs
- counting
- understanding time
- matching digital and analog times
- using nonstandard units of measurement

Test-taking Skills

- following oral directions
- listening carefully
- considering every answer choice
- identifying and using key words, figures, or numbers to find the answer
- marking the right answer as soon as it is found
- referring to a graphic
- taking the best guess when unsure of the answer

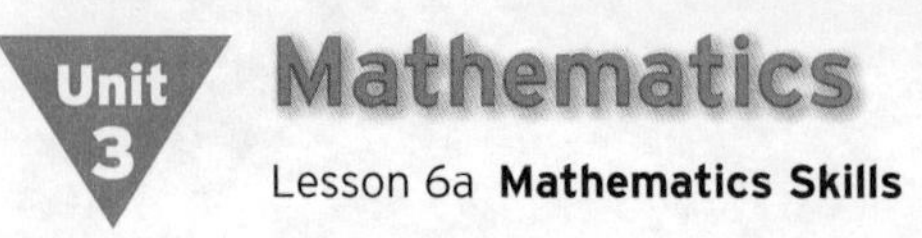

Lesson 6a **Mathematics Skills**

- **Listen carefully. Think about the question while you look at the answer choices.**
- **Listen for key words and numbers.**
- **As soon as you know which answer is right, mark it and get ready for the next item.**
- **If you aren't sure which answer is correct, take your best guess.**

Unit 3 Lesson 6a **Mathematics Skills** 55

Sample

Distribute scratch paper to the students.

Say Turn to Lesson 6a, on page 55. The page number is at the bottom of the page on the right. There are pictures for the Sample item.

Check to see that the students have found the right page.

Say In this lesson, you will do different kinds of mathematics problems. When you answer a question, mark the circle for the answer you think is right. Be sure your answer circle is completely filled in with a dark mark. Don't make any other marks in your book. If you have to work a problem, use the scratch paper I gave you. Put your finger under the sample.

Check to see that the students have found the sample.

Say Listen to the problem while you look at the sample. Rudy has one dollar. He used it to buy a book. After he paid for the book, he got three pennies back. Which book did he buy? *(pause)* The second answer choice is correct because the book cost ninety-seven cents. Mark the circle for the second answer. Be sure your answer circle is completely filled in with a dark mark.

Check to see that the students have marked the correct circle.

★TIPS

Say Now let's look at the tips.

Read the tips aloud to the students.

Say It is important that you listen carefully to the directions and look at all the answer choices before picking the one you think is correct. Important words and numbers I say, plus the numbers and pictures on the page, will help you find the answer. Another tip you should keep in mind is to mark the right answer as soon as you decide which choice it is. This will give you a chance to get ready for the next item. Once you have marked an answer, don't think about it any more. It is better to pay close attention to the next item rather than go back and change items you already marked. If you are not sure which answer choice is correct, take your best guess. It is better to guess than to leave an answer blank.

Look at the next page, page 56.

Check to be sure the students have found the right page.

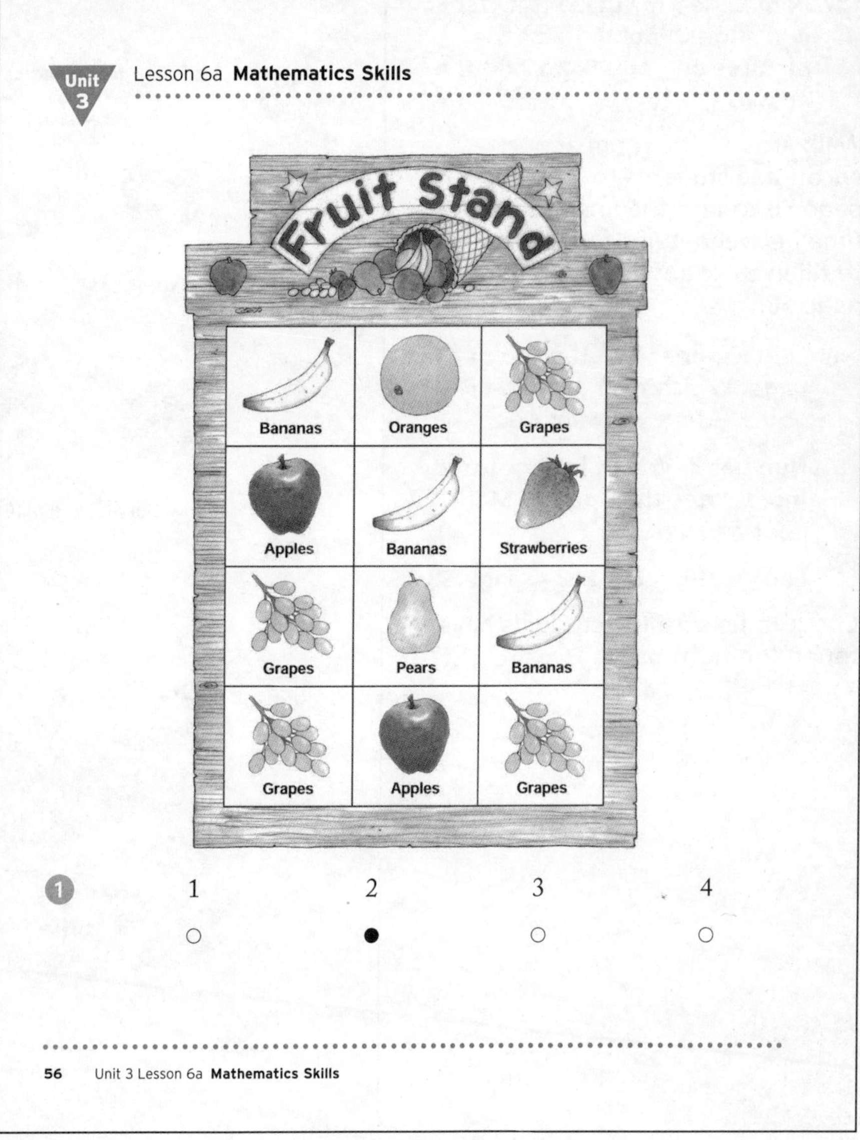

Practice

Say Now you will do some Practice items. Listen carefully to what I say while you look at each item. If you like, you can work the problem on the scratch paper I gave you. Mark the circles for your answers and make sure you fill in your answer circles completely with dark marks. Completely erase any marks for answers you change. Do you have any questions? Let's begin.

Allow time between items for the students to fill in their answers.

Say Tenisha's mother wanted to serve fruit in addition to cookies and birthday cake at a party. She asked each child at the party to draw a picture of the fruit he or she liked best. Look at the pictures. Use the pictures to answer Numbers 1 through 3.

Put your finger on Number 1. How many children liked apples best? Mark your answer.

Turn to the next page, page 57.

Check to be sure the students have found the right page.

Say **Remember, for these two items, you should look back at the pictures on page 56 to find the answers.**

Walk around the room and encourage students to look back to page 56 to find the answers. Allow time between items for the students to fill in their answers and check page 56.

Say **Find Number 2 at the top of the page. Which fruit got the most votes? Mark your answer.**

Number 3. Which fruit got two more votes than pears? Mark your answer.

Look at the next page, page 58.

Check to be sure the students have found the right page.

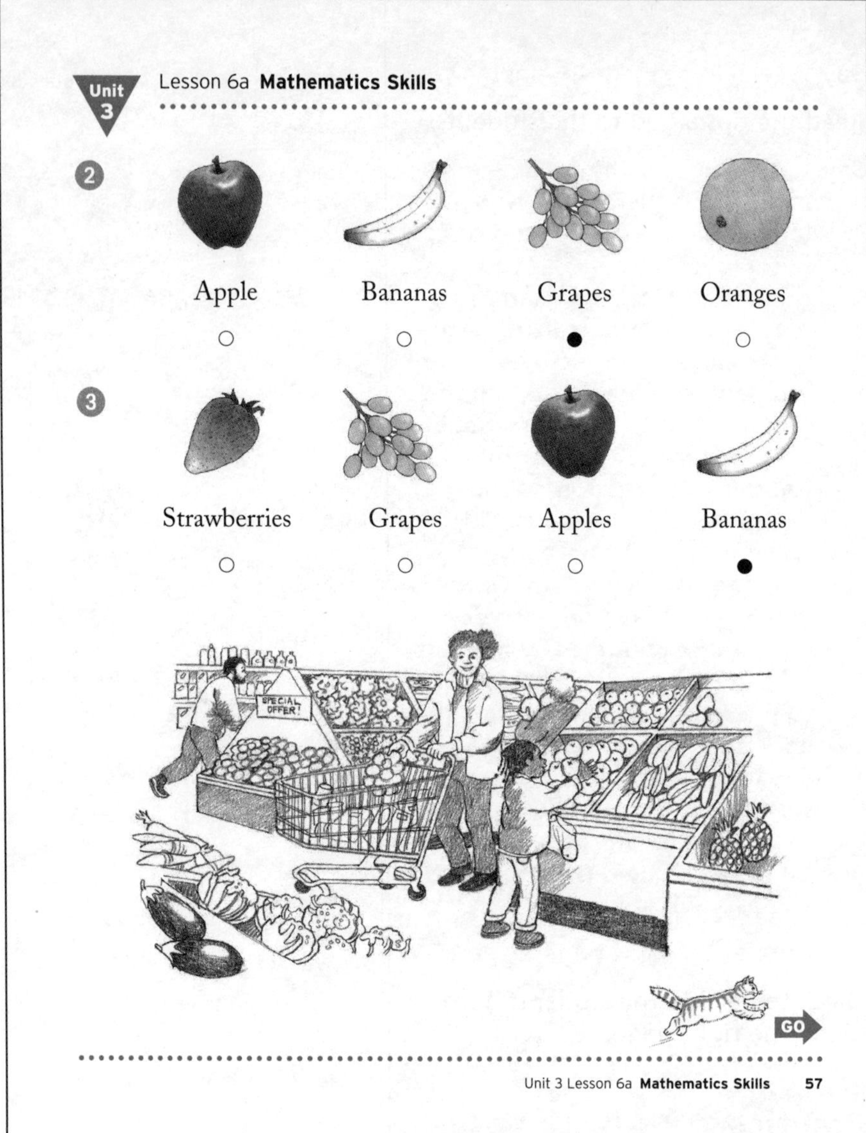

Unit 3 Lesson 6a **Mathematics Skills**

2

Apple	Bananas	Grapes	Oranges
○	○	●	○

3

Strawberries	Grapes	Apples	Bananas
○	○	○	●

Unit 3 Lesson 6a **Mathematics Skills** 57

Say Find Number 4 at the top of the page. The children lined up to play "Pin the Tail on the Donkey." Find the sixth child in line. Mark your answer.

Number 5. Look at the large clock. This was the time that Tenisha's party started. If the party lasted for two and one half hours, what did the clock look like when the party ended? Mark your answer.

Pause for a moment.

Say Look at the next page, page 59.

Check to be sure the students are working on the right page.

Say The next two items are a little different. Find Number 6 at the top of the page. Look at the digital clock at the top of the page. Find the round clock that shows the same time as the digital clock. Mark your answer.

Number 7. Look at the postage stamps and the objects beside the stamps. Find the object that is three postage stamps tall. Mark your answer.

It's time to stop. You have finished Lesson 6a.

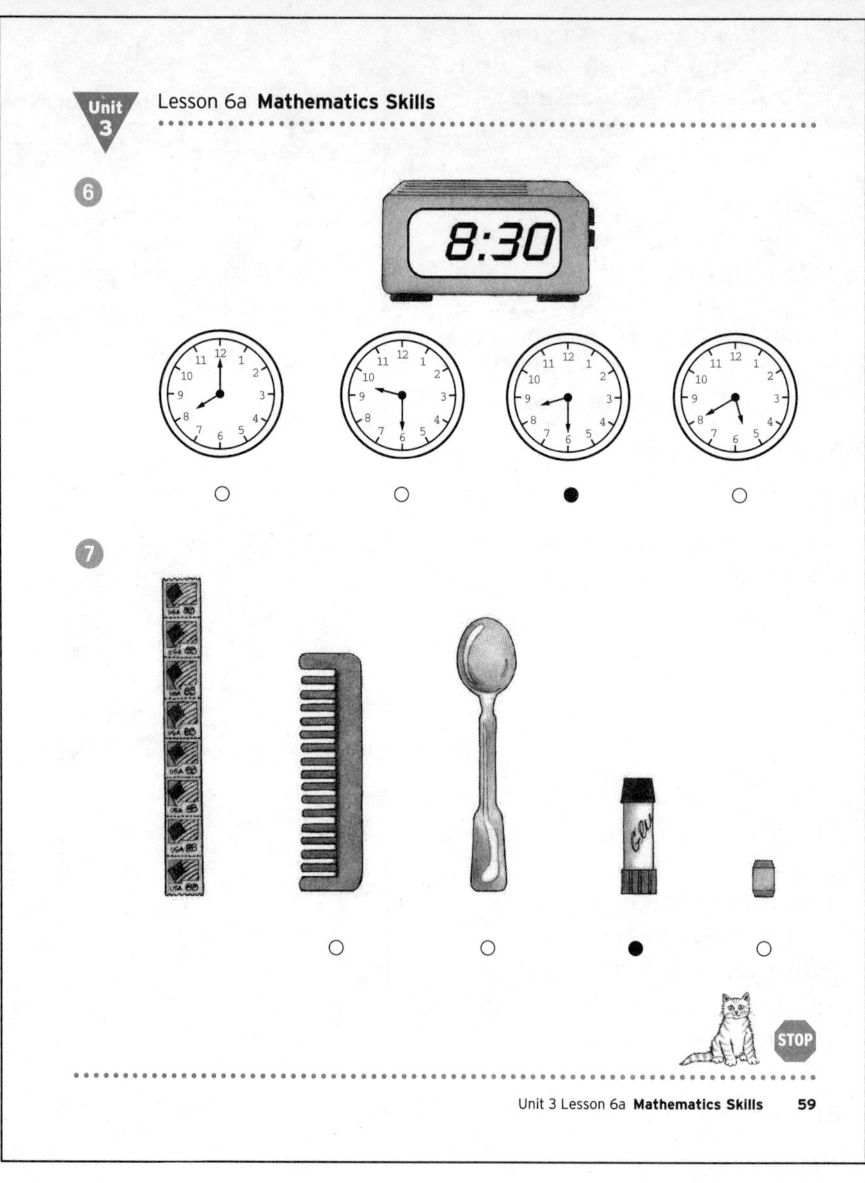

Review the answers with the students. Work through each item as a class activity, demonstrating the principle that underlies each. Emphasize how important it is to refer to the illustration to do Numbers 1 through 3. Note whether any of the item types were particularly easy or difficult. Try to determine through a group discussion whether the students' incorrect answers were the result of being unfamiliar with the format of the items or the content on which the items were based. This will help you plan future instruction.

Have the students indicate completion of the lesson by entering their score for this activity on the progress chart at the beginning of the book. Provide the students whatever help is necessary to record their scores.

Lesson 6b Mathematics Skills

Focus

Mathematics Skills
- understanding volume
- understanding the base-ten system
- understanding the value of coins
- matching shape patterns
- counting
- naming numerals
- recognizing basic shapes
- understanding number sentences
- solving word problems

Test-taking Skills
- following oral directions
- listening carefully
- considering every answer choice
- identifying and using key words, figures, or numbers to find the answer
- marking the right answer as soon as it is found
- referring to a graphic
- taking the best guess when unsure of the answer

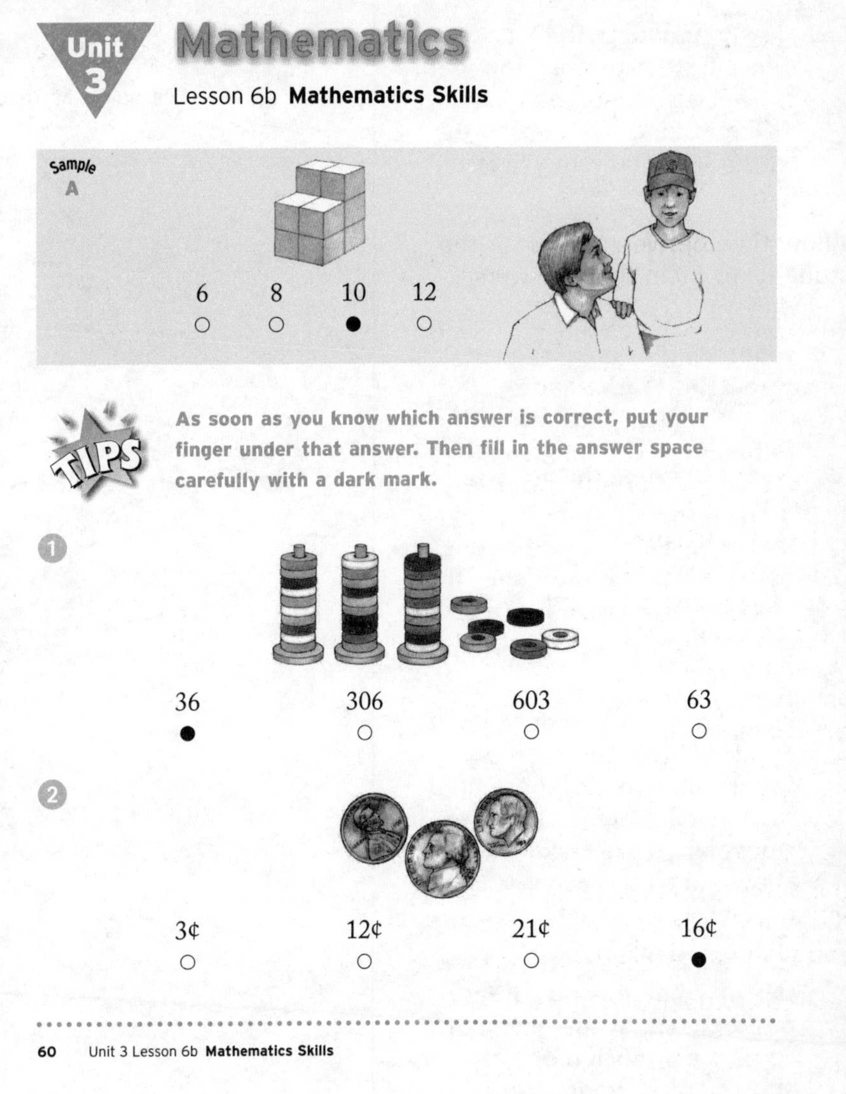

Sample A

Distribute scratch paper to the students.

Say Open your book to Lesson 6b on page 60. There are pictures and numbers on the page.

Check to see that the students have found the right page.

Say In this lesson, you will solve more mathematics problems. When you answer a question, mark the circle for the answer you think is right. Be sure your answer circle is completely filled in with a dark mark. Put your finger under Sample A at the top of the page.

Check to see that the students have found Sample A.

Say Listen carefully. Look at the tower made of blocks. How many blocks in all are in the tower? *(pause)* The third answer is correct because the tower has ten blocks. Mark the circle under *ten*. Be sure your answer circle is completely filled in with a dark mark.

Check to see that the students have marked the correct circle. If necessary, draw the tower of blocks on the board and explain why ten is the correct answer.

TIPS

Say Now let's look at the tips.

Read the tips aloud to the students.

Say As soon as you know which answer is correct, put your finger under that answer. Then fill in the answer space carefully with a dark mark.

Practice

Say Now you will do the Practice items. Listen carefully to what I say because there are many different kinds of items in this lesson. Are you ready? Let's begin.

Allow time between items for the students to fill in their answers.

Say The local bookstore is sponsoring a contest called Parents as Mathematics Partners. Ricky entered with his father, who will be giving him mathematics problems. Every time he solves a problem, his father gives him another one. If he solves all the problems, the bookstore will give him a $5.00 gift certificate to buy a book of his choice.

Put your finger under Number 1. It is below the tips. Ricky's father showed him these hard candies with holes in the center. How many hard candies are shown in all? Mark your answer.

Number 2. Ricky's father took this much money out of his pocket. Look at the group of coins. How much money is shown? Mark your answer.

Look at the next page, page 61.

Check to be sure the students have found the right page.

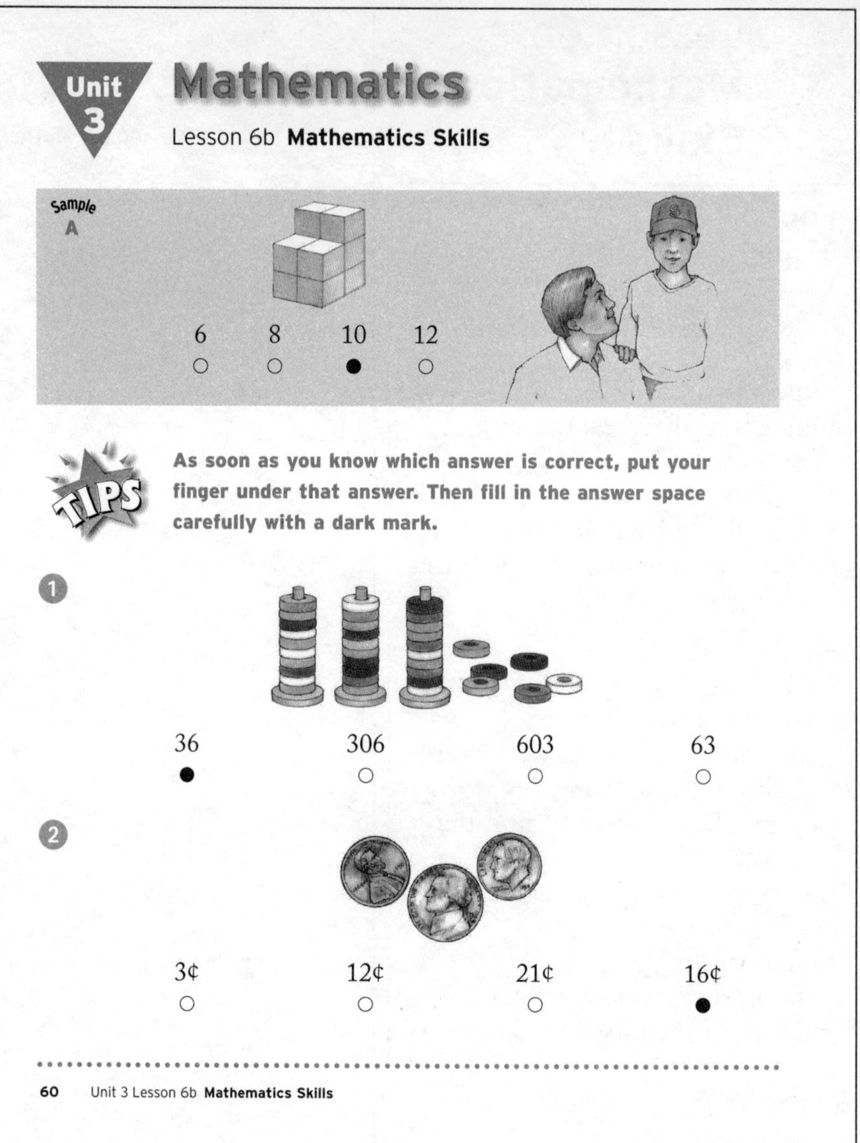

Say Find Number 3 at the top of the page. Look at the pattern in the box. Which of the answer choices has the same kind of pattern? Mark your answer.

Number 4. Look at the pictures. Find the picture that shows a group of eight. Mark your answer.

Look at the next page, page 62.

Check to be sure the students have found the right page.

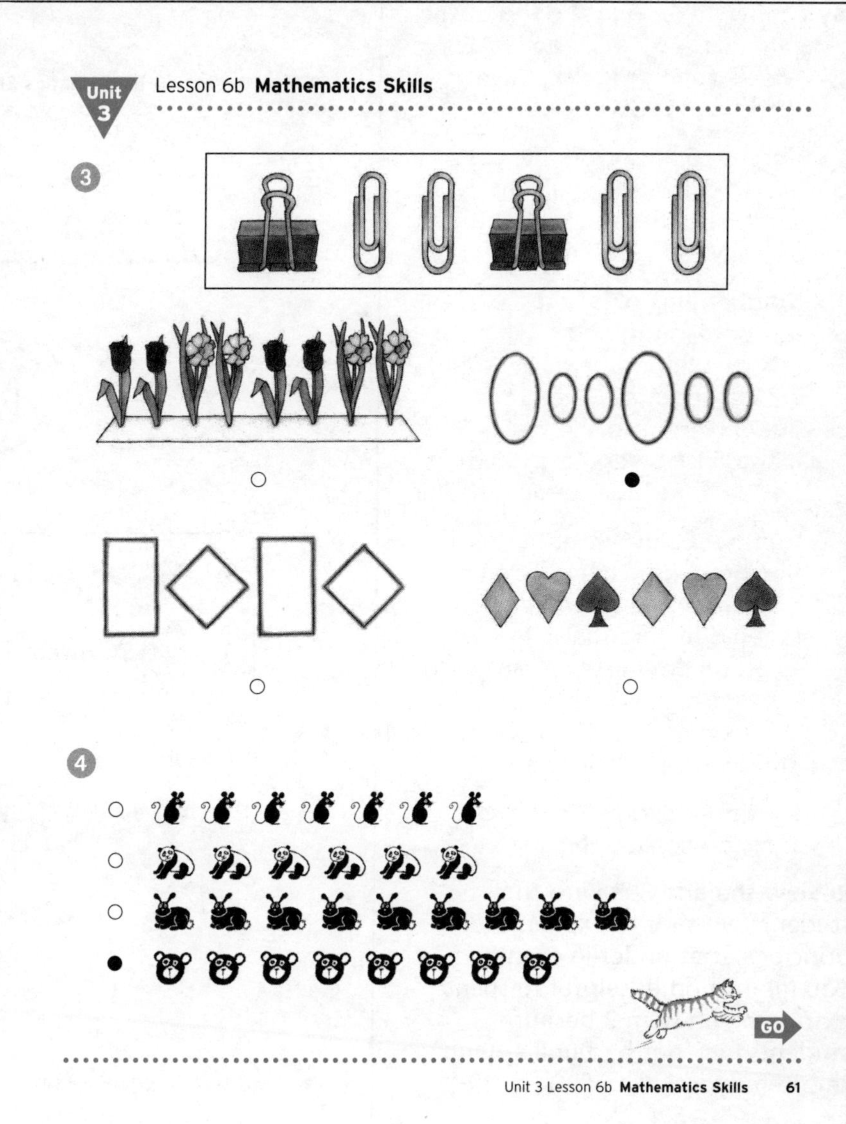

Say Find Number 5 at the top of the page. Look at the numbers. Which number is sixty-seven? Mark your answer.

Number 6. Ricky's father asked him to draw a triangle inside a circle. Find the shape that Ricky drew. Mark your answer.

Number 7. Look at the sentences in the box. Listen to this problem. Nine ducks stood on the edge of a lake. Four ducks went into the water. How many ducks were left standing on the edge? Mark your answer.

Number 8. Ricky's father took him bowling. There were ten pins standing before Ricky bowled his first ball. He knocked down seven pins with his first ball. Which picture shows how many pins were left standing? Mark your answer.

It's time to stop. You have finished Lesson 6b.

Review the answers with the students. Be sure to explain the principles that underlie each item. You might find it helpful to spend extra time on item 3 because students may not be familiar with this item type.

Have the students indicate completion of the lesson by entering their score for this activity on the progress chart at the beginning of the book. Provide the students whatever help is necessary to record their scores.

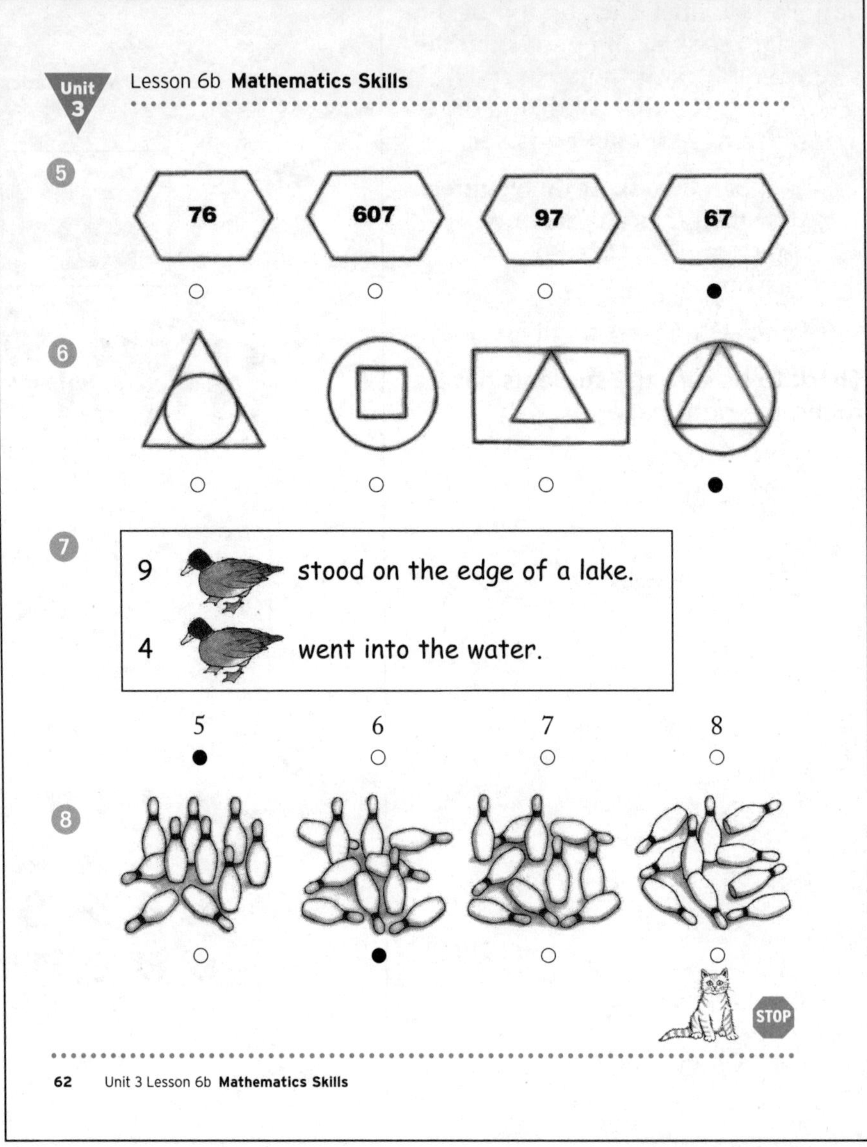

Unit 3 Test Yourself: Mathematics

Focus

Mathematics Skills
- recognizing lines of symmetry
- counting
- recognizing basic shapes
- using charts and graphs
- counting by fours
- following geometric directions
- understanding place value
- matching shape patterns
- using nonstandard units of measurement
- solving word problems

Test-taking Skills
- following oral directions
- listening carefully
- considering every answer choice
- identifying and using key words, figures, or numbers to find the answer
- marking the right answer as soon as it is found
- referring to a graphic
- taking the best guess when unsure of the answer

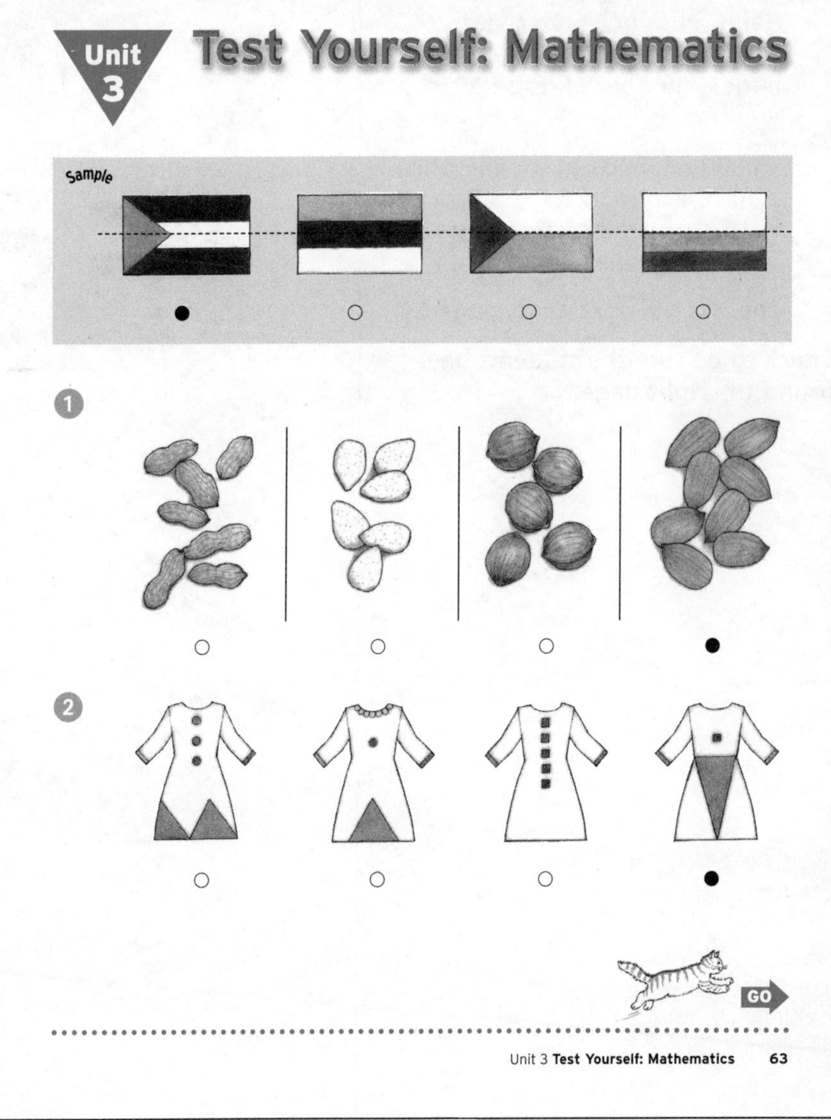

This lesson simulates an actual test-taking experience. Therefore, it is recommended that the directions be read verbatim and the suggested procedures be followed.

Directions

Administration Time: approximately 35 minutes

Distribute scratch paper to the students.

Say **Look at the Test Yourself lesson on page 63.**

Check to be sure the students have found the right page. Point out to the students that this is not a real test and that they will score it themselves to see how well they are doing.

Say **This lesson will check how well you remember the mathematics you practiced in other lessons. Put your finger under the sample at the top of the page. You can use the scratch paper I gave you to solve problems if you think it will help. Mark only your answers in your book.**

Look at the flags. Which flag can be folded on the dashed line so the parts match? *(pause)* **The first answer is correct. Fill in the circle under the first answer. Be sure the circle is completely filled in with a dark mark.**

Check to see that the students have marked the correct circle.

Say Now you are going to do more items. Put your finger under Number 1. Which group has the largest number of nuts? Mark your answer.

Number 2. Look at the pictures. Which picture of a dress has both a triangle and a square on it? Mark your answer.

Look at the next page, page 64.

Check to be sure the students have found the right page.

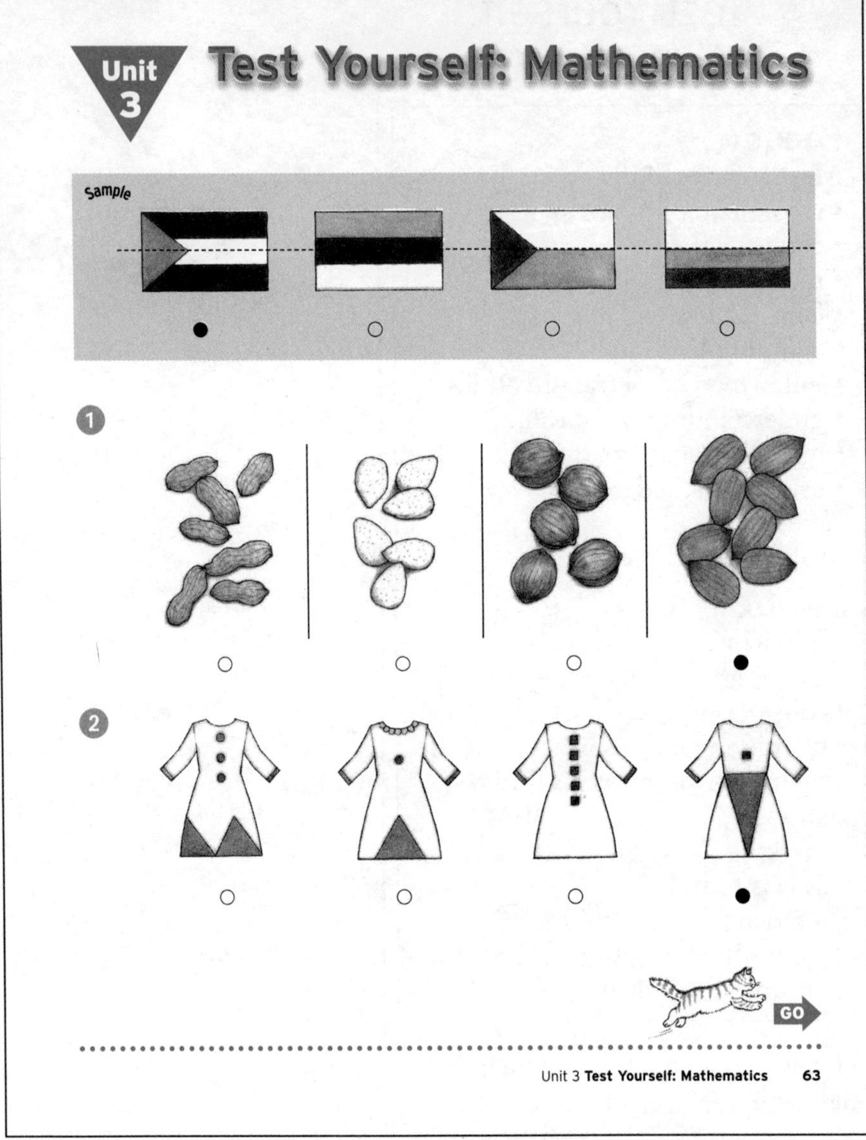

Say Listen to this story. Sam, Mindy, Paul, and Sasha are members of the book club. The graph shows how many books each friend read this week. Use the graph to answer Numbers 3 and 4.

Number 3. Which friend read the fewest books? Mark your answer.

Number 4. Which two friends read the same number of books? Mark your answer.

Look at the next page, page 65.

Check to be sure the students have found the right page.

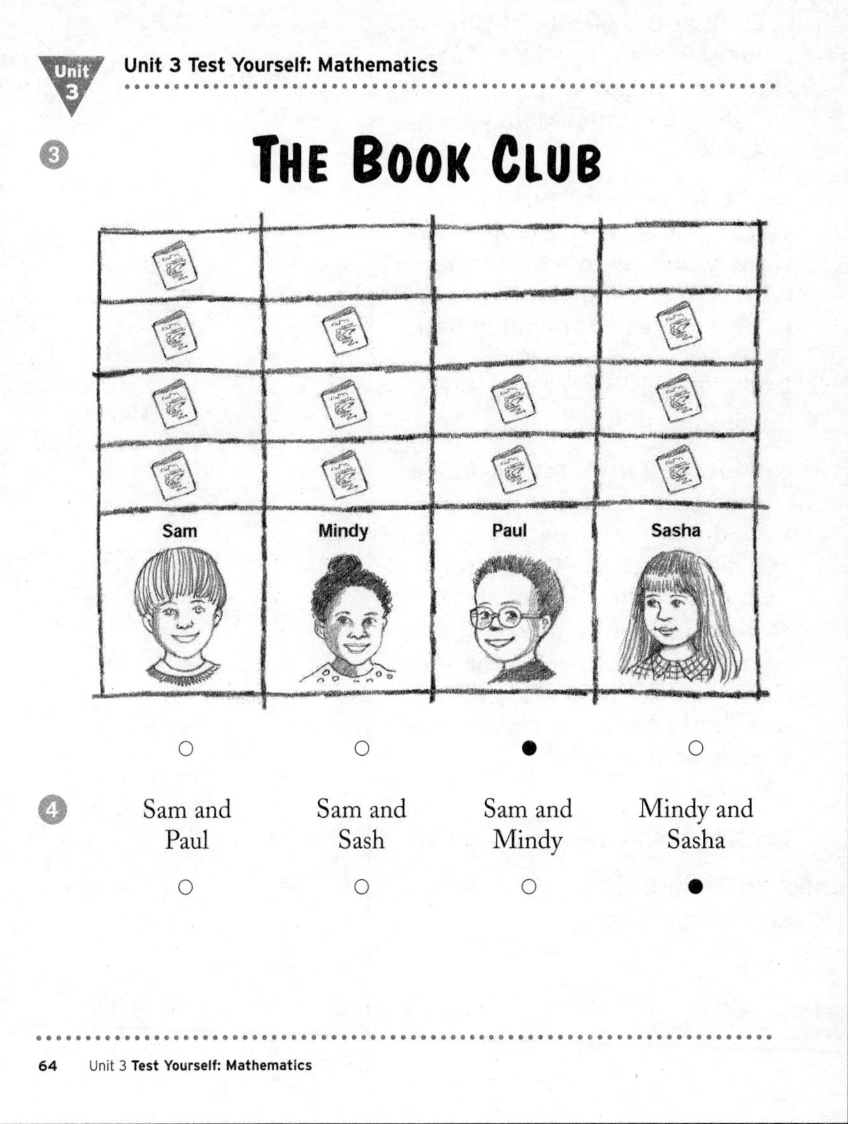

Unit 3 Unit 3 Test Yourself: Mathematics

3 **THE BOOK CLUB**

4 Sam and Paul | Sam and Sash | Sam and Mindy | Mindy and Sasha

64 Unit 3 **Test Yourself: Mathematics**

Say Put your finger under Number 5. Look at the picture of the students counting jelly beans. Find the student who is counting by fours. Mark your answer.

Move down to the pictures of pieces of paper. These pictures show you how to make a shape with two equal parts. Begin by folding a piece of paper in half. Then draw one half of the shape. Cut along the line and unfold the shape.

Number 6. Barry's father took a square piece of paper and folded it in half. Next, he cut on the diagonal from the bottom right corner to the top left corner. He then removed the two pieces of paper on the top right. Finally, he unfolded the remaining paper. Find the shape that remained. Mark your answer.

Look at the next page, page 66.

Check to be sure the students have found the right page.

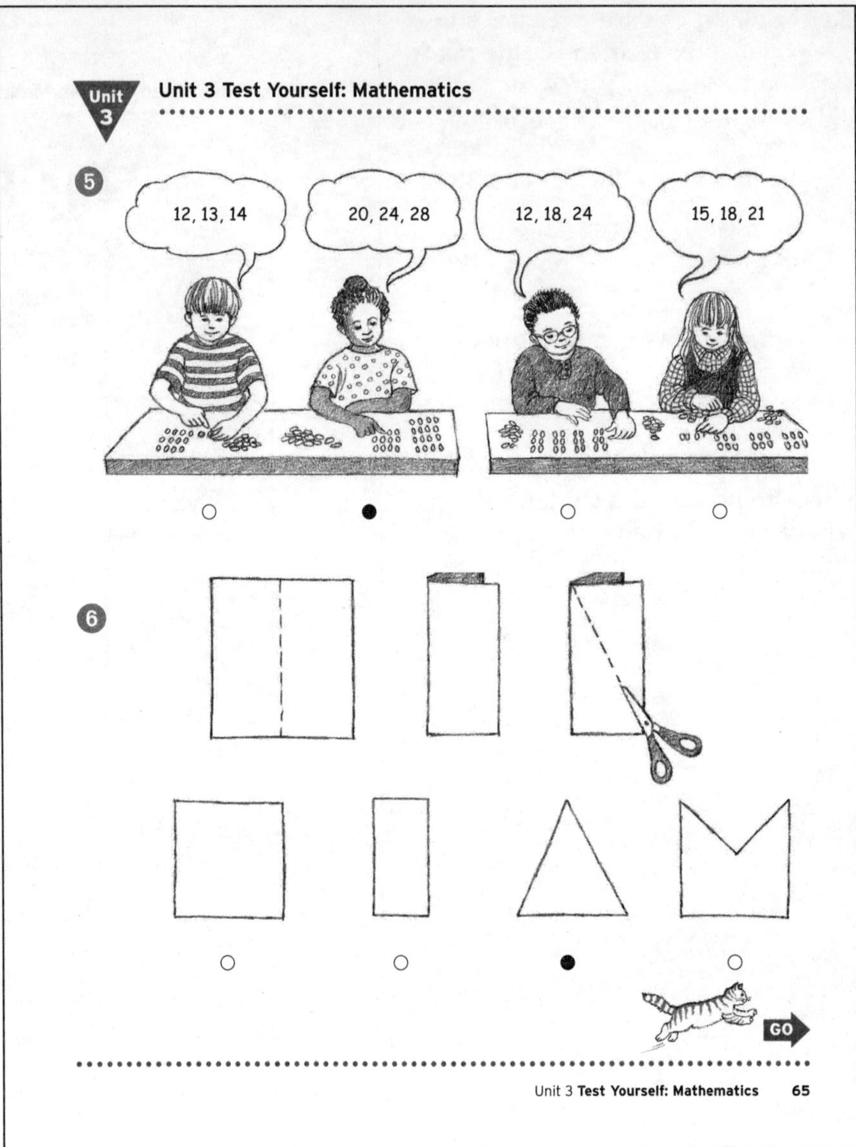

Say Look at the table and the children. The table has tally marks that show the coins that Sam, Mindy, Paul, and Sasha have. We will use this table to answer Numbers 7 and 8.

Number 7. Find the child that has the most coins. Mark your answer.

Number 8. Look at the table again. Find the child that has both a dime and a quarter. Mark your answer.

Look at the next page, page 67.

Check to be sure the students have found the right page.

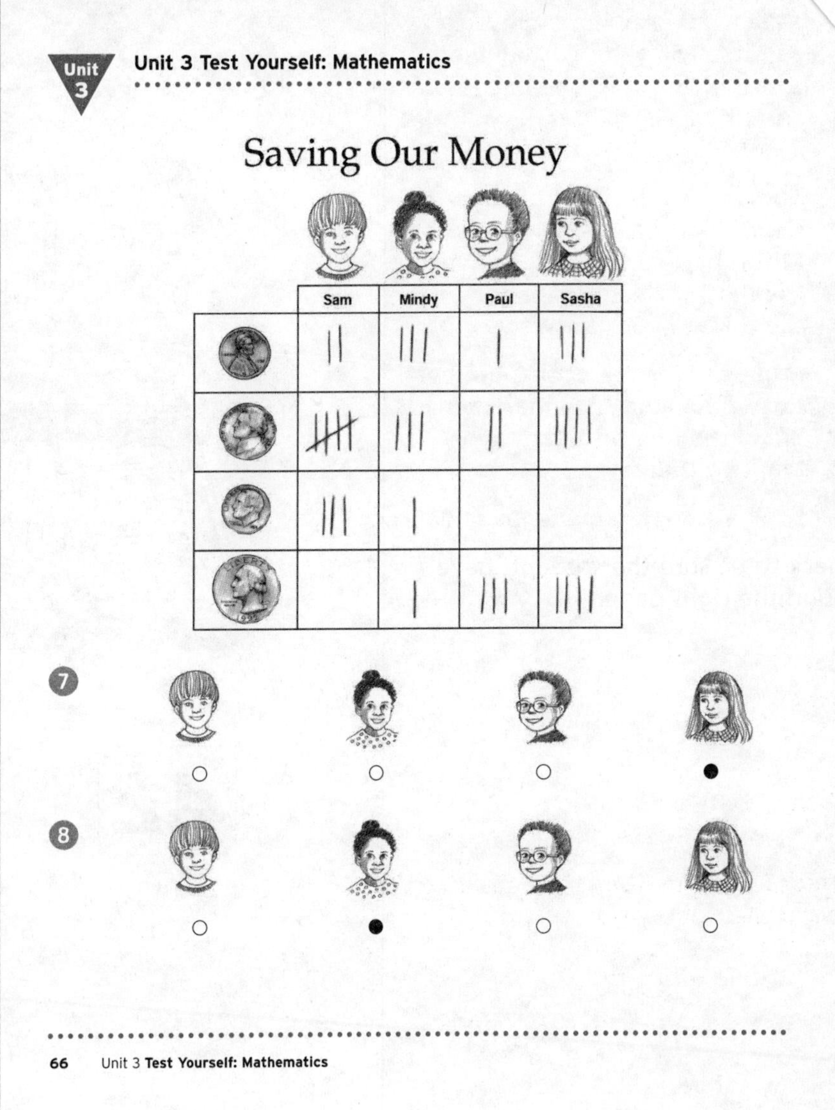
Unit 3 Test Yourself: Mathematics

Saving Our Money

<table>
<tr><th></th><th>Sam</th><th>Mindy</th><th>Paul</th><th>Sasha</th></tr>
<tr><td>(penny)</td><td>||</td><td>|||</td><td>|</td><td>|||</td></tr>
<tr><td>(nickel)</td><td>𝍸</td><td>|||</td><td>||</td><td>||||</td></tr>
<tr><td>(dime)</td><td>|||</td><td>|</td><td></td><td></td></tr>
<tr><td>(quarter)</td><td></td><td>|</td><td>|||</td><td>||||</td></tr>
</table>

7

8

66 Unit 3 **Test Yourself: Mathematics**

Say Find Number 9 at the top of the page. Look at the pictures. If you cut along the dotted line, which of these would have two parts that match? Mark your answer.

Number 10. Here is a picture of the inside of a desk drawer. Which part of the desk drawer has the smallest number of clips? Mark your answer.

Number 11. Look at the number forty-two. Find how many tens are in the number forty-two. Mark your answer.

Look at the next page, page 68.

Check to be sure the students have found the right page.

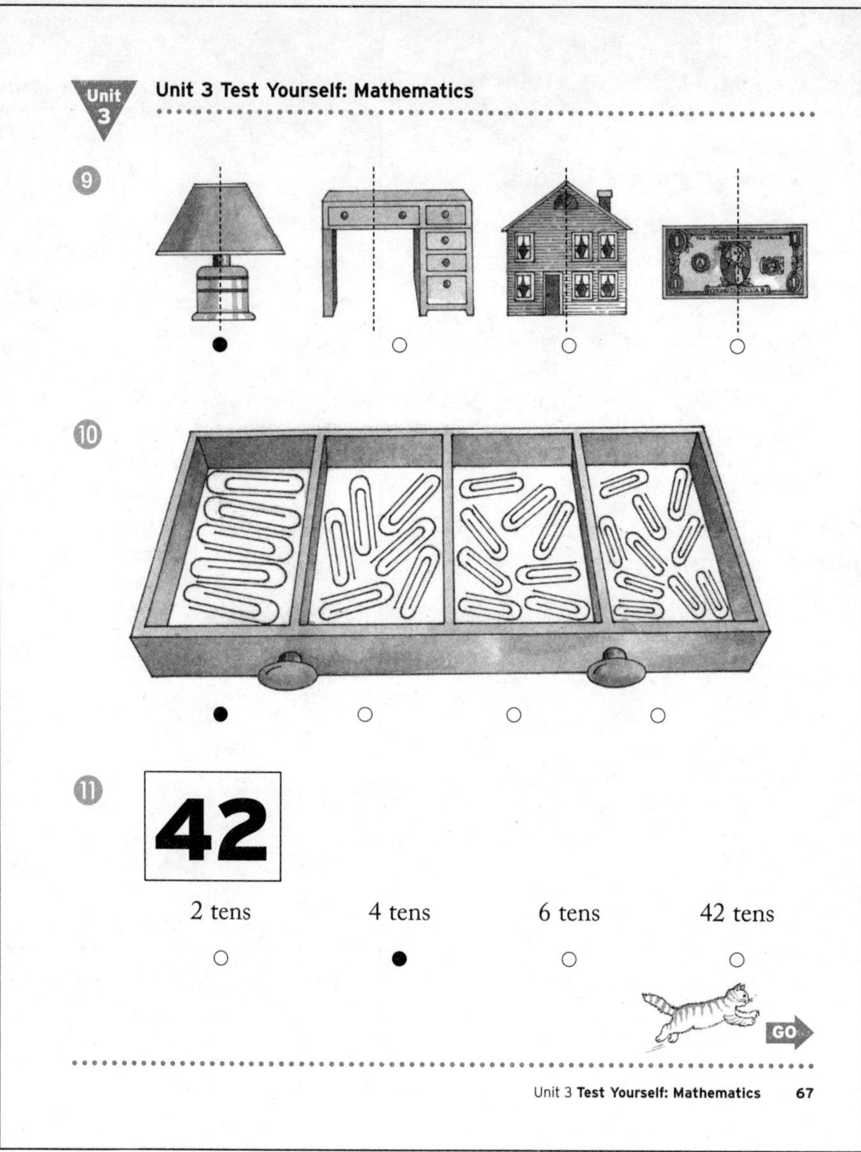

Say Number 12. Ann made a letter pattern. Which of the picture patterns that follow have the same kind of pattern as the letter pattern? Mark your answer.

Look at the next page, page 69.

Check to be sure the students have found the right page.

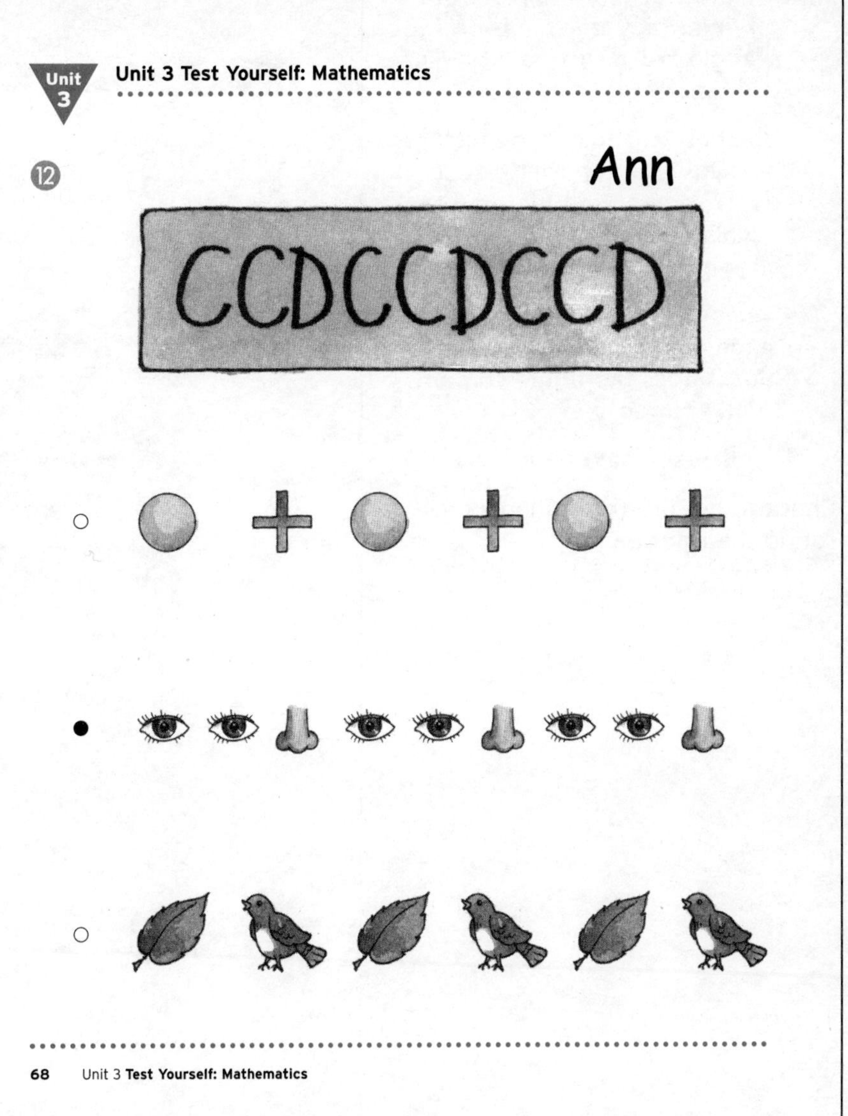

Unit 3 **Unit 3 Test Yourself: Mathematics**

12

Ann

CCDCCDCCD

68 Unit 3 **Test Yourself: Mathematics**

Say Number 13. Which picture of a serving of ice cream has both a triangle and a circle on it? Mark your answer.

Number 14. Look at the pictures of roads. The top road equals twelve steps. Find the road that equals six steps. Mark your answer.

Number 15. Look at the figure made of blocks. How many blocks does the figure contain? Mark your answer.

Look at the next page, page 70.

Check to be sure the students have found the right page.

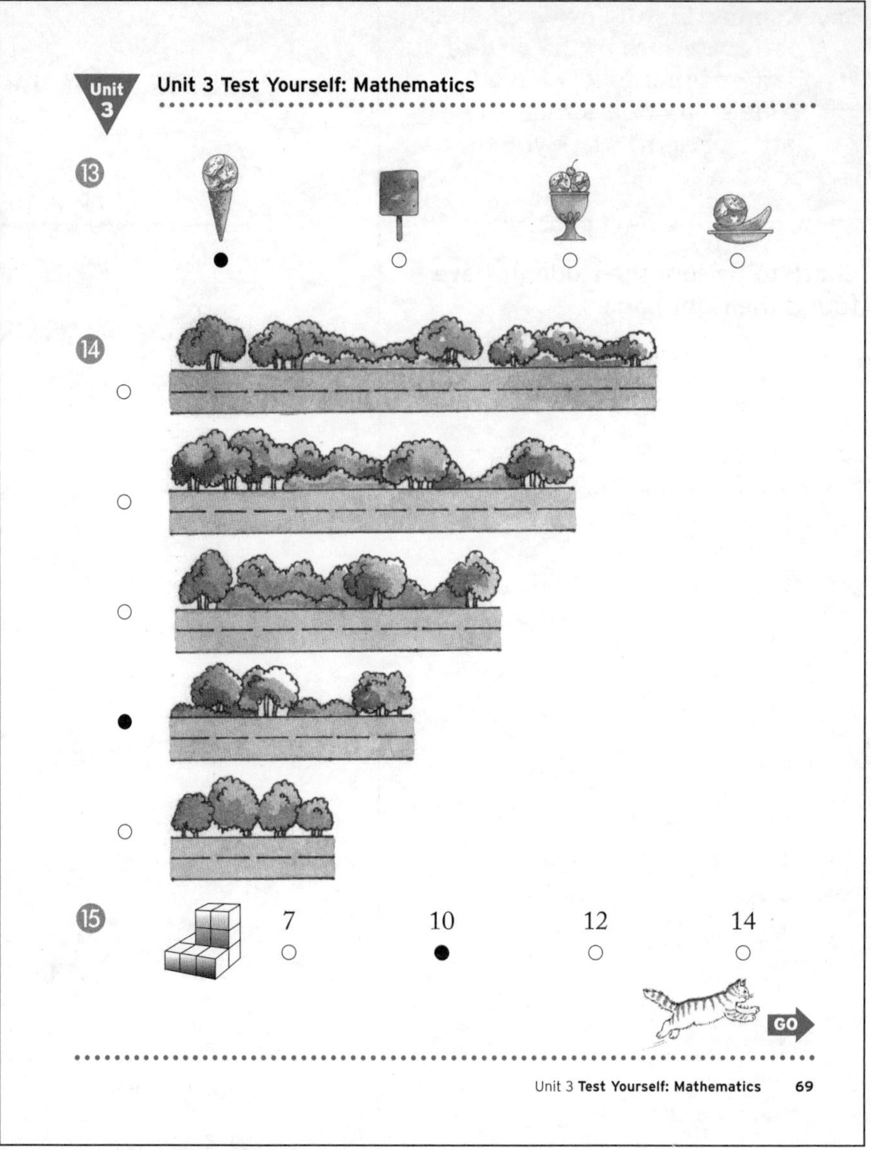

Say **Number 16. Twelve classmates celebrated after they finished playing the "Brain Stretch" game. They got to choose how they would spend the last three minutes of class time. Everyone went outside at first. Then four of the students came back inside. How many students stayed outside?**

It's time to stop. You have completed the Test Yourself lesson.

Review the answers with the students. Have the students indicate completion of the lesson by entering their score for this activity on the progress chart at the beginning of the book. Provide the students whatever help is necessary to record their scores.

To the Teacher:

The Test Practice unit provides the students with an opportunity to apply the reading, language arts, basic skills, mathematics, and test-taking skills practiced in the lessons of this book. It is also a final practice activity to be used prior to administering the *TerraNova* CTBS. By following the step-by-step instructions on the subsequent pages, you will be able to simulate the structured atmosphere in which achievement tests are given. Take time to become familiar with the administrative procedures before the students take the tests.

Preparing for the Tests

1. **Put a "Testing—Do Not Disturb" sign on the classroom door to eliminate unnecessary interruptions.**
2. **Make sure the students are seated a comfortable distance from each other and that their desks are clear.**
3. **Provide each student with sharpened pencils with erasers. Have an extra supply of pencils available. For the mathematics items, provide each student with scratch paper.**
4. **Distribute the students' books.**
5. **Encourage the students with a "pep talk."**

Scheduling the Tests

Each test should be administered in a separate session. Two sessions may be scheduled for the same day if a sufficient break in time is provided between sessions.

Test	Administration Time (minutes)
1 Reading and Language Arts	60
2 Basic Skills	60
3 Mathematics	70

Administering the Tests

1. Read the "Say" copy verbatim to the students and follow all instructions given.
2. Make sure the students understand the directions for each test before proceeding.
3. Move about the classroom during testing to see that the students are following the directions. Make sure the students are working on the correct page and are marking their answers properly.
4. Without distracting the students, provide test-taking tips at your discretion. If you notice a student is working independently and is unable to answer a question, encourage him or her to skip the question and go on to the next one. If students finish the test before time is called, suggest they go back to any skipped questions within that part of the test. However, do not provide help with the content of any question.

Unit 4

Test 1 Reading and Language Arts

Administration Time: 60 minutes in two sessions

Part 1

Say **Turn to the Test Practice section of your book on page 71. There are pictures on this page. This is Test 1, Reading and Language Arts Part 1.**

Check to see that the students have found page 71.

Say **This test will check how well you remember the reading and language arts skills you learned. Remember to make sure that the circles for your answer choices are completely filled in. Press your pencil firmly so your marks come out dark. Completely erase any marks for answers you change.**

Find Sample A at the top of the page. Listen carefully. Look at the words. Find the word that has the same <u>beginning</u> sound as "tail ... tail." *(pause)* **The second answer, *toy,* is correct because it begins with the same sound as *tail.* Fill in the circle under the word *toy.* Be sure your answer circle is completely filled in with a dark mark and that you have marked the correct answer circle.**

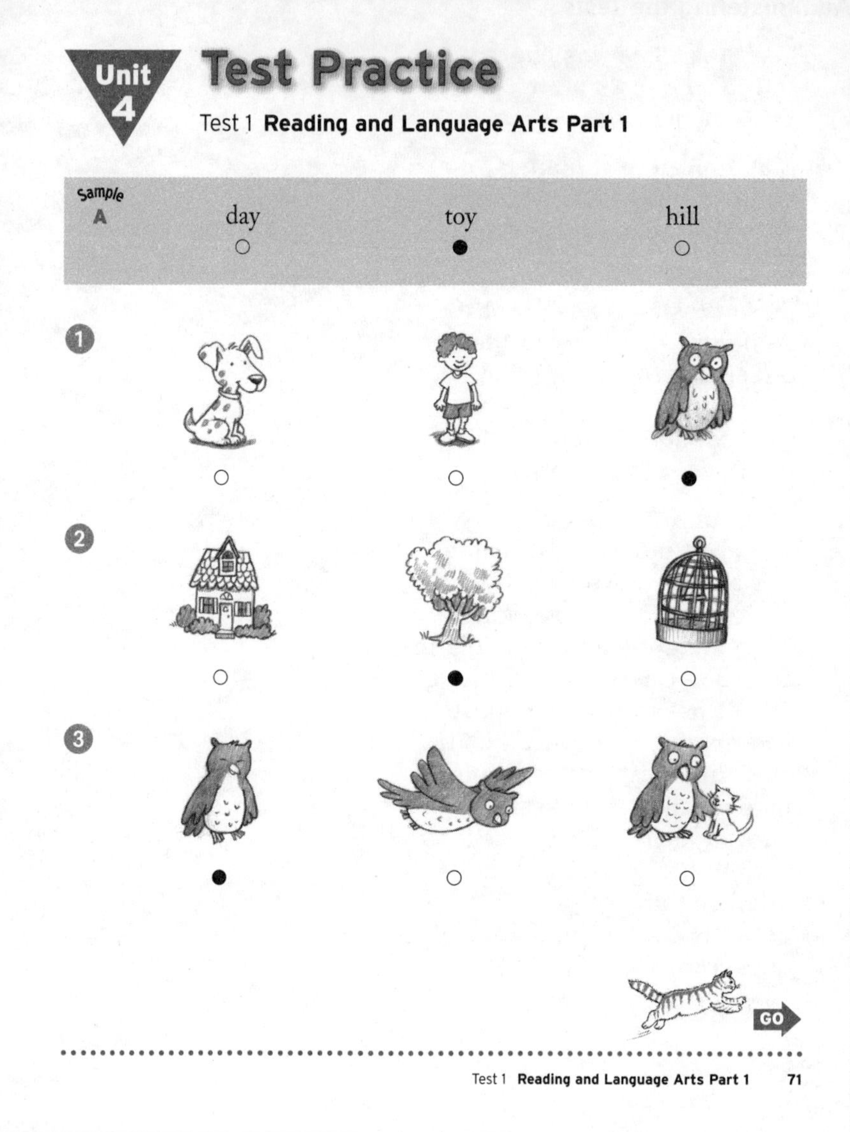

Unit 4 **Test Practice**

Test 1 **Reading and Language Arts Part 1**

Sample A — day ○ toy ● hill ○

1 ○ ○ ●

2 ○ ● ○

3 ● ○ ○

GO

Test 1 **Reading and Language Arts Part 1** 71

Check to see that the students have correctly filled in their answer circles with a dark mark.

Say **Now you will answer more questions. There are different kinds of questions in this activity, so it is important to listen carefully to what I say. Fill in the circle under the answer you think is right. If you are not sure which answer is correct, fill in the circle under the answer you think might be right. Are you ready? Let's begin.**

Allow time between items for the students to mark their answers. Walk around the room to make sure the students understand what they are supposed to do.

Say At home, Tom's mother reads a poem called "Walter the Wise." Look at me and listen carefully while I read the first part of the poem. Then you will answer some questions about what I've read.

Walter the owl lives in a tree.

He always looks so wise.

He sometimes hoots with a funny voice

And always looks with two round eyes.

Put your finger on Number 1. Look at the pictures. Who is Walter? Find the picture that shows "Who is Walter?" Mark your answer.

Number 2. Look at the pictures. Where does Walter live? Find the picture that shows "Where does Walter live?" Mark your answer.

Number 3. Look at the pictures. What does Walter do during the day? Find the picture that shows "What does Walter do during the day?" Mark your answer.

Look at the next page, page 72.

Check to be sure the students have found the right page.

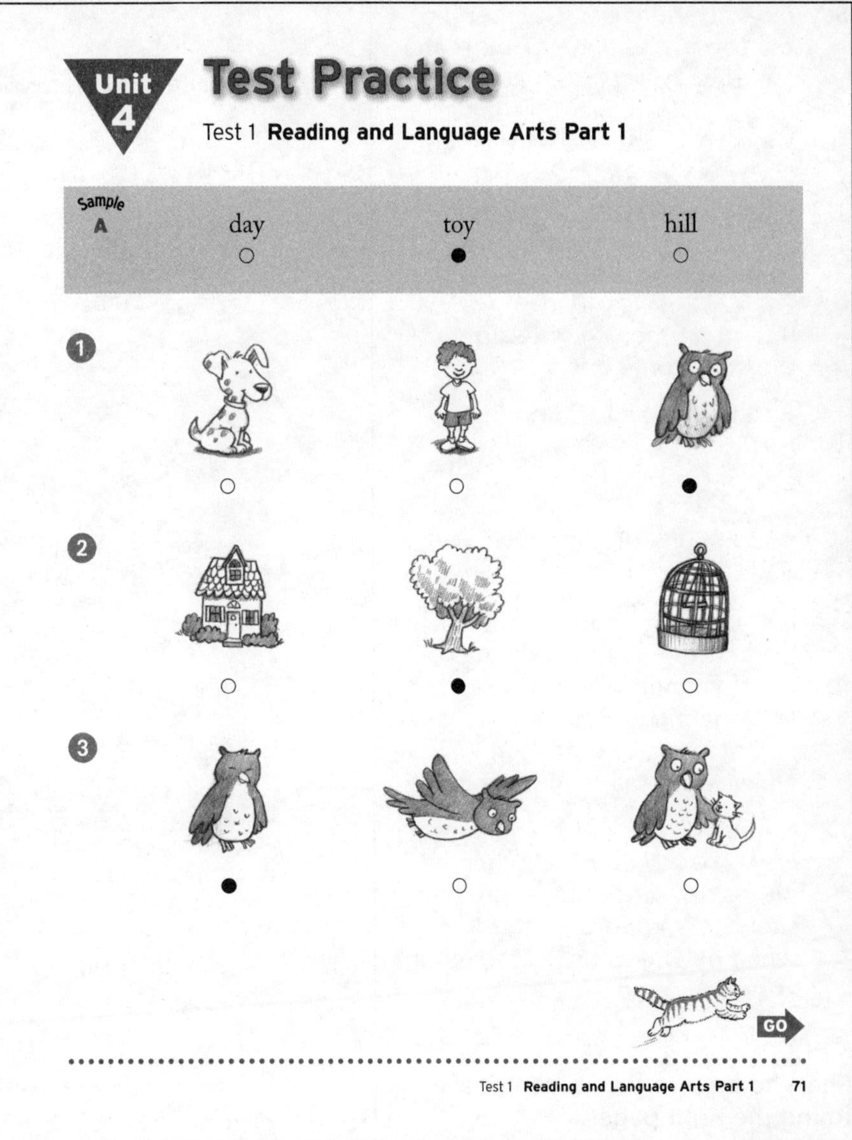

Say Put your finger on Number 4 at the top of the page. Look at the pictures. Where does Walter get cozy? Find the picture that shows "Where does Walter get cozy?" Mark your answer.

Here is the last part of the poem. Look at me. Listen carefully.

But when the sun goes down, the stars come out

And the moon is riding high.

Walter wakes up and stretches his wings

And happily flies up into the sky!

Put your finger on Number 5. Look at the pictures. What is in the sky when Walter wakes up? Find the picture that shows "What is in the sky when Walter wakes up?" Mark your answer.

Number 6. Look at the pictures. How does Walter feel when he wakes up? Find the picture that shows "How does Walter feel when he wakes up?" Mark your answer.

Look at the next page, page 73.

Check to be sure the students have found the right page.

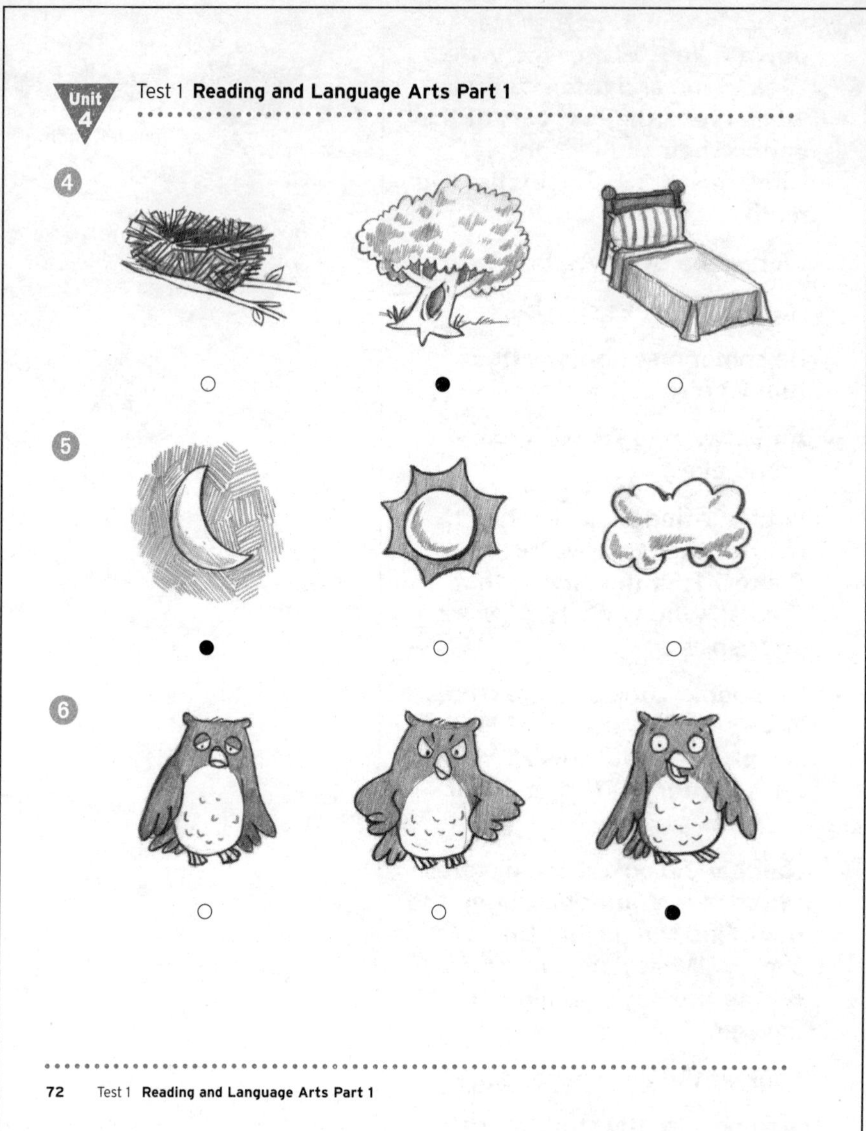

Say Now you'll answer some questions about beginning sounds.

Number 7. After Tom's mother read the poem, Tom fell asleep on the floor. Find the word that has the same beginning sound as "floor ... floor." Mark your answer.

Number 8. Another story in the book of poetry is about a duck. Find the word that has the same beginning sound as "duck ... duck." Mark your answer.

Number 9. This question is a little different. Listen to this sentence: Tom slept for a long time. Find the word "time ... time." Mark your answer.

Number 10. Listen to this sentence: A loud noise came out of the kitchen. The noise made Tom wake up. Find the word "noise ... noise." Mark your answer.

Number 11. Listen to this sentence: Tom's mother was making the noise. She was getting ready to wash the dishes. Find the word "wash ... wash." Mark your answer.

Look at the next page, page 74.

Check to be sure the students have found the right page.

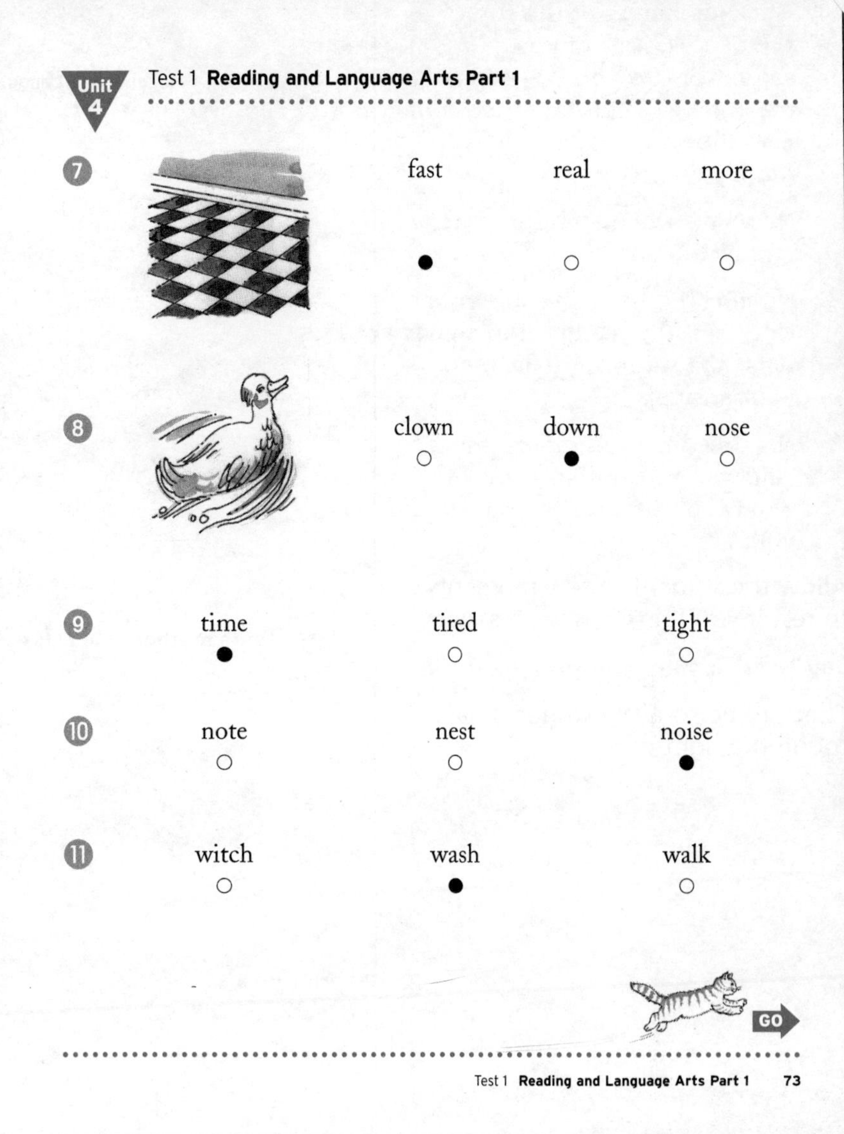

Unit 4
Test 1 Reading and Language Arts Part 1
7
fast
real
more
8
clown
down
nose
9
time
tired
tight
10
note
nest
noise
11
witch
wash
walk
GO
Test 1 Reading and Language Arts Part 1
73

Say Find Number 12 at the top of the page. Listen to this sentence: "Do you want to help me in here?" Mother asked Tom. Find the word "here ... here." Mark your answer.

Now you will match sentences and pictures.

Number 13. Read the sentence. Now find the picture that shows what the sentence tells. Mark your answer.

Number 14. Read the sentence. Find the picture that shows what the sentence tells. Mark your answer.

Allow the students a few moments to rest if you think it is necessary.

Say Look at the next page, page 75.

Check to be sure the students have found the right page.

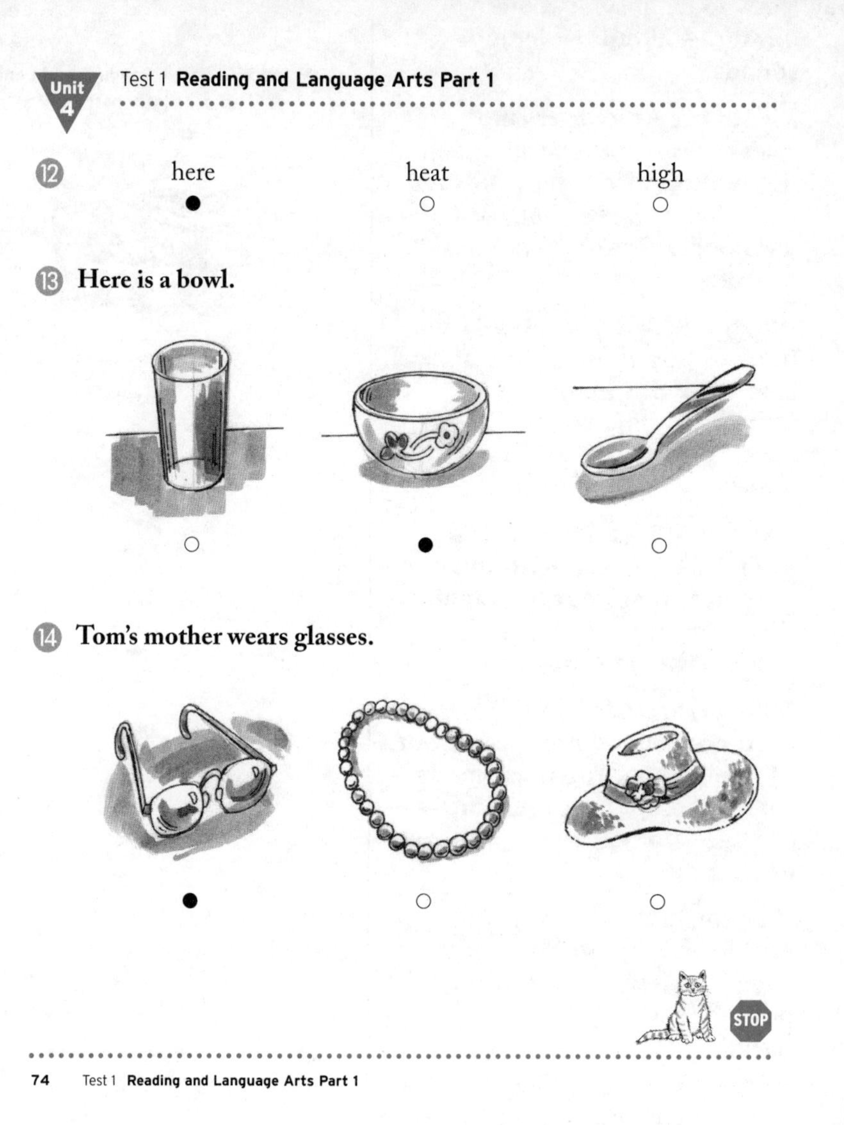

Unit 4
Test 1 Reading and Language Arts Part 1
12
here
heat
high
13 Here is a bowl.
14 Tom's mother wears glasses.
STOP
74 Test 1 Reading and Language Arts Part 1

Say After Tom finished helping with the dishes, he read a book. The book was about a boy named Earl who had a pet turtle. Look at me and listen carefully while I read the first part of the story to you.

When Earl brought his turtle home, he took it out back. He gently set the turtle next to the pond. "You need a name," said Earl. He closed his eyes and tried to think of a good name for his turtle.

Put your finger on Number 15. Where did the boy set the turtle? Find the picture that shows "Where did Earl set the turtle?" Mark your answer.

Number 16. What does the turtle in this story need? Find the word that shows "What does the turtle in this story need?" Mark your answer.

Number 17. The story says that the boy closed his eyes. Find the sentence that tells why the boy closed his eyes. Mark your answer.

Look at me and listen while I read the rest of the story.

Earl felt something tickle his toe. Earl opened his eyes. The turtle was trying to eat his toe! He thought it was a pink worm. "I know," said Earl. "I'll call you Snapper."

Put your finger on Number 18. What is this story mostly about? Look at the words. Find the words that answer "What is this story mostly about?" Mark your answer.

Look at the next page, page 76.

Check to be sure the students have found the right page.

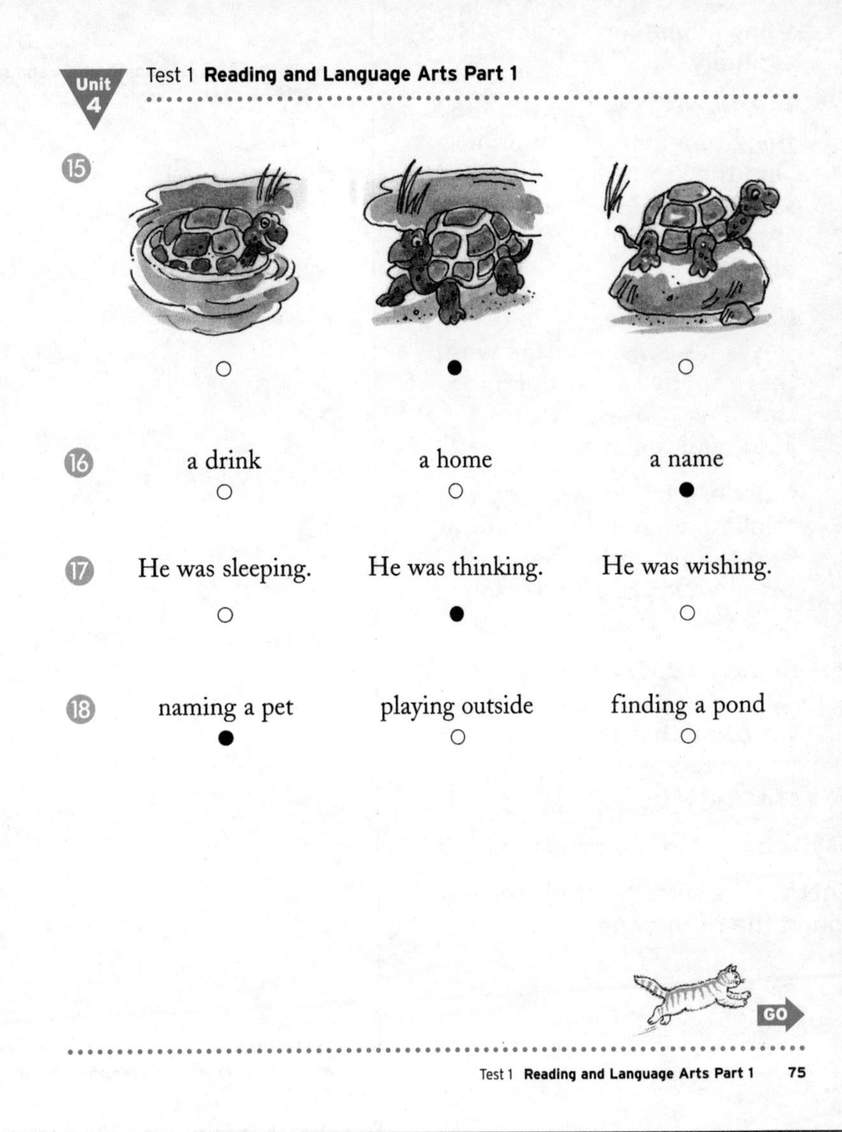

Unit 4
Test 1 Reading and Language Arts Part 1
15
16 a drink a home a name
17 He was sleeping. He was thinking. He was wishing.
18 naming a pet playing outside finding a pond
GO
Test 1 Reading and Language Arts Part 1 75

Say Now you will do some items using beginning sounds. Listen carefully.

Number 19. The boy tried to think of a name for the turtle. Find the word that has the same beginning sound as "think ... think." Mark your answer.

Number 20. The boy in the story closes his eyes. Find the word that has the same beginning sound as "closes ... closes." Mark your answer.

Number 21. The boy tried to think of a name for the turtle. Find the word that has the same vowel, or middle, sound as "tried ... tried."

Number 22. The boy decides to call the turtle Snapper. Find the word that has the same vowel, or middle, sound as "call ... call."

Say Look at the next page, page 77.

Check to be sure the students have found the right page.

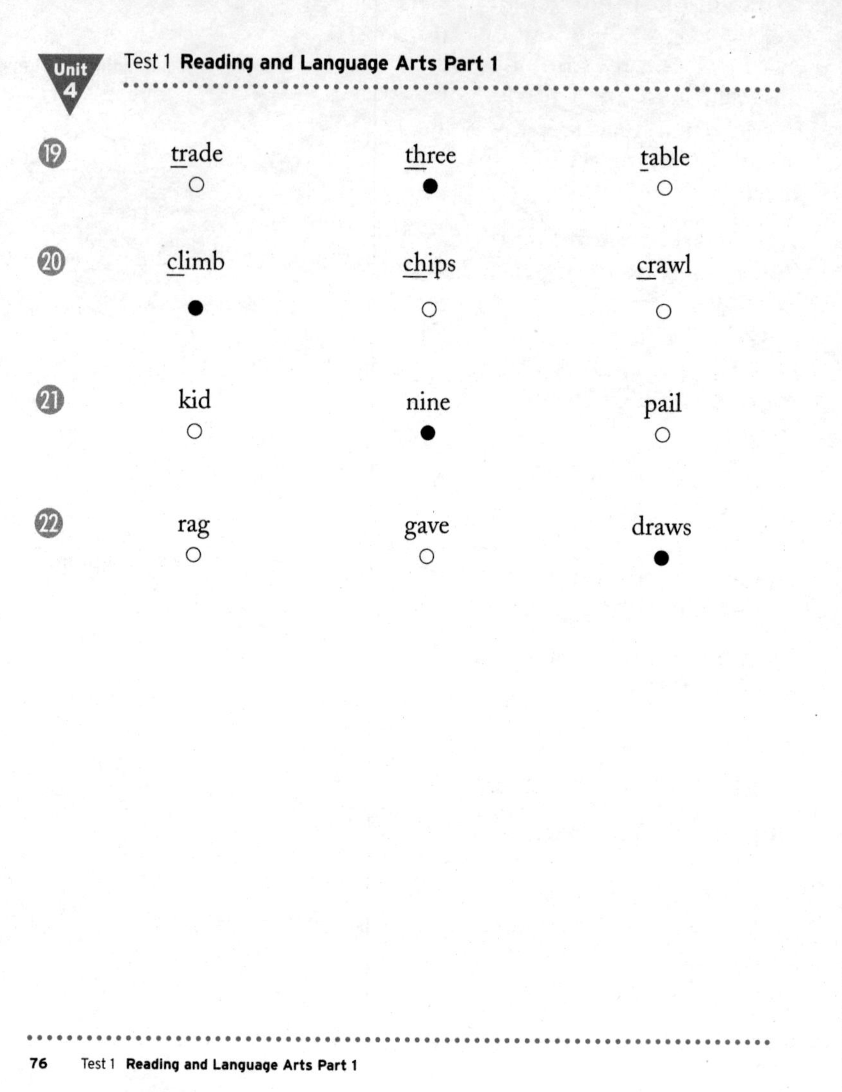

Unit 4 Test 1 **Reading and Language Arts Part 1**

19	trade ○	three ●	table ○
20	climb ●	chips ○	crawl ○
21	kid ○	nine ●	pail ○
22	rag ○	gave ○	draws ●

76 Test 1 **Reading and Language Arts Part 1**

Say Chris wrote a letter to his grandmother to thank her for a gift. Look at the letter while you do Numbers 23 through 26. Listen carefully to what I say.

Allow time between items for the students to fill in their answers.

Say Put your finger on Number 23. Read the words. Which punctuation mark comes at the end? Mark your answer.

Number 24. Read the sentence. Which punctuation mark comes at the end? Mark your answer.

Number 25. Read the sentence. Find the part of the sentence that needs a capital letter. Mark your answer.

Number 26. Read the words. Find the part that needs a punctuation mark. Mark your answer.

Allow the students to take a break at this point.

Say Look at the next page, page 78.

Check to be sure the students have found the right page.

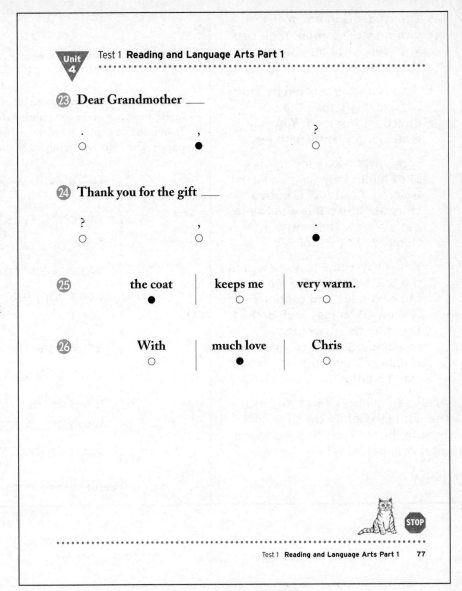

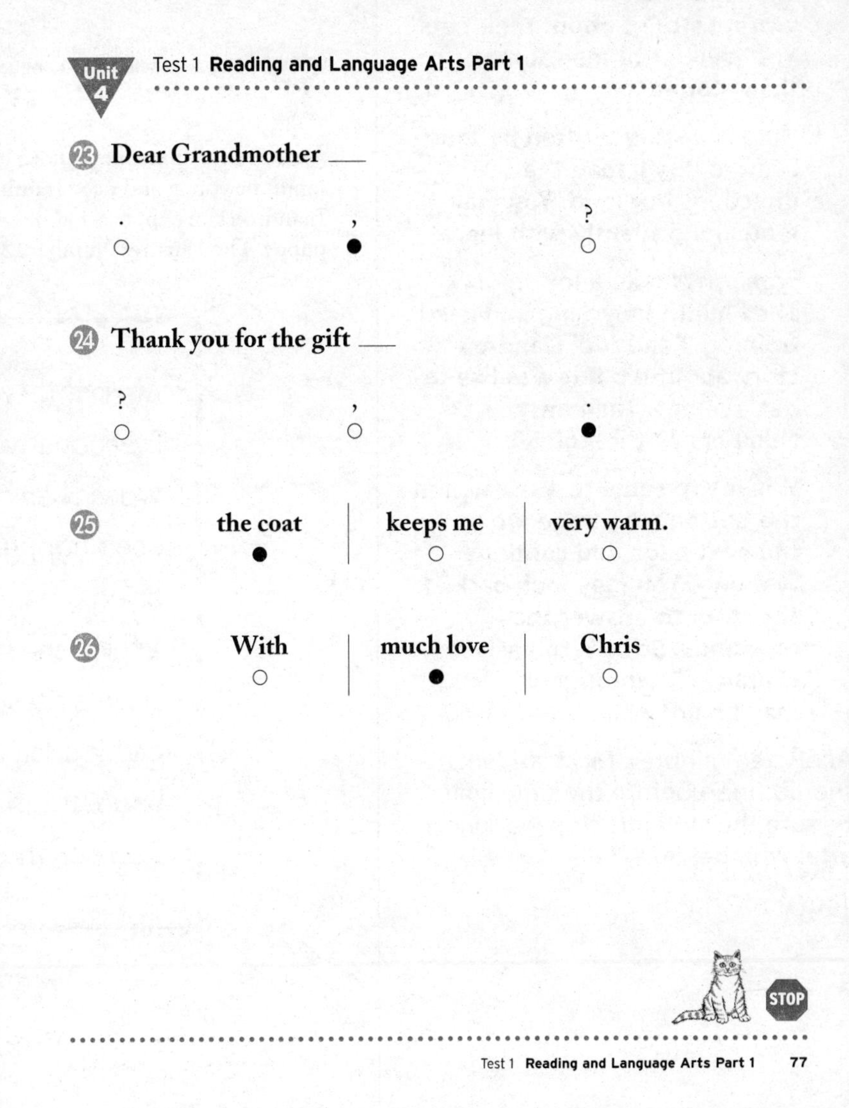

Unit 4 Test 1 **Reading and Language Arts Part 1**

23 Dear Grandmother ___

.	,	?
○	●	○

24 Thank you for the gift ___

?	,	.
○	○	●

	the coat	keeps me	very warm.
25	●	○	○

	With	much love	Chris
26	○	●	○

STOP

Test 1 **Reading and Language Arts Part 1** 77

Say The students in Room 10 are writing stories about their pets. You will get to read some of their stories.

Here is a story written by Jodi Liandro. I will read the directions out loud. You may read along silently with me.

Some pets take a lot of work. They might be young and need training. Read Jodi Liandro's story about what it was like to get a puppy. Then answer Numbers 27 through 30.

When you come to a GO sign at the bottom of a page, go on to the next page and continue working. You may look back at the story to answer the questions. Be sure to answer Numbers 27 through 30. You may begin.

Allow ten minutes. Most students should finish before the time limit. Be sure the students stop working after Number 30.

Directions: Some pets take a lot of work. They might be young and need training. Read Jodi Liandro's story about what it was like to get a puppy. Then answer Numbers 27 through 30.

At first it was hard.
Everyone was in bed. Popie was in her crate. She did not seem happy. She cried and cried.
I think she missed her mom.
It was so sad. The crying got louder. Put a pillow on my head. It did not help. Then, Dad set the crate in my bed.

27 When was Popie crying?

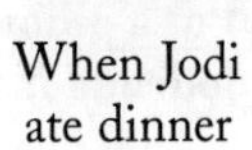

When Jodi ate dinner	When Jodi was at school	When Jodi was in bed
○	○	●

28 What does Jodi use after the crying gets louder?

- ○ a crate
- ● a pillow
- ○ a cookie

29 Which of these probably will help Popie stop crying the next time?

- ● being with someone
- ○ staying with another dog
- ○ getting out of the crate

Say Stop working. Put your finger on Number 31. For Numbers 31 through 34, we will read the questions together. For each question, fill in the circle that goes with the answer you choose.

Number 31. "Put a pillow on my head" is not a complete sentence. What could Jodi add if she wanted to make it a complete sentence? Mark your answer.

Number 32. Read the sentence. Then read the answer choices below it. Find the answer choice that correctly changes the sentence into a question. Mark your answer.

Say Look at the next page, page 81.

Check to be sure the students have found the right page.

30 **Which of these is the best name for the story?**

- ○ Naming Popie
- ● A Puppy's Cries
- ○ Tears on the Pillow

31 **Put a pillow on my head is not a complete sentence. What could Jodi add if she wanted to make it a complete sentence?**

__________ put a pillow on my head.

- ○ Them
- ○ Us
- ● I

32 **Popie is Jodi's puppy.**

- ○ Jodi's puppy Popie is?
- ○ Jodi's Popie is puppy?
- ● Is Popie Jodi's puppy?

Say Put your finger on Number 33 at the top of the page. Read the story. Part of the story is missing. Find the sentence that best completes the story. Mark your answer.

Move down to Number 34. Read the story. Find the sentence that best completes the story. Mark your answer.

We're going to stop now. We will do more reading and language arts items later. Check to see that you have completely filled in your answer circles with dark marks. Make sure that any marks for answers you changed have been completely erased. Now you may close your books.

Collect the students' books. Distribute them again when you continue. This can be later in the same day or on a different day.

33 **Rick likes sports.**

He plays basketball.

____

- ● He runs in races.
- ○ He reads books.
- ○ He draws pictures.

34 **I had a garden.**

I planted seeds there.

____

- ○ I like to help cook.
- ● Then I watered them.
- ○ My house is small.

Part 2

Distribute the students' books and be sure they have pencils.

Say Open your books to page 82. You are going to do another reading and language arts activity. Remember to make sure the circles for your answer choices are completely filled in. Press your pencil firmly so that your marks come out dark. Completely erase any marks for answers you change.

Find Sample B at the top of the page. Listen carefully. Look at the sentence. Some of the words are missing. Find the words that make the sentence complete. *(pause)* The second answer, *was windy*, is correct because it completes the sentence correctly. Fill in the circle under the second answer. Be sure your answer circle is completely filled in with a dark mark and that you have marked the correct answer circle.

Check to see that the students have correctly filled in their answer circles with a dark mark.

Say We will begin with a story you will read on your own.

Read the whole story. Then answer Numbers 35 through 39.

You may look back at the story to answer the questions. Be sure to answer Numbers 35 through 39. When you come to a GO sign at the bottom of a page, go on to the next page and continue working. When you come to the STOP sign after Number 39, wait for me to tell you what to do next. You may begin.

Allow ten minutes. Walk around the room to make sure the students understand what they are supposed to do. Be sure the students stop working after Number 39.

Unit 4
Test Practice
Test 1 Reading and Language Arts Part 2

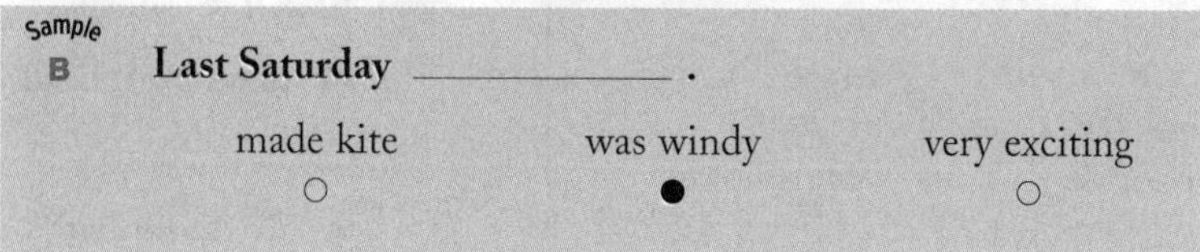

Sample B
Last Saturday ______ .
made kite
was windy
very exciting

Directions: This story is about how Ant and Bird helped one another. Read the whole story. Then answer Numbers 35 through 39.

Ant and Bird

One day Ant walked near a river. Maybe she was looking for food. Or, maybe she just wanted to walk. No one knows for sure. But the sun was bright, and Ant could not see very well. She fell right into the water.

82 Test 1 **Reading and Language Arts Part 2**

Ant tried to climb back out. The rocks were slippery. Bird flew by and saw Ant. At first, Bird thought Ant would make a tasty snack. But Bird had just eaten breakfast. He felt sorry for Ant. He swooped down and dropped a leaf into the water. Ant hopped on and floated to land.

That was enough adventure for one day. Ant started the journey home. In the forest, she saw Bird again. A man was trying to catch Bird with a net. Ant knew just what to do. She bit the man's foot. The man yelled and dropped his net. And Bird got away.

35 **What was Ant doing at the beginning of the story?**

- ○ She was looking for food.
- ○ She was going for a swim.
- ● She was walking by a river.

36 **What caused Ant to fall?**

- ● The sun was bright.
- ○ A leaf got in her way.
- ○ The rocks were wet.

37 **Bird thought**

Ant would make a tasty snack.

What does this mean?

- ○ Ant looked like a fish.
- ○ Ant carried good treats.
- ● Ant might be good to eat.

38 **After getting out of the river, Ant started the journey home. Journey means about the same as**

○ song ● trip ○ path

Say You can stop working now. We will do the rest of the questions together. For each question, fill in the circle that goes with the answer you choose.

For Numbers 40 and 41, find the word for each blank that best completes the story. Read the whole story in the box. Be sure to answer Numbers 40 and 41. Mark your answers.

Allow time for the students to fill in their answers.

Say Look at the next page, page 87.

Check to be sure the students have found the right page.

39 **What was Ant doing at the beginning of the story?**

- ● Ant saves Bird from trouble.
- ○ Ant goes home with Bird.
- ○ Ant gets caught inside a net.

Directions: **For Numbers 40 and 41, find the word for each blank that best completes the story.**

> The man with the net worked in a (40). He wanted to (41) birds and learn about them.

40
- ○ train
- ● zoo
- ○ pool

41
- ● study
- ○ ride
- ○ swim

Allow time between items for the students to fill in their answers.

Say For Numbers 42 and 43, find the word for each blank that best completes the story. Read the whole story in the box. Be sure to answer Numbers 42 and 43. Mark your answers.

Move down to Number 44. Find the word that can take the place of "Ant and Bird" in the sentence. Mark your answer.

Number 45. Find the sentence that is written correctly. Mark your answer.

Look at the next page, page 88.

Check to be sure the students have found the right page.

Directions: For Numbers 42 and 43, find the word for each blank that best completes the story.

> As Bird flew away, he saw a (42) in the woods.
>
> It was a good place to (43) fish.

42
- ○ tree
- ○ cave
- ● lake

43
- ● catch
- ○ buy
- ○ swim

44 **Ant and Bird are at home in the woods.**
- ○ She
- ○ We
- ● They

45
- ● Bird and Ant help each other now.
- ○ Bird help Ant every day.
- ○ One time, Bird help Ant's family.

Say The students in Room 10 are learning how to write letters. Look at Misty's letter to her cousin Nancy as you answer Numbers 46 through 49.

Allow time between items for the students to fill in their answers.

Say Put your finger on Number 46. Read the words. Which punctuation mark comes at the end? Mark your answer.

Number 47. Read the sentence. Which punctuation mark comes at the end? Mark your answer.

Number 48. Read the sentence. Find the part of the sentence that needs a capital letter. Mark your answer.

Number 49. Read the words. Find the part that needs a capital letter. Mark your answer.

Allow the students to take a break at this point.

Say Look at the next page, page 89.

Check to be sure the students have found the right page.

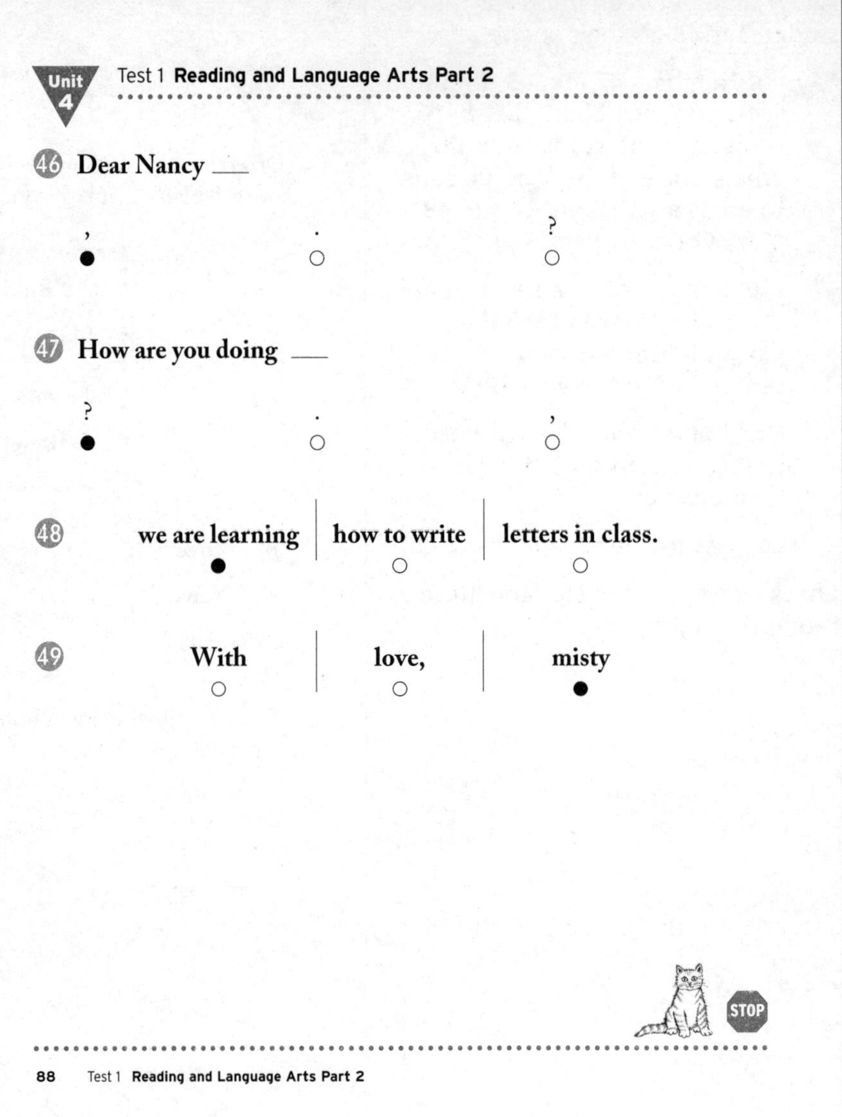

Allow time between items for the students to fill in their answers.

Say Put your finger on Number 50. Listen to this sentence: We will eat some apples. Find the word "eat ... eat." Mark your answer.

Put your finger on Number 51. Listen to this sentence: The clown has a funny face. Find the word "face ... face." Mark your answer.

Now you will do some items about sentences. You will read the sentence and choose the picture that shows what the sentence tells.

Number 52. Read the sentence. Find the picture that shows what the sentence tells. Mark your answer.

Number 53. Read the sentence. Find the picture that shows what the sentence tells. Mark your answer.

Look at the next page, page 90.

Check to be sure the students have found the right page.

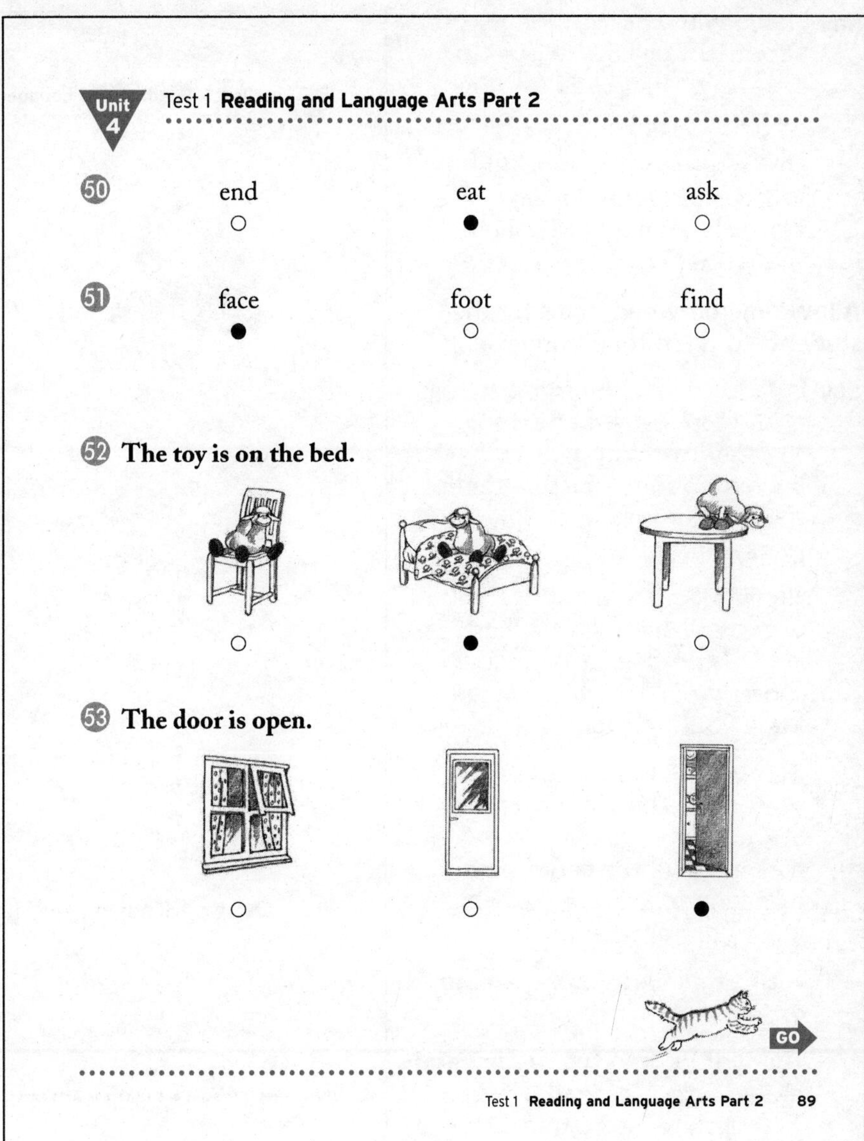

Unit 4 Test 1 **Reading and Language Arts Part 2**

50 end ○ eat ● ask ○

51 face ● foot ○ find ○

52 **The toy is on the bed.**

○ ● ○

53 **The door is open.**

○ ○ ●

GO

Test 1 **Reading and Language Arts Part 2** 89

Say Now I will read you a story about two children. Listen to the story. Then I will ask you questions about it.

One morning Steven and his little sister were playing in the yard. They saw a bird land on the fence beside the house.

Allow time between items for the students to fill in their answers.

Say Put your finger on Number 54 at the top of the page. Look at the pictures. Who was with Steven? Find the picture that shows who was with Steven. Mark your answer.

Number 55. Look at the pictures. Where did the bird land? Find the picture that shows where the bird landed. Mark your answer.

Number 56. Look at the sentences. The story says that Steven and his sister were playing. Find the sentence that tells where they were playing. Mark your answer.

Look at me and listen to more of the story.

The bird flew to the ground and picked up some dead grass. Then it flew into a tree. Steven said that the bird was building a nest.

Put your finger on Number 57. What is this story mostly about? Look at the words. Find the words that answer the question "What is this story mostly about"? Mark your answer.

It's time to stop. You have completed this part of the Test Practice. Check to see that you have completely filled in your answer circles with dark marks. Make sure that any marks for answers you changed have been completely erased.

Unit 4 Test 1 **Reading and Language Arts Part 2**

54 ○ ● ○

55 ○ ● ○

56 They were in the yard. ● They were in school. ○ They were on the steps. ○

57 two friends ○ playing a game ○ what a bird did ●

STOP

90 Test 1 **Reading and Language Arts Part 2**

Review the items with the students. Have students indicate completion of the lesson by entering their score for this activity on the progress chart at the beginning of the book. Provide the students whatever help is necessary to record their scores. Then collect the students' books if this is the end of the testing session.

Unit 4 Test 2 Basic Skills

Administration Time: 60 minutes

Distribute scratch paper to the students for the computation items.

Say Turn to the Test Practice section of your book on page 91. This is Test 2, Basic Skills.

Check to see that the students have found page 91.

Say This test will check how well you remember word study, vocabulary, and computation skills. Find Sample A at the top of the page. Listen carefully. Look at the words. Find the word that has the same beginning sound as "pat ... pat." *(pause)* The second answer, *pen*, is correct. *Pat* and *pen* begin with the same sound. Mark the circle for the second answer. Be sure your answer circle is completely filled in with a dark mark.

Check to see that the students have filled in the correct answer circle.

Say Now you will do the Test Practice items. Listen carefully to what I say because there are many different kinds of items in this part. Are you ready? Let's begin.

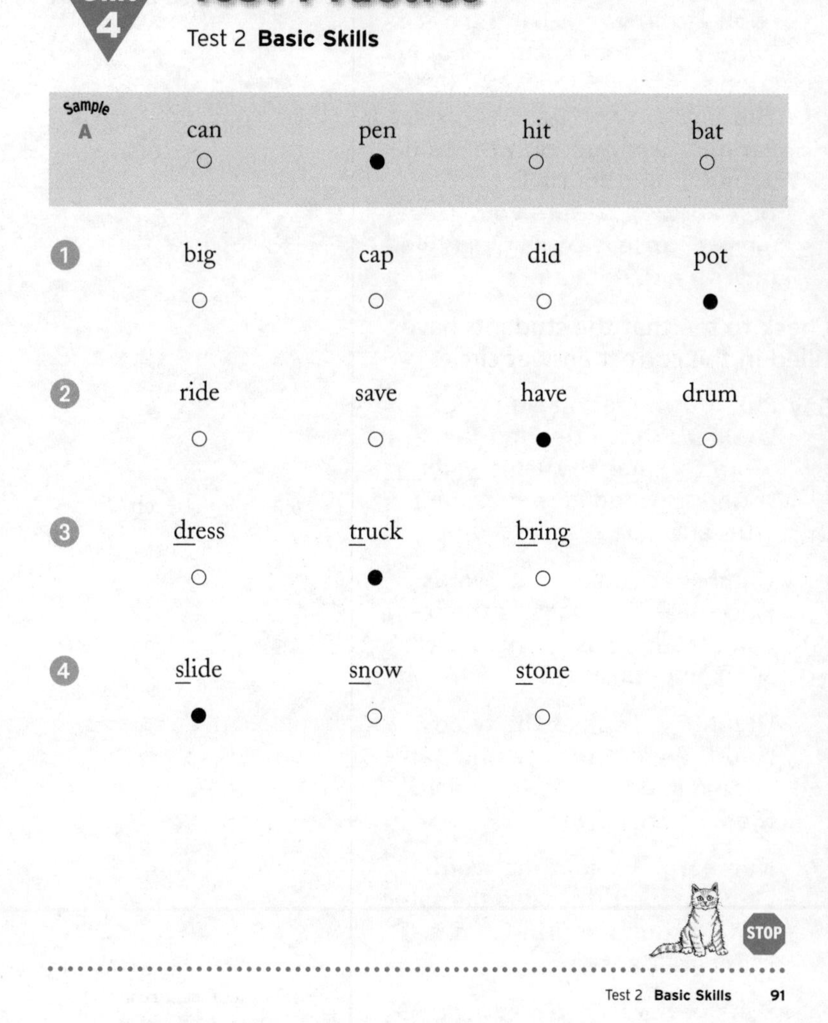

Allow time between items for the students to fill in their answers.

Say Put your finger beside Number 1. Look at the four words. Find the word that has the same beginning sound as "pig ... pig." Mark your answer.

Number 2. Look at the words. Find the word that has the same beginning sound as "hide ... hide." Mark your answer.

Number 3. Look at the words. The beginning part of each word is underlined. This is the part of the word I want you to listen to. Find the word that has the same beginning sound as "try ... try." Mark your answer.

Put your finger beside Number 4. Find the word that has the same beginning sound as "slow ... slow." Mark your answer.

Look at the next page, page 92.

Check to be sure the students have found the right page.

Say Find Sample B at the top of the page. These questions are a little different. Listen carefully. Look at the words. Find the word that has the same ending sound as "far ... far." *(pause)* The first answer, *bear*, is correct. *Far* and *bear* end with the same sound. Mark the circle for the first answer. Be sure your answer circle is completely filled in with a dark mark.

Check to see that the students have filled in the correct answer circle.

Say Put your finger on Number 5. Look at the words. Find the word that has the same ending sound as "road ... road." Mark your answer.

Number 6. Look at the words. Find the word that has the same ending sound as "park ... park." Mark your answer.

Number 7. Look at the words. Find the word that has the same ending sound as "dish ... dish." Mark your answer.

Number 8. Look at the words. Find the word that has the same ending sound as "ring ... ring." Mark your answer.

Look at the next page, page 93.

Check to be sure the students have found the right page.

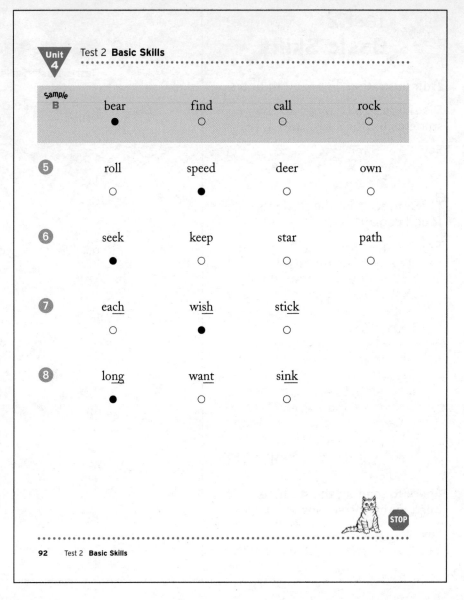

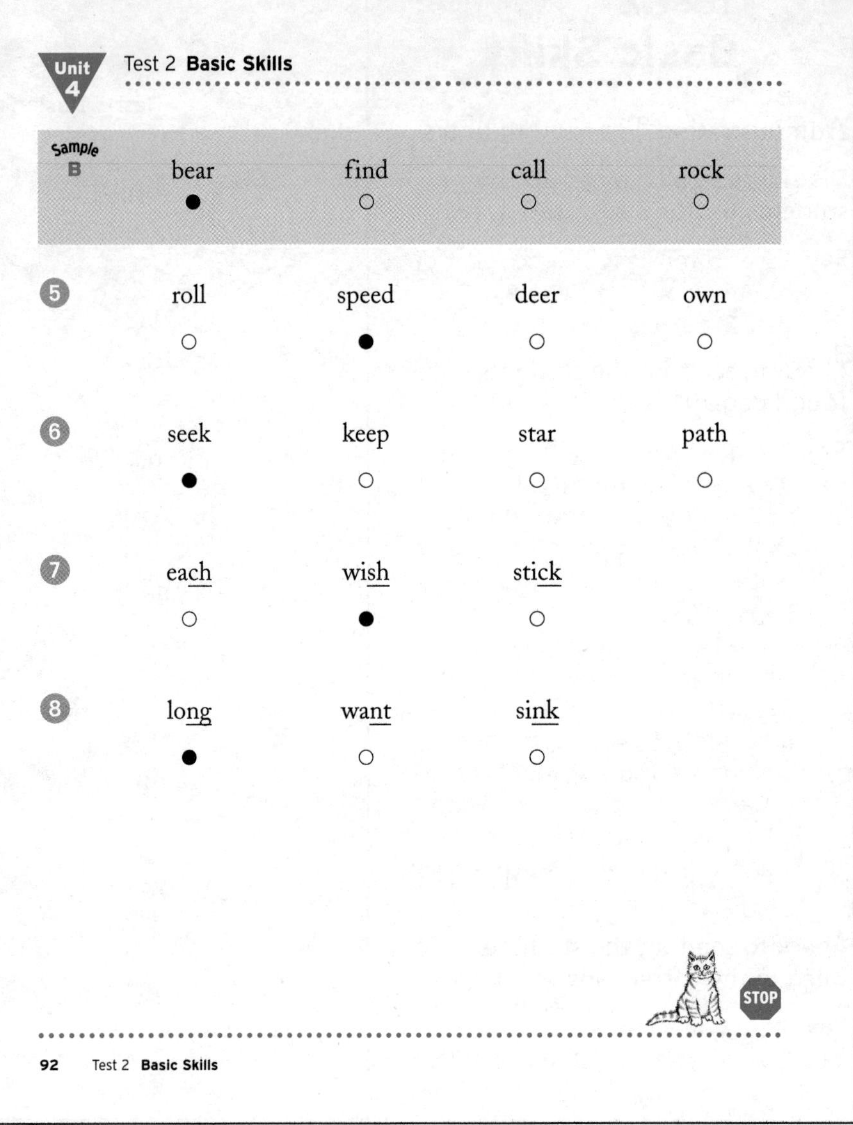

Say Put your finger on Sample C at the top of the page. Look at the picture of the pan and the words beside it. Which word has the same vowel sound (middle sound) as "pan ... pan"? *(pause)* The correct answer is *have*. Mark the circle under the last answer. Be sure your answer circle is completely filled in with a dark mark.

Check to see that the students have filled in the correct answer circle.

Say Remember, for these items, listen only for the vowel sound. This is the sound in the middle of the word. You must be sure to ignore the beginning and ending sounds.

Allow time between items for the students to fill in their answers.

Say Put your finger on Number 9 Look at the step. Find the word that has the same vowel sound (middle sound) as "step ... step." Mark your answer.

Number 10. Look at the path. Find the word that has the same vowel sound (middle sound) as "path ... path." Mark your answer.

Number 11. Look at the hose. Find the word that has the same vowel sound (middle sound) as "hose ... hose." Mark your answer.

Number 12. Look at the street. Find the word that has the same vowel sound (middle sound) as "street ... street." Mark your answer.

Look at the next page, page 94.

Check to be sure the students have found the right page.

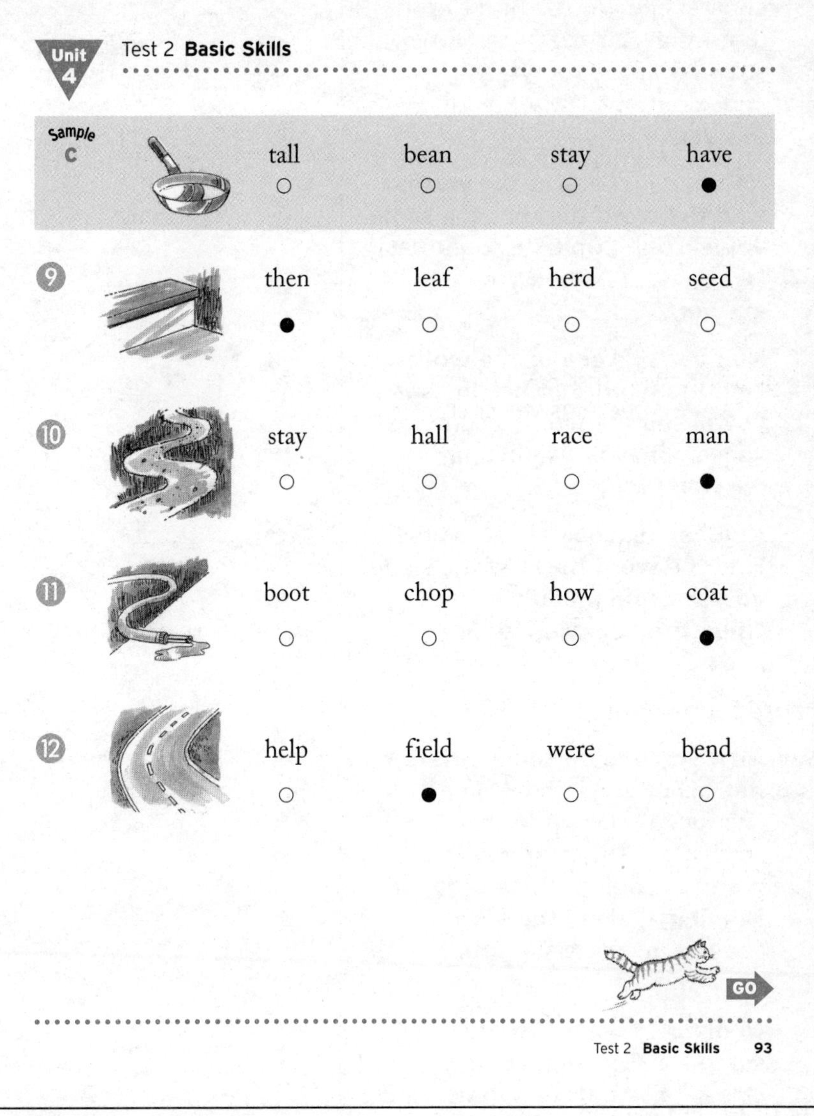

Say Put your finger on Number 13. Look at the words. Find the word that has the same vowel sound (middle sound) as "book ... book." Mark your answer.

Number 14. Look at the words. Find the word that has the same vowel sound (middle sound) as "lock ... lock." Mark your answer.

Number 15. Look at the words. Find the word that has the same vowel sound (middle sound) as "have ... have." Mark your answer.

Number 16. Look at the words. Find the word that has the same vowel sound (middle sound) as "blue ... blue." Mark your answer.

Pause for a moment.

Say Now you will do some different items. Put your finger on Number 17. Listen to this sentence: "The bear was in the woods." Look at the words for Number 17. Find the word "bear ... bear." Mark your answer.

Number 18. Listen to this sentence: "He walked down the street." Look at the words. Find the word "down ... down." Mark your answer.

Number 19. Listen to this sentence: "The birds sat in the tree." Look at the words. Find the word "sat ... sat." Mark your answer.

Number 20. Listen to this sentence. "Do you play hide and seek?" Look at the words. Find the word "seek ... seek." Mark your answer.

Say Look at the next page, page 95.

Check to be sure the students have found the right page.

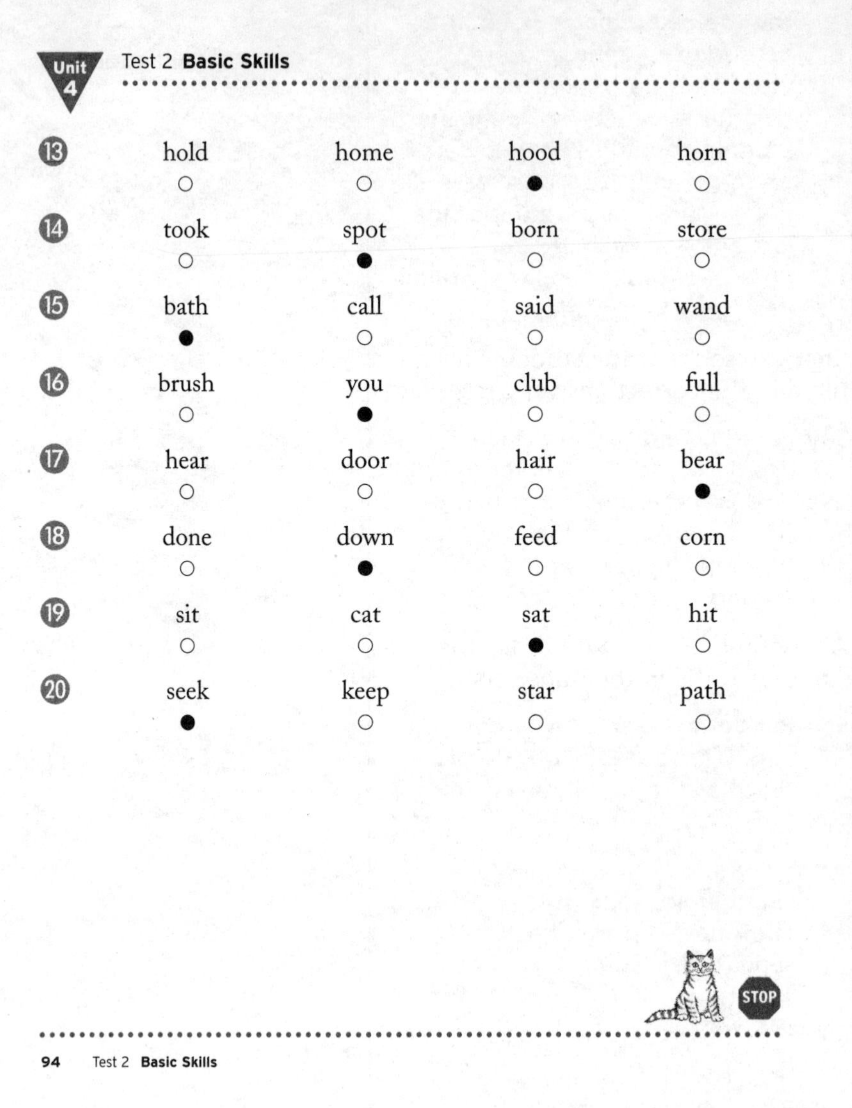

Unit 4 Test 2 **Basic Skills**

13	hold ○	home ○	hood ●	horn ○
14	took ○	spot ●	born ○	store ○
15	bath ●	call ○	said ○	wand ○
16	brush ○	you ●	club ○	full ○
17	hear ○	door ○	hair ○	bear ●
18	done ○	down ●	feed ○	corn ○
19	sit ○	cat ○	sat ●	hit ○
20	seek ●	keep ○	star ○	path ○

STOP

94 Test 2 **Basic Skills**

Say Find Sample D at the top of the page. Listen carefully. Look at the words. Find the word that means "something that you play ... something that you play." *(pause)* The correct answer is *game*. Mark the circle for the second answer. Be sure your answer circle is completely filled in with a dark mark.

Check to see that the students have marked the correct circle. For the following items, allow time between items for the students to fill in their answers.

Say Now you will do more items like Sample D. Put your finger beside Number 21. Look at the words. Find the word that names "something that grows on a tree ... something that grows on a tree." Mark your answer.

Number 22. Look at the words. Find the word that names "a thing to sit on ... a thing to sit on." Mark your answer.

Number 23. Look at the words. Find the word that names "something that is funny ... something that is funny." Mark your answer.

Number 24. Look at the words. Find the word that names "something to write on ... something to write on." Mark your answer.

Number 25. Look at the words. Find the word that names "something you wear on your hands ... something you wear on your hands." Mark your answer.

Allow the students a moment to rest.

Say Look at the next page, page 96.

Check to be sure the students have found the right page.

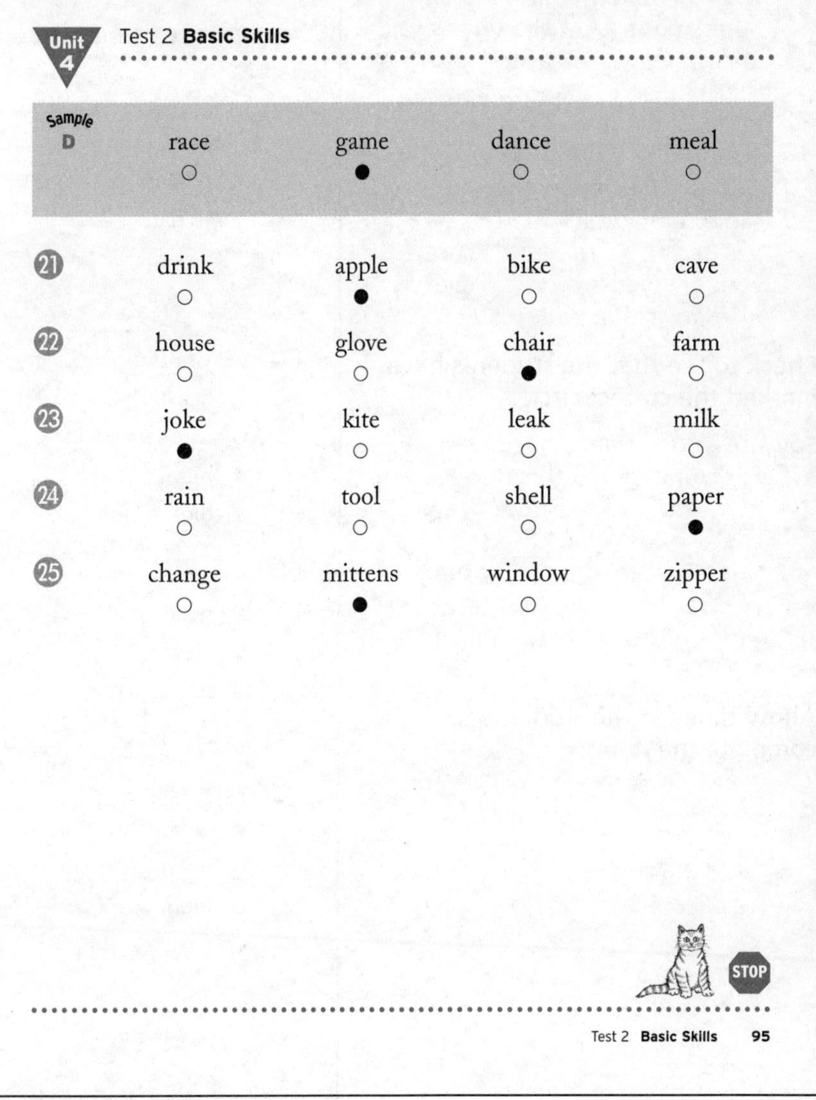

Say Find Sample E. Read the phrase with the underlined word and think about what the word means. Now look at the answers. Which answer means about the same as the underlined word? *(pause)* The right answer is *hat*. *Cap* and *hat* mean about the same thing. Mark the circle beside the word *hat*. Be sure your answer circle is completely filled in with a dark mark.

Check to see that the students have marked the correct circle.

Say Put your finger on Number 26. For Numbers 26 through 33, mark the circle for the answer that means about the same as the underlined word in the phrase. Start working now. Work until you come to the STOP sign after Number 33.

Allow time for the students to complete the items.

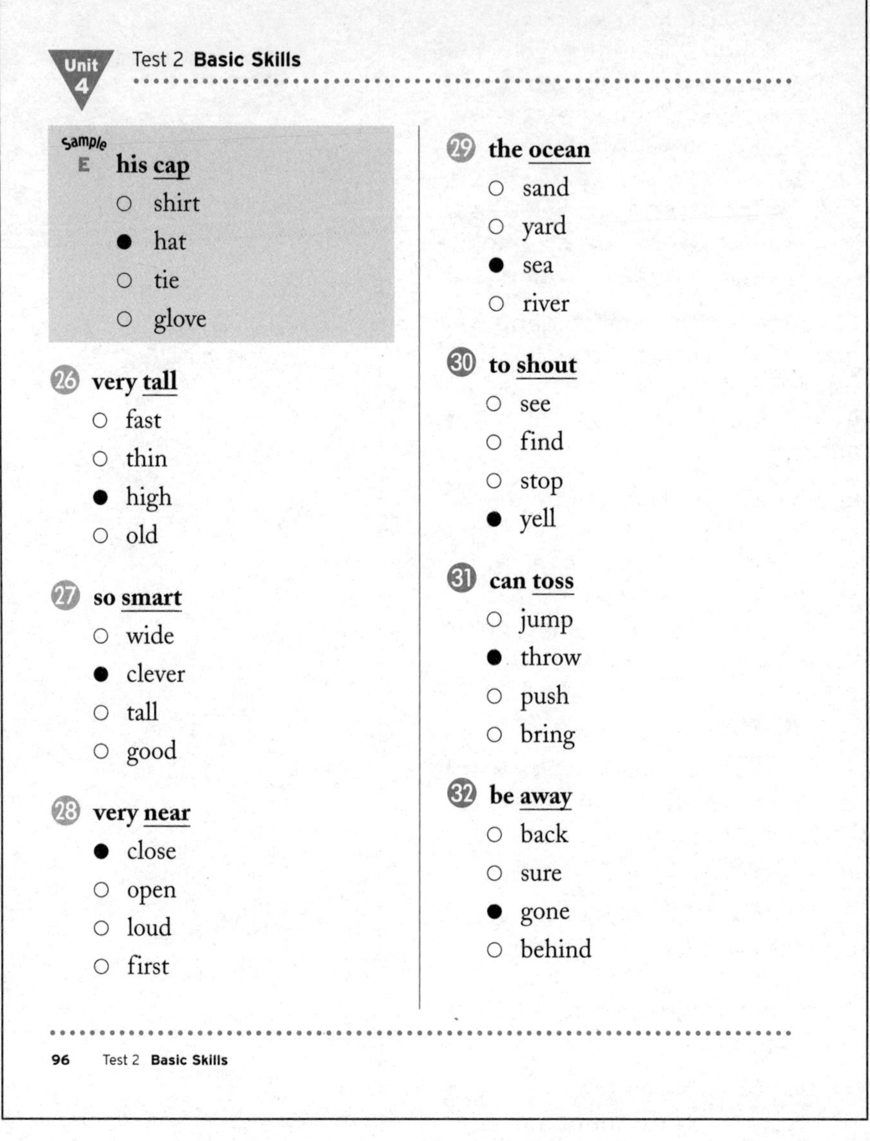

Unit 4 Test 2 **Basic Skills**

Sample E **his cap**
- ○ shirt
- ● hat
- ○ tie
- ○ glove

26 **very tall**
- ○ fast
- ○ thin
- ● high
- ○ old

27 **so smart**
- ○ wide
- ● clever
- ○ tall
- ○ good

28 **very near**
- ● close
- ○ open
- ○ loud
- ○ first

29 **the ocean**
- ○ sand
- ○ yard
- ● sea
- ○ river

30 **to shout**
- ○ see
- ○ find
- ○ stop
- ● yell

31 **can toss**
- ○ jump
- ● throw
- ○ push
- ○ bring

32 **be away**
- ○ back
- ○ sure
- ● gone
- ○ behind

96 Test 2 **Basic Skills**

Say You should be on page 97. Find Sample F in the middle of the page. Read the story to yourself while I read it out loud. There is a blank in the story. When I come to the blank, I will say the word "blank."

Dad added blank to my bath. It made lots of bubbles.

Now look at the answer choices. Which answer choice fits best in the blank? *(pause)* The correct answer is *soap*. Mark the circle for the last answer. Be sure your answer circle is completely filled in with a dark mark.

Check to see that the students have filled in the correct answer circle.

Say Now you will do more items like Sample F. Read the story to yourself while I read it out loud. Find the answer that fits best in the blank.

Number 34. Listen carefully. "The soup had too much blank. It tasted like ocean water." Mark your answer.

Number 35. Listen carefully. "Nomi could not hear the teacher. The students next to her were blank." Mark your answer.

Look at the next page, page 98.

Check to be sure the students have found the right page.

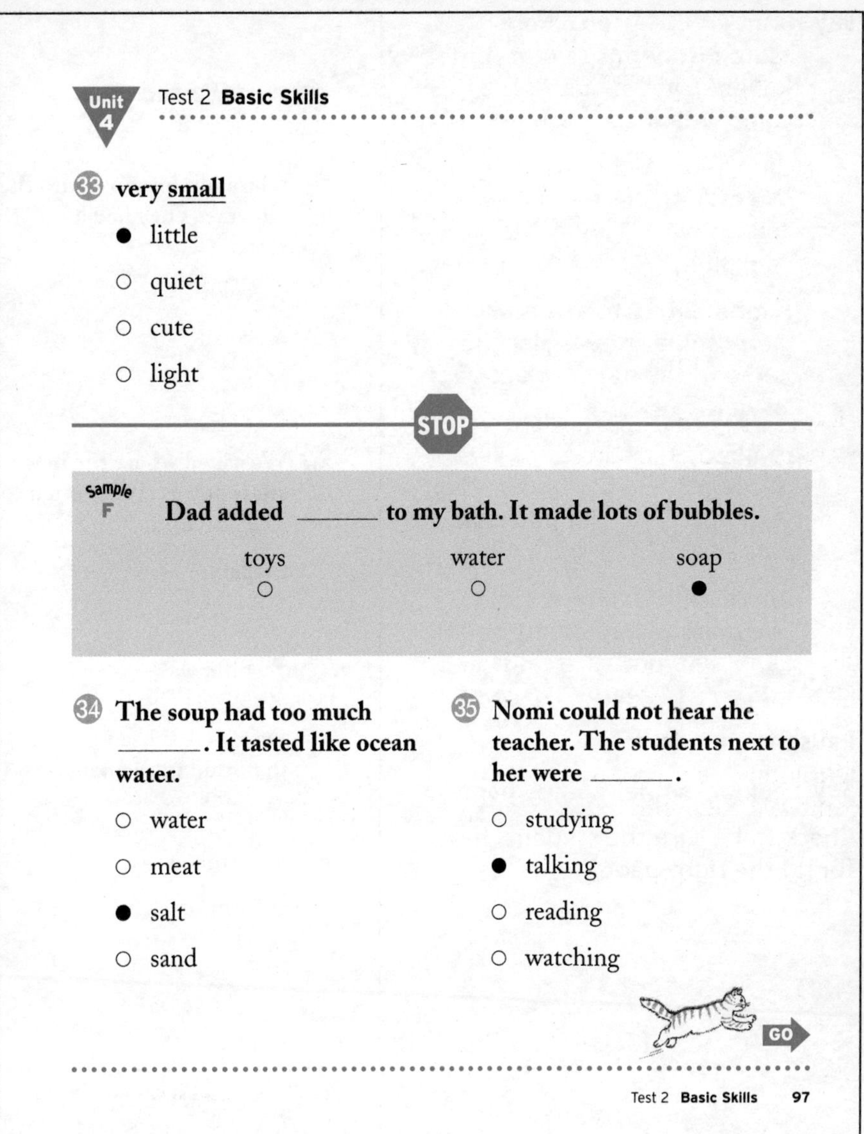

Unit 4 Test 2 **Basic Skills**

33 **very small**

- ● little
- ○ quiet
- ○ cute
- ○ light

STOP

Sample F **Dad added ______ to my bath. It made lots of bubbles.**

toys	water	soap
○	○	●

34 **The soup had too much ______. It tasted like ocean water.**

- ○ water
- ○ meat
- ● salt
- ○ sand

35 **Nomi could not hear the teacher. The students next to her were ______.**

- ○ studying
- ● talking
- ○ reading
- ○ watching

GO

Test 2 **Basic Skills** 97

Say Number 36. Listen carefully. "Clara put her nose into the flowers. They had a sweet blank." Mark your answer.

Number 37. Listen carefully. "We asked where the new student was. We wanted to blank him." Mark your answer.

Number 38. Listen carefully. "Derry's dad used a blank to pound in the nails." Mark your answer.

Number 39. Listen carefully. "Wade made a big blank when he jumped into the pool." Mark your answer.

Number 40. Listen carefully. "We read a story about a sea blank who buried a chest of gold coins." Mark your answer.

Pause for a moment.

Say Look at the next page, page 99.

Check to be sure the students have found the right page.

36 **Clara put her nose into the flowers. They had a sweet ______.**

- ○ color
- ● smell
- ○ look

37 **We asked where the new student was. We wanted to ______ him.**

- ○ pass
- ○ drop
- ● meet

38 **Derry's dad used a ______. to pound in the nails.**

- ○ saw
- ● hammer
- ○ drill

39 **Wade made a big ______. when he jumped into the pool.**

- ● splash
- ○ slide
- ○ punch

40 **We read a story about a sea ______ who buried a chest of gold coins.**

- ○ butcher
- ○ fireman
- ● pirate

Say In the next part of the Test Practice, you will show how well you can solve arithmetic problems. Listen very carefully to what I say. When you answer a question, fill in the circle for the answer you think is right. Don't write anything else on the page. If you want to work a problem, use the scratch paper I gave you. Find Sample G at the top of the page.

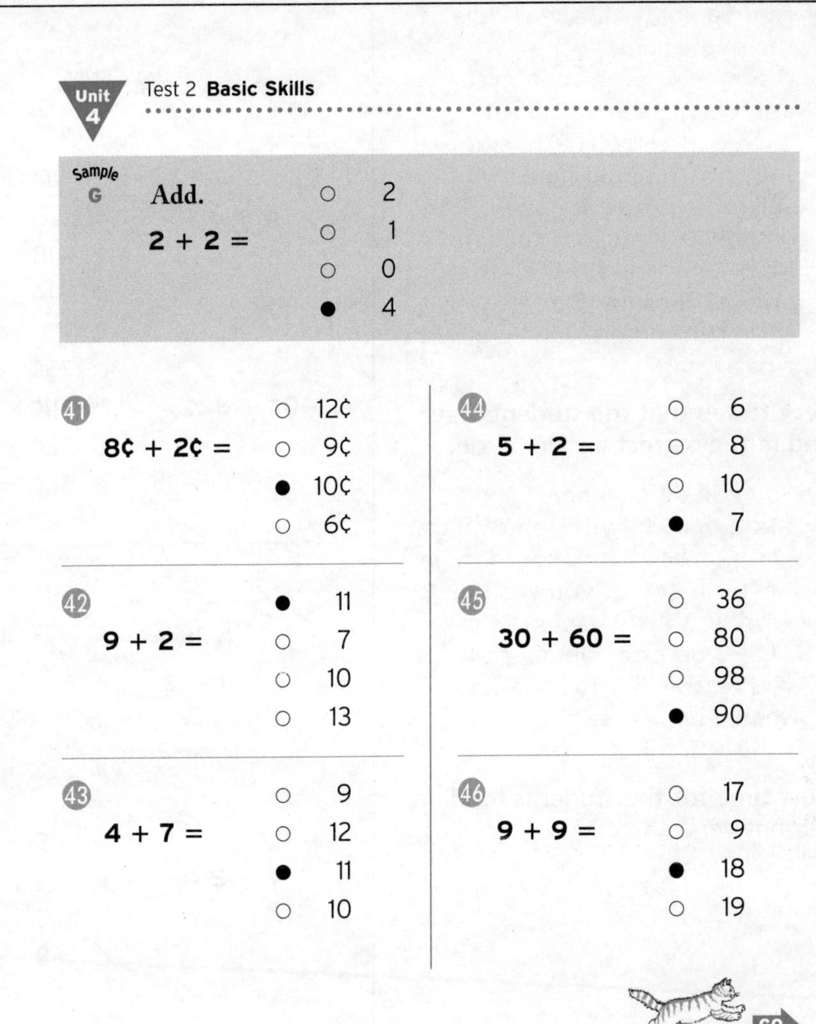

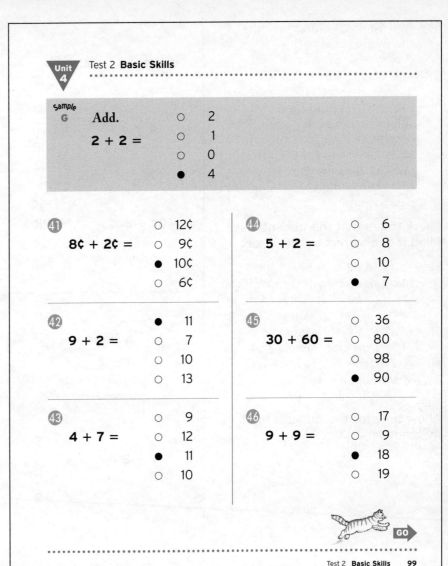

Unit 4 Test 2 **Basic Skills**

Sample G **Add.**

2 + 2 =

- ○ 2
- ○ 1
- ○ 0
- ● 4

41 **8¢ + 2¢ =**

- ○ 12¢
- ○ 9¢
- ● 10¢
- ○ 6¢

42 **9 + 2 =**

- ● 11
- ○ 7
- ○ 10
- ○ 13

43 **4 + 7 =**

- ○ 9
- ○ 12
- ● 11
- ○ 10

44 **5 + 2 =**

- ○ 6
- ○ 8
- ○ 10
- ● 7

45 **30 + 60 =**

- ○ 36
- ○ 80
- ○ 98
- ● 90

46 **9 + 9 =**

- ○ 17
- ○ 9
- ● 18
- ○ 19

GO

Test 2 **Basic Skills** 99

Check to see that the students have found Sample G.

Say Look at the addition problem and the numbers beside it. Which answer is the solution to the problem? *(pause)* The last answer, *4*, is correct. Mark the circle for the last answer. Be sure your answer circle is completely filled in with a dark mark.

Check to see that the students have marked the correct circle.

Say You will do Numbers 41 through 50 by yourself. You can work on scratch paper to solve the problems, if you wish. Mark only one circle for each item. Make sure the circle is completely filled in and remember to press your pencil firmly so your mark comes out dark. Do not write anything except your answer choices in your book. Completely erase any marks for answers you change. When you come to the GO sign at the bottom of the page, go on to the next page. Work until you come to the STOP sign after Number 50. Are you ready? You may begin. Remember, these are addition items.

Allow time for the students to fill in their answers. Walk around the room to make sure the students stop after Number 50.

Say Find Sample H in the middle of the page. Look at the subtraction problem and the numbers beside it. Which answer is correct? You may use the scratch paper I gave you to solve the problem. *(pause)* The second answer, *2*, is correct. Mark the circle for the second answer. Be sure your answer circle is completely filled in with a dark mark.

Check to see that the students have filled in the correct answer circle.

Say You will do Numbers 51 through 60 by yourself. You can work on scratch paper to solve the problems, if you wish. Work until you come to the STOP sign after Number 60. Are you ready? You may begin. Remember, these are subtraction items.

Allow time for the students to fill in their answers.

47 **8 + 3 =**
- ○ 12
- ● 11
- ○ 18
- ○ 14

49 **2 + 4 + 3 =**
- ○ 7
- ● 9
- ○ 11
- ○ 8

48 **40¢ + 32¢ =**
- ○ 75¢
- ○ 11¢
- ● 72¢
- ○ 54¢

50 **12¢ + 52¢ =**
- ○ 44¢
- ○ 60¢
- ● 64¢
- ○ 62¢

STOP

Sample H **Subtract.**

4 − 2 =
- ○ 4
- ● 2
- ○ 6
- ○ 1

51 **7 − 2 =**
- ○ 9
- ● 5
- ○ 2
- ○ 8

52 **13 − 6 =**
- ○ 4
- ○ 9
- ● 7
- ○ 6

53 **8 − 5 =**
- ● 3
- ○ 13
- ○ 4
- ○ 5

Say It's time to stop. You have completed Test 2. Check to see that you have completely filled in your answer circles with dark marks. Make sure that any marks for answers you changed have been completely erased. Now you may close your books.

Review the items with the students. Have the students indicate completion of the lesson by entering their score for this activity on the progress chart at the beginning of the book. Provide the students whatever help is necessary to record their scores. Then collect the students' books if this is the end of the testing session.

Unit 4 Test 2 **Basic Skills**

54 **20 − 20 =**
- ○ 40
- ○ 2
- ● 0
- ○ 22

55 **56¢ + 5¢ =**
- ○ 51¢
- ○ 65¢
- ● 61¢
- ○ 55¢

56 **12 − 4 =**
- ○ 6
- ● 8
- ○ 10
- ○ 7

57 **57 − 16 =**
- ○ 51
- ○ 46
- ○ 31
- ● 41

58 **17 − 9 =**
- ● 8
- ○ 9
- ○ 7
- ○ 6

59 **45¢ − 35¢ =**
- ○ 15¢
- ● 10¢
- ○ 20¢
- ○ 5¢

60 **16 − 8 =**
- ○ 7
- ○ 11
- ● 8
- ○ 10

Test 2 **Basic Skills** 101

Unit 4 Test 3 **Mathematics**

Administration Time: 70 minutes in two sessions

Distribute scratch paper to the students.

Part 1

Say **Turn to the Test Practice section of your book on page 102. This is Test 3, Mathematics Part 1.**

Check to see that the students have found page 102.

Say **This test will check how well you solve mathematics problems. Remember to make sure that the circles for your answer choices are completely filled in. Press your pencil firmly so your marks come out dark. Completely erase any marks for answers you change. Do not write anything except your answer choices in your book.**

Find Sample A at the top of the page. Look at the answers and listen carefully. Which answer shows counting by twos? *(pause)* **The second answer is correct because it shows counting by twos. Mark the circle under the second answer. Be sure the circle is completely filled in with a dark mark and that you have marked the correct answer circle.**

Check to see that the students have marked the correct circle.

Say **Now you will do more mathematics problems. Put your finger on Number 1. Do the problems on this page by yourself. When you come to the STOP sign after Number 4, stop working and wait for me to tell you what to do. Are you ready? You may begin.**

Allow time for the students to fill in their answers. Walk around the room to make sure the students stop after Number 4.

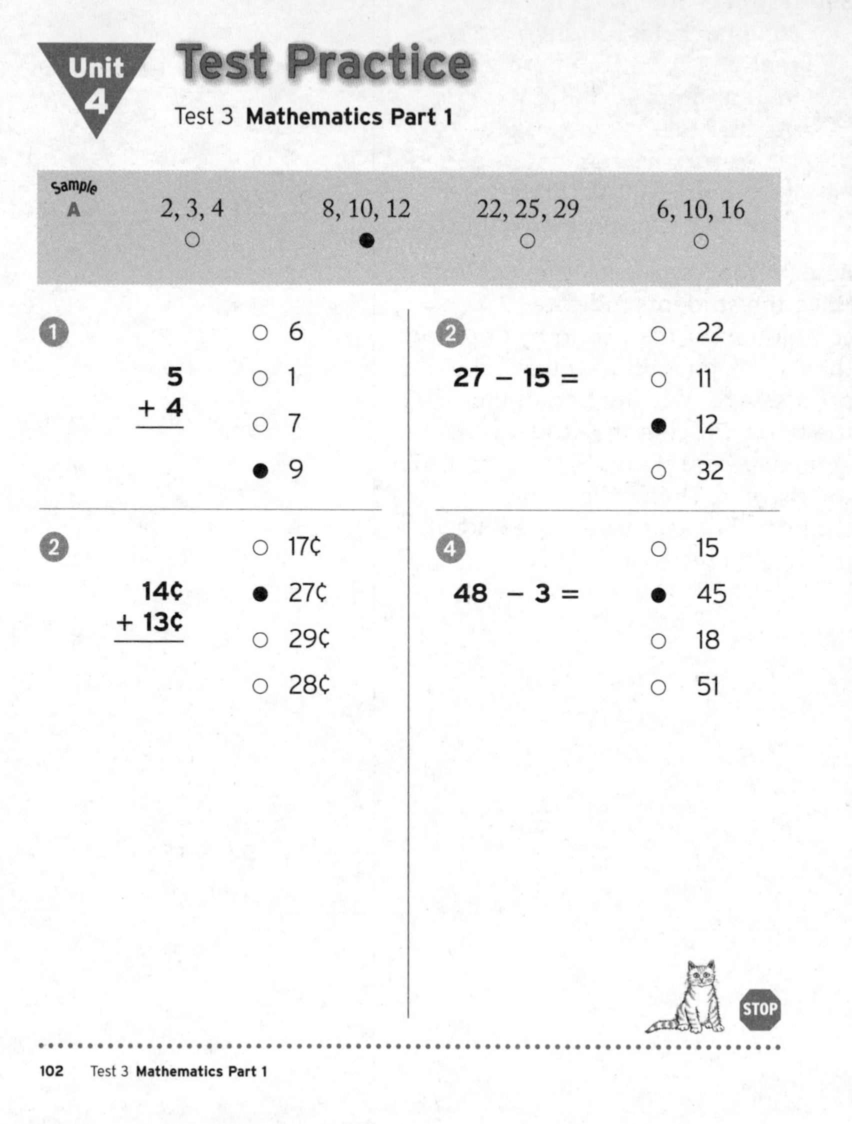

Unit 4 **Test Practice**

Test 3 **Mathematics Part 1**

Sample A

2, 3, 4	8, 10, 12	22, 25, 29	6, 10, 16
○	●	○	○

1 $5 + 4$
- ○ 6
- ○ 1
- ○ 7
- ● 9

2 $27 - 15 =$
- ○ 22
- ○ 11
- ● 12
- ○ 32

2 14¢ + 13¢
- ○ 17¢
- ● 27¢
- ○ 29¢
- ○ 28¢

4 $48 - 3 =$
- ○ 15
- ● 45
- ○ 18
- ○ 51

STOP

102 Test 3 **Mathematics Part 1**

Say **Look at the next page, page 103.**

Check to be sure the students have found the right page.

Say **Put your finger on Number 5. Listen carefully. On his way home from school, Ethan picked up some leaves. At home, he laid the leaves on the table. Find the graph that shows the correct number of each kind of leaf on the table. Mark your answer.**

Look at the next page, page 104.

Check to be sure the students have found the right page.

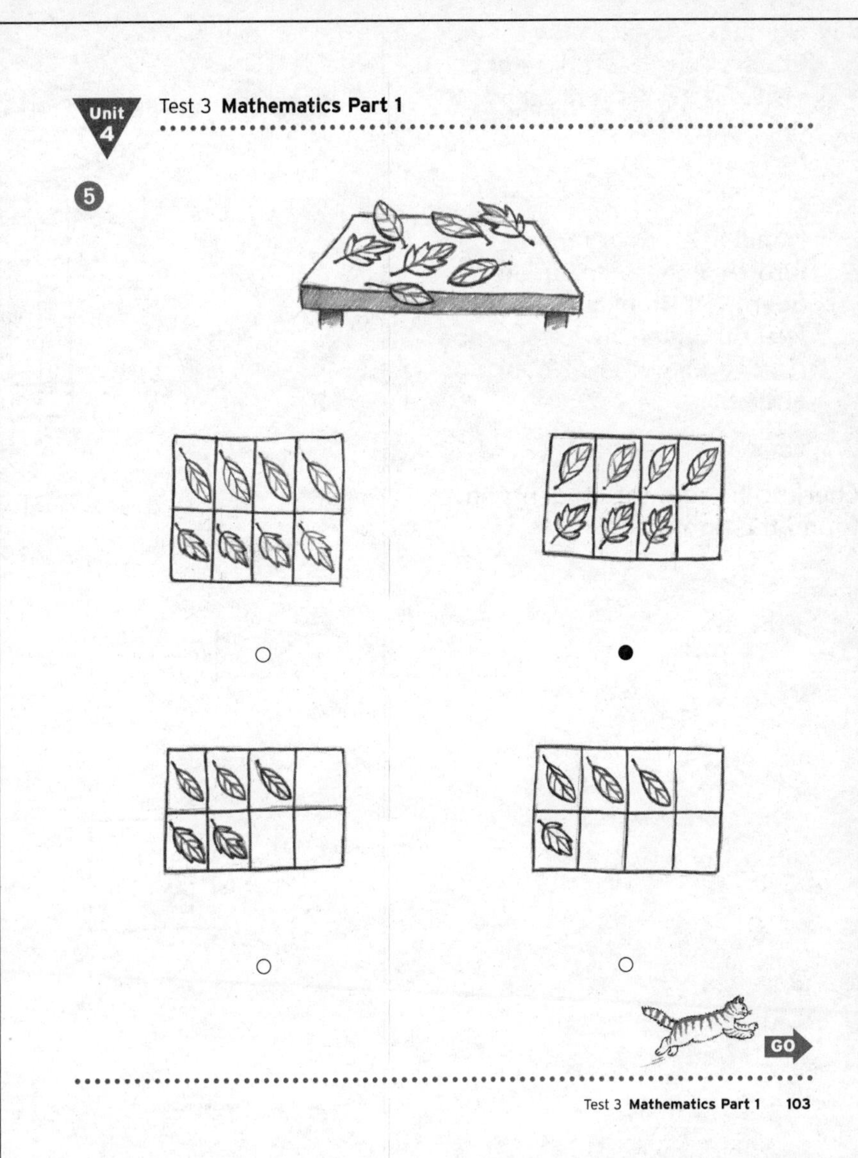

Say Number 6. Look at the calendar. Ethan's class has a different visitor every Friday. Choose the date when Ethan's class will have a visitor. Mark your answer.

Number 7. Ethan's teacher wrote some letters on the board. Which picture shows the letter B under the letter A and next to the letter C? Mark your answer.

Look at the next page, page 105.

Check to be sure the students have found the right page.

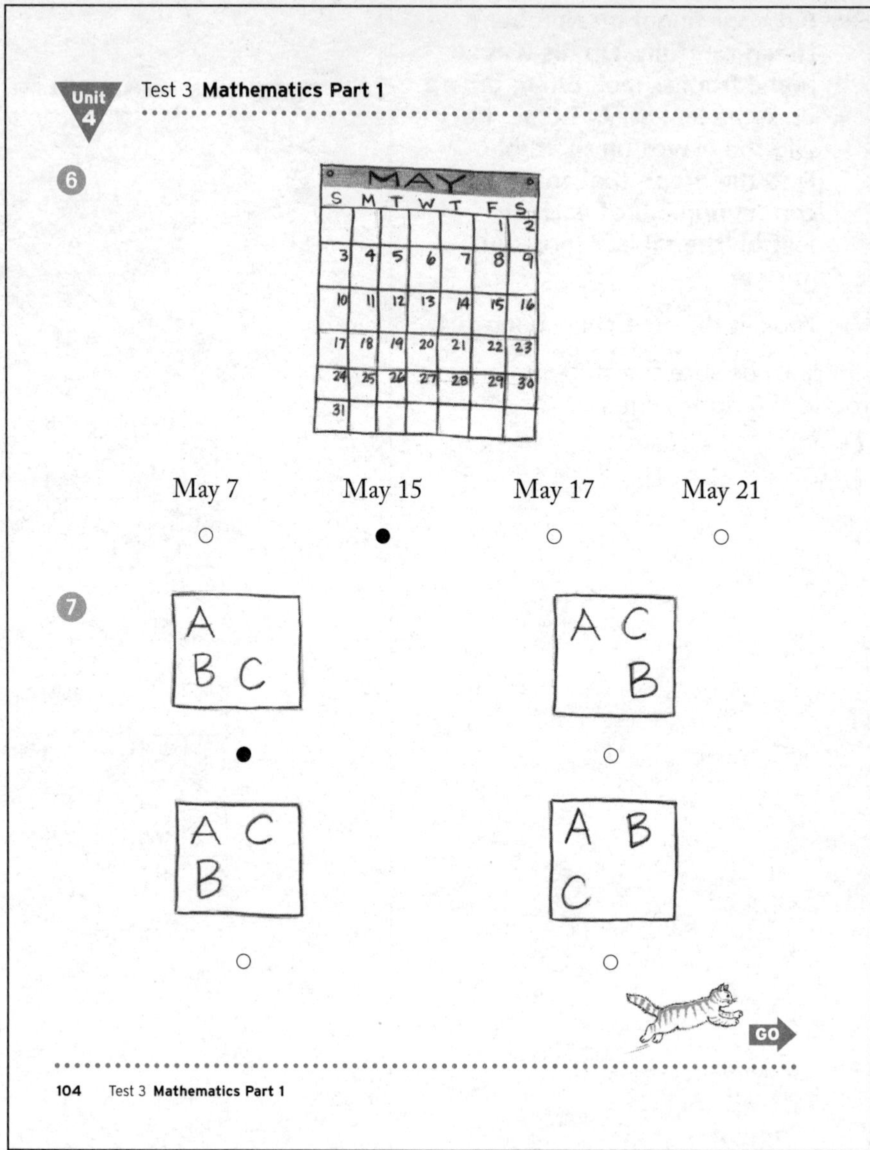

Say **Number 8. Ethan's teacher drew this pattern of shapes on the board. If the pattern continued, what would the next shape be? Mark your answer.**

Number 9. Look at the pattern again. If the pattern continued until there were fourteen shapes in all, what would the last shape be? Mark your answer.

Look at the next page, page 106.

Check to be sure the students have found the right page.

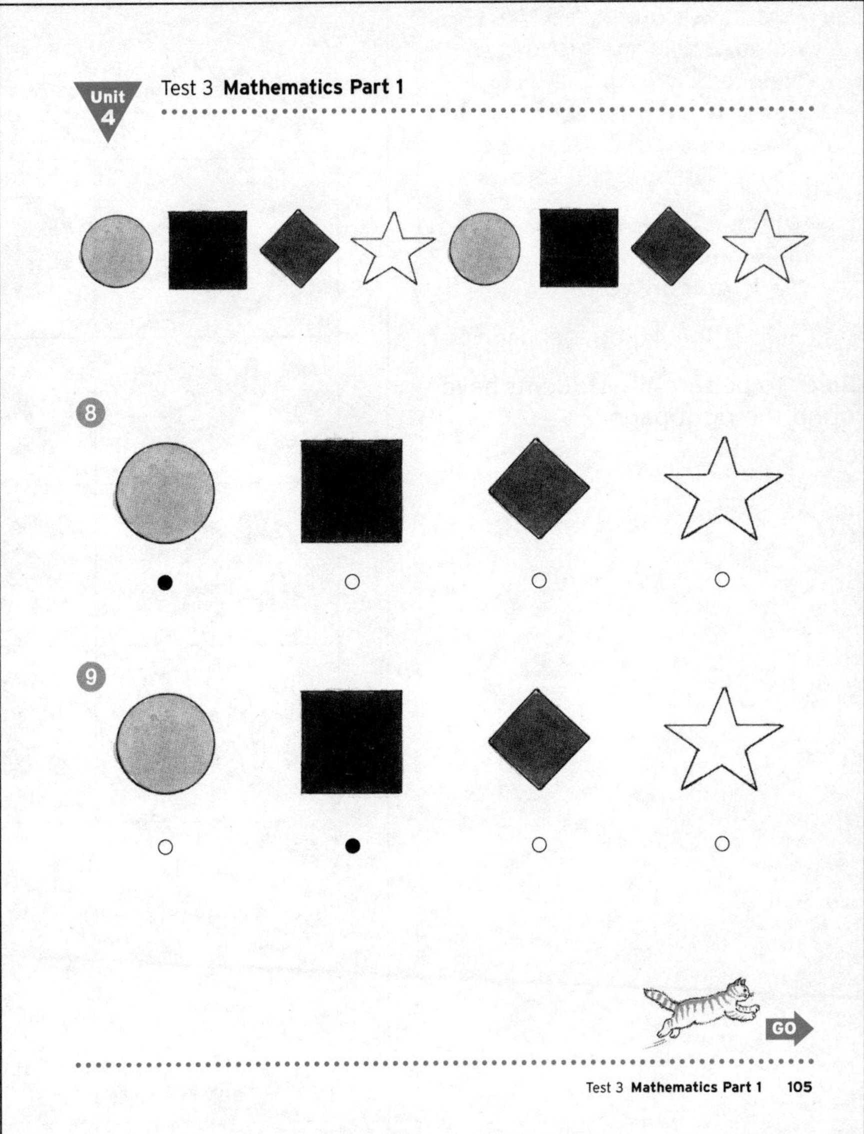

Say Ethan's teacher asked the students to draw pictures of their families. All the pictures were put on one wall. Look at the pictures. Use them to answer Numbers 10 through 12.

Number 10. How many students have families with five people? Mark your answer.

Look at the next page, page 107.

Check to be sure the students have found the right page.

10

1	2	3	4
○	●	○	○

Say Number 11. What size family do most students have? Mark your answer.

Number 12. Which family is the only family of its size?

Look at the next page, page 108.

Check to be sure the students have found the right page.

Say Number 13. Look at the first clock. This was what the clock looked like when the students went out for recess. Recess lasted for 15 minutes. What did the clock look like when the students came inside? Mark your answer.

Number 14. Then the students hung up their coats on hooks by the door. Find the ninth coat from the door. Mark your answer.

Look at the next page, page 109.

Check to be sure the students have found the right page.

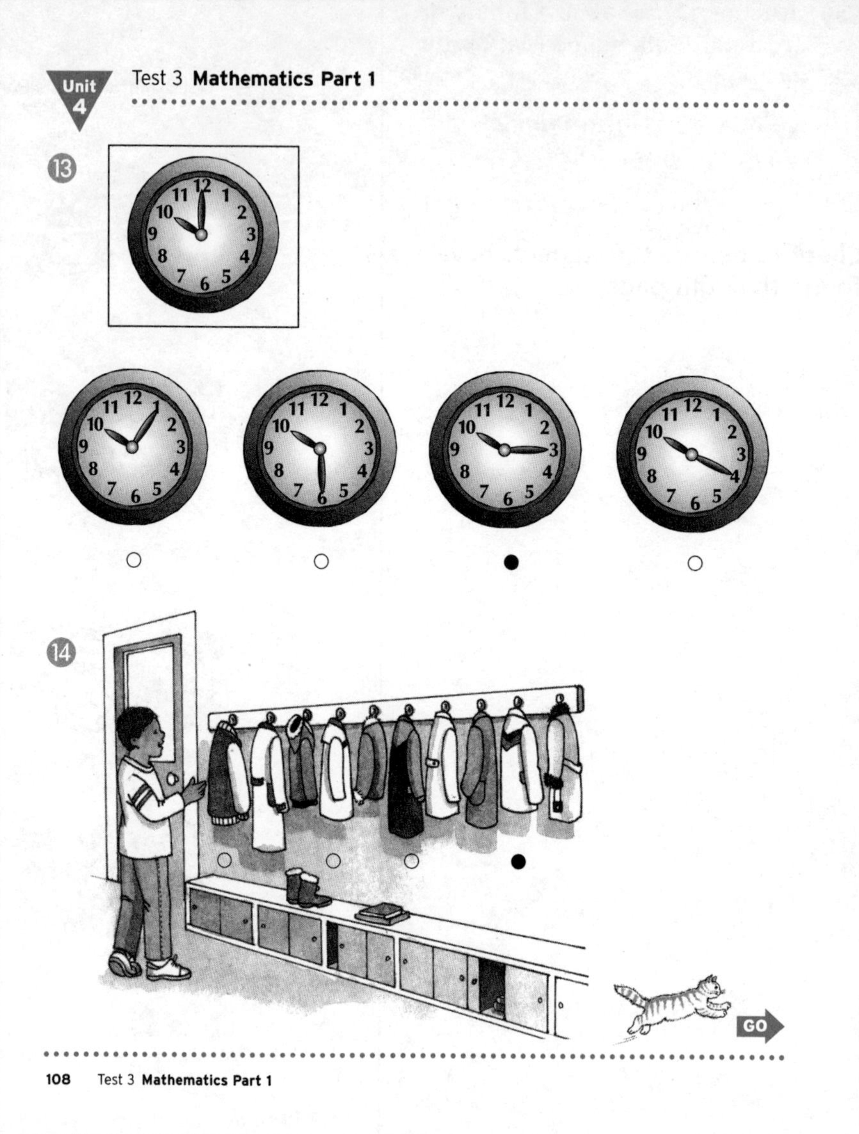

Say Number 15. Look at the pattern in the box at the top of the page. Which of these answer choices has the same kind of pattern? Mark your answer.

Number 16. Look at the pennies and the other items. Find the item that is two pennies long. Mark your answer.

Look at the next page, page 110.

Check to be sure the students have found the right page.

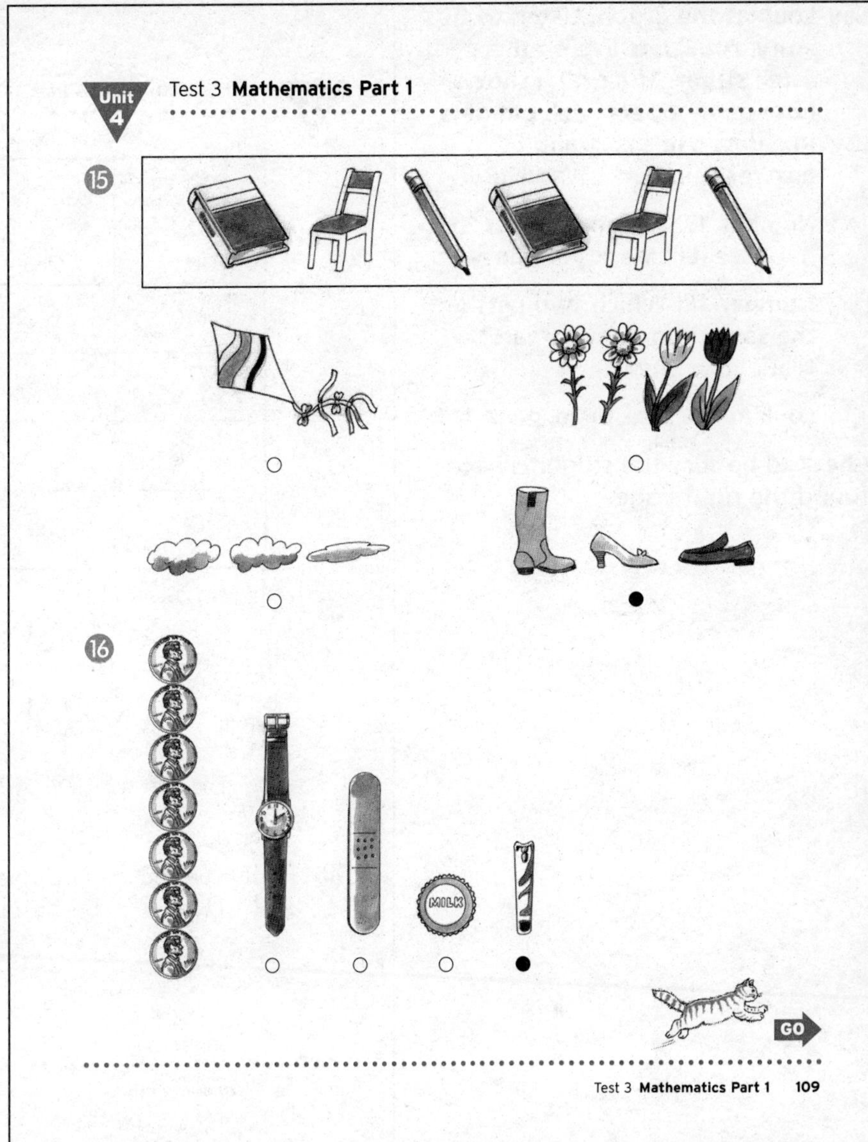

Say Look at the graph. Listen to this story. Four pets live on the same street. The graph shows how many treats each pet gets in a day. Use the graph to answer Numbers 17 and 18.

Number 17. Which pet gets the most treats? Mark your answer.

Number 18. Which two pets get the same number of treats? Mark your answer.

Look at the next page, page 111.

Check to be sure the students have found the right page.

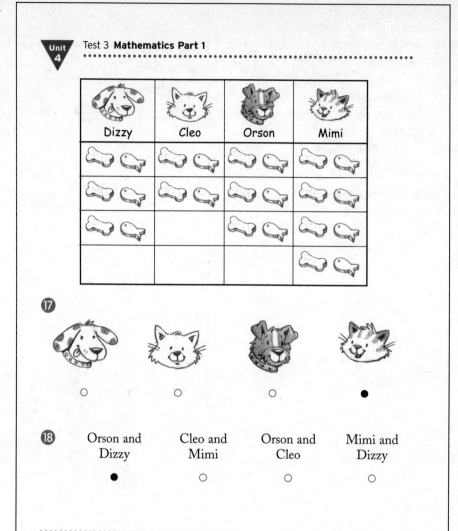

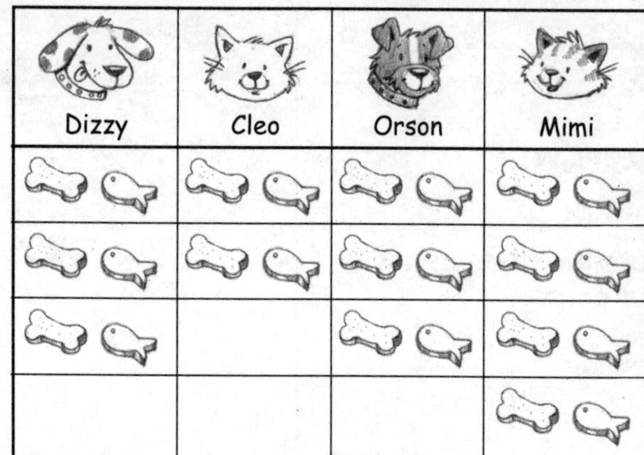

17

○ ○ ○ ●

18

Orson and Dizzy	Cleo and Mimi	Orson and Cleo	Mimi and Dizzy
●	○	○	○

Say Ethan's teacher cut out a perfect pine tree with a folded piece of paper and some scissors. She folded the paper in half. Then she drew one half of the tree next to the fold. Finally, she cut along the line she drew. When she unfolded the shape, she had a pine tree. Everyone got to try this using different shapes.

Number 19. Look at the picture of the paper Ethan cut. Find the shape he made. Mark your answer.

Number 20. Ethan's teacher put some items on a big table. There were coins, beans, paper clips, sunflower seeds, and other small things. She wanted the students to use the items to practice counting in different ways. Read what the students said while they were counting. Who counted by twos? Mark your answer.

Look at the next page, page 112.

Check to be sure the students have found the right page.

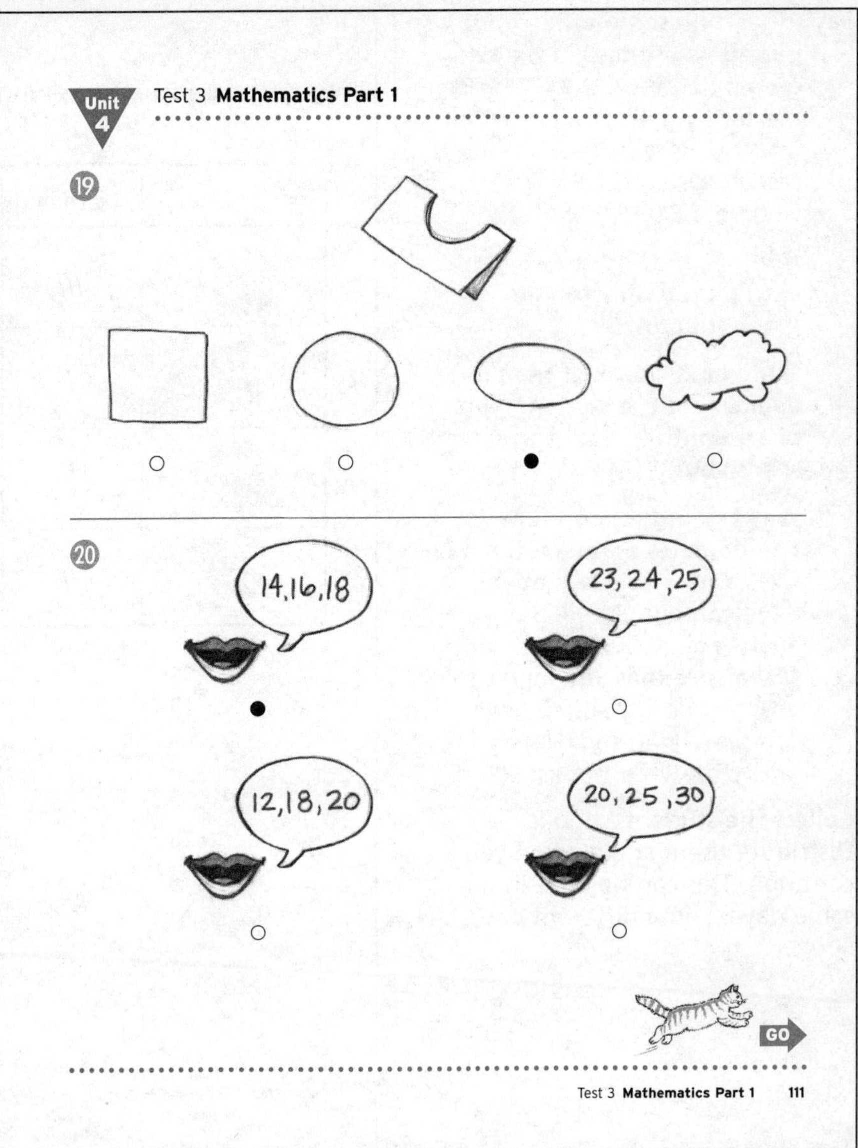

Say Ethan and some other students picked vegetables in the school garden. Look at the table. There are tally marks that show how many vegetables each student picked. Use this table to answer Numbers 21 and 22.

Number 21. Find the student who picked only tomatoes. Mark your answer.

Number 22. Look at the table again. Find the student who picked both lettuce and carrots. Mark your answer.

We're going to stop now. We will do more mathematics items later. Check to see that you have completely filled in your answer circles with dark marks. Make sure that any marks for answers you changed have been completely erased. Now you may close your books.

Collect the students' books. Distribute them again when you continue. This can be later in the same day or on a different day.

	Ethan	Sammy	Carter	Ned
(tomato)	///	/	////	
(beets)	/	///		
(lettuce)	/			/
(carrots)	//	///		

21 Ethan ○ Sammy ○ Carter ● Ned ○

22 Ethan ● Sammy ○ Carter ○ Ned ○

Part 2

Distribute the students' books and be sure they have pencils and scratch paper.

Say Open your books to page 113. You are going to solve more mathematics problems. Remember to make sure that the circles for your answer choices are completely filled in. Press your pencil firmly so your marks come out dark. Completely erase any marks for answers you change.

Now you are going to do some work with stories about Ann and a few other students. Listen carefully as I tell you what to do. When Ann came back from lunch, the teacher gave the class a sheet of math problems to do.

Do Numbers 23 through 25 for Ann. When you come to the STOP sign after Number 25, wait for me to tell you what to do next. You may begin.

Allow time for the students to fill in their answers.

Say Put your finger on Number 26. Listen to this story. Hannah had three crackers. A friend gave her five more. Look at the number sentences. Which number sentence tells how many crackers Hannah has now? Mark your answer.

Look at the next page, page 114.

Check to be sure the students have found the right page.

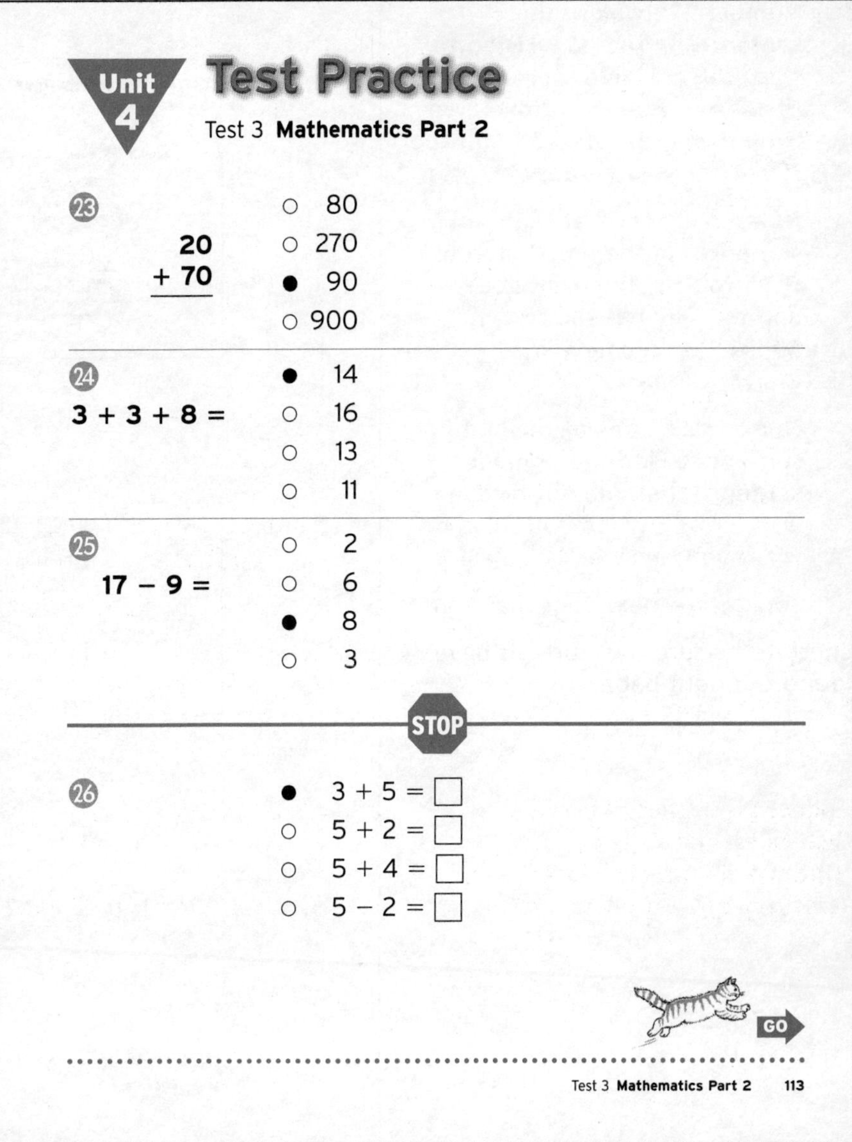

Unit 4 **Test Practice**

Test 3 **Mathematics Part 2**

23

$$\begin{array}{r} 20 \\ +\ 70 \\ \hline \end{array}$$

○ 80
○ 270
● 90
○ 900

24 **3 + 3 + 8 =**

● 14
○ 16
○ 13
○ 11

25 **17 − 9 =**

○ 2
○ 6
● 8
○ 3

STOP

26

● 3 + 5 = □
○ 5 + 2 = □
○ 5 + 4 = □
○ 5 − 2 = □

GO

Test 3 **Mathematics Part 2** 113

Say Number 27. Look at the sentences in the box. Listen to this problem. Five cars were on the street. Two cars drove away. How many cars were left on the street? Mark your answer.

Number 28. Look at the sentences in the box. Listen to this problem. Ida has three apples. Joey has six. How many apples do they have in all? Mark your answer.

Number 29. Look at the number sentences. Find the number sentence that will not have an answer of 2 when you solve it. Mark your answer.

Look at the next page, page 115.

Check to be sure the students have found the right page.

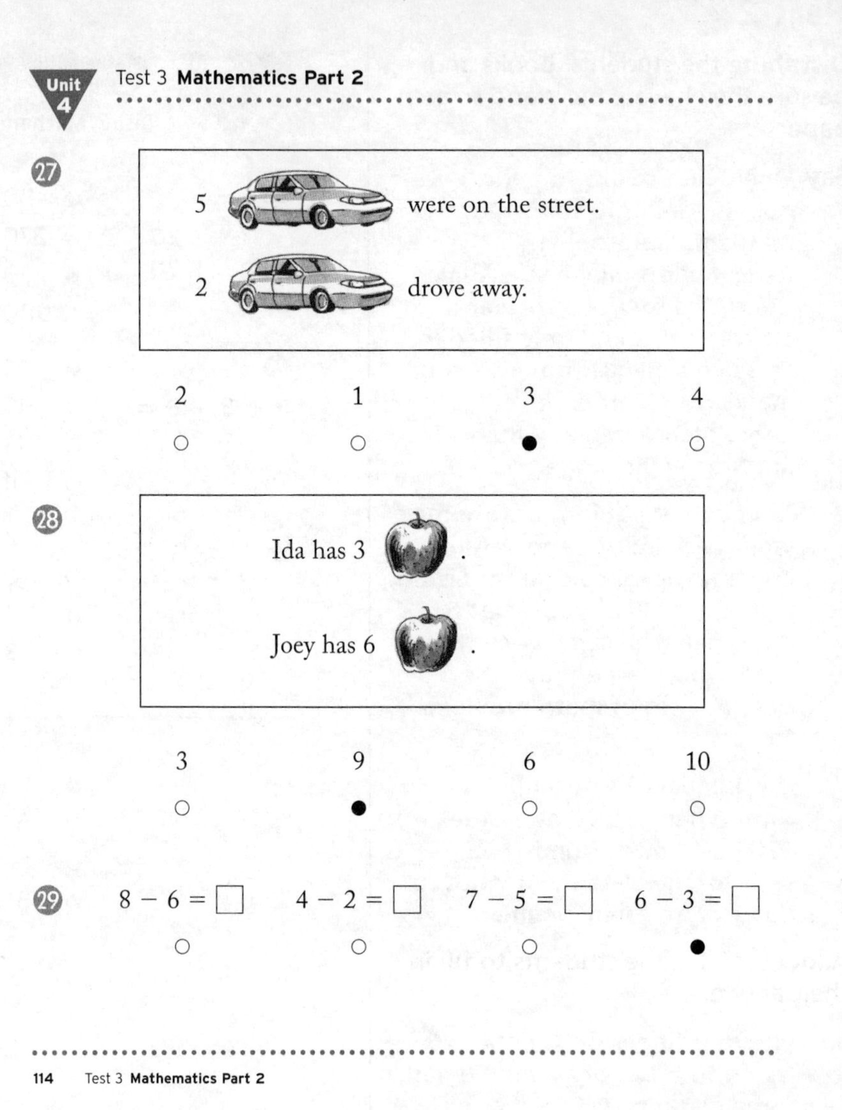

Say Number 30. Ann's teacher pointed to a digital clock on her desk. Then she asked the students to draw a clock with a round face with the time that was showing on the digital clock. Find the drawing that matches the time on the digital clock. Mark your answer.

Number 31. There was some change in Ann's backpack. Look at the money she took out of her backpack. Find how much money there was. Mark your answer.

Look at the next page, page 116.

Check to be sure the students have found the right page.

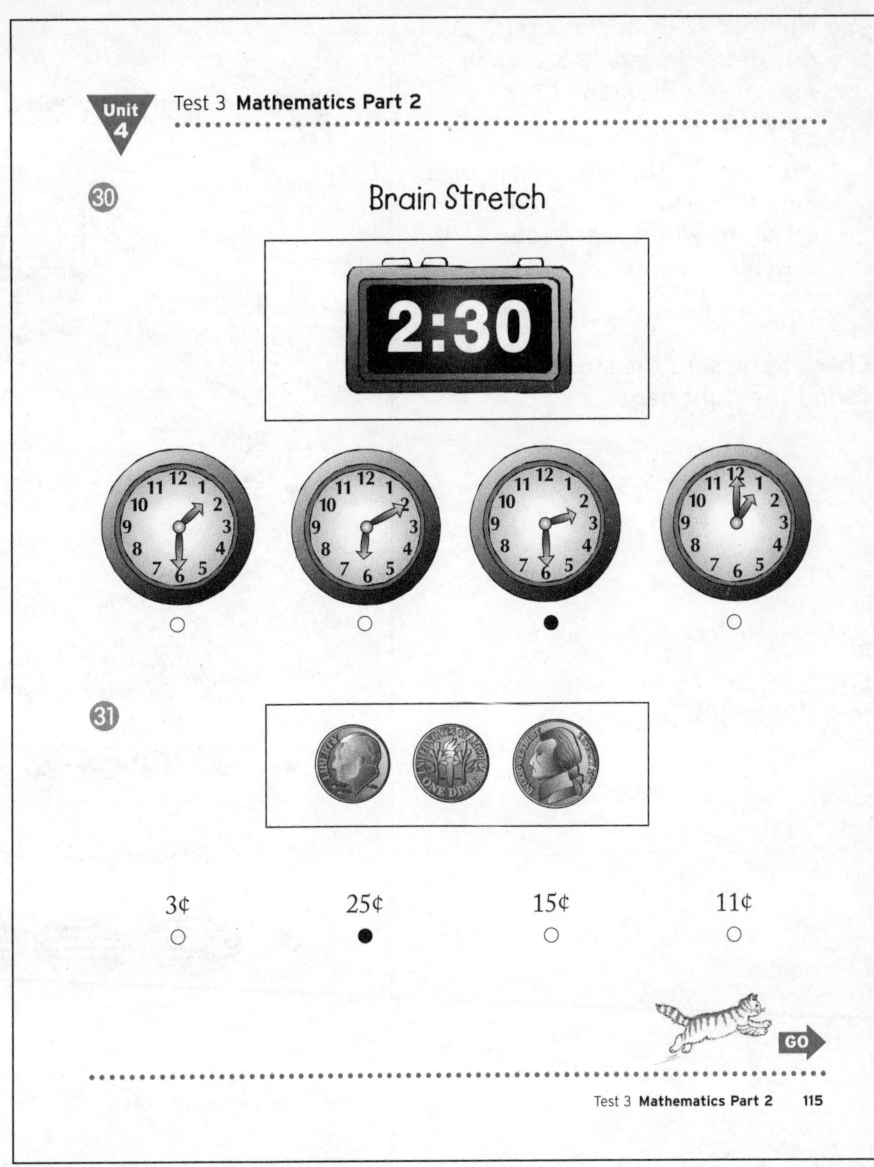

Say Number 32. Ann's teacher put out these erasers. How many erasers are there in all? Mark your answer.

Number 33. Look at the pictures. Find the picture that shows a group of eight. Mark your answer.

Look at the next page, page 117.

Check to be sure the students have found the right page.

32
- ○ 73
- ○ 307
- ● 37
- ○ 703

33

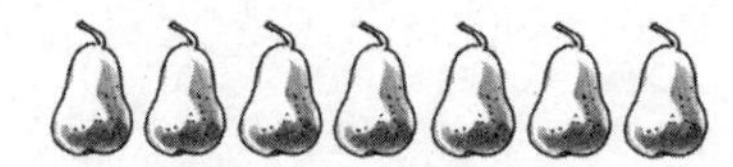

Say Number 34. Ann's teacher told the class a story. There were eight flies sitting on the edge of an open window. Five of the flies smelled something interesting and flew away. Which picture shows how many flies were left sitting on the edge of the window? Mark your answer.

Number 35. Look at the answers. Find the number seventy-six. Mark your answer.

Number 36. The teacher asked Ann to draw a triangle on top of a square. Find what Ann drew. Mark your answer.

Number 37. Look at the story inside the box. Listen to this problem. There were eight pizzas at the dinner party. Six of the pizzas were eaten. How many pizzas were left? Mark your answer.

Look at the next page, page 118.

Check to be sure the students have found the right page.

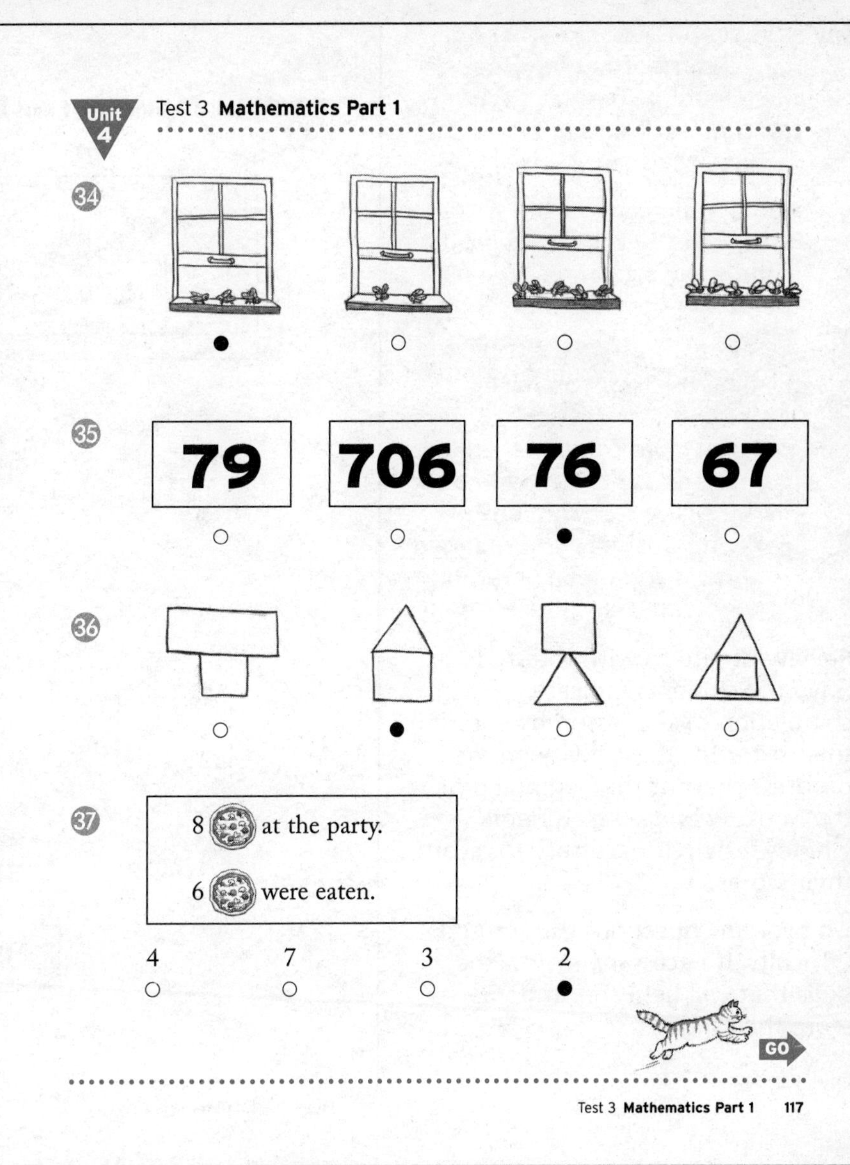

Say Number 38. Ann's teacher held up a picture of her yard. Look at the picture of the yard. What is the shortest thing in the picture? Mark your answer.

Number 39. Look at the shape in the box. Find the answer that is the same size and shape as the one in the box. Mark your answer.

It's time to stop. You have completed Test 3. Check to see that you have completely filled in your answer circles with dark marks. Make sure that any marks for answers you changed have been completely erased. Now you may close your books.

Review the items with the students. Have the students indicate completion of the lesson by entering their score for this activity on the progress chart at the beginning of the book. Provide the students whatever help is necessary to record their scores.

Go over any questions that caused difficulty. If necessary, review the skills that will help the students score their highest.

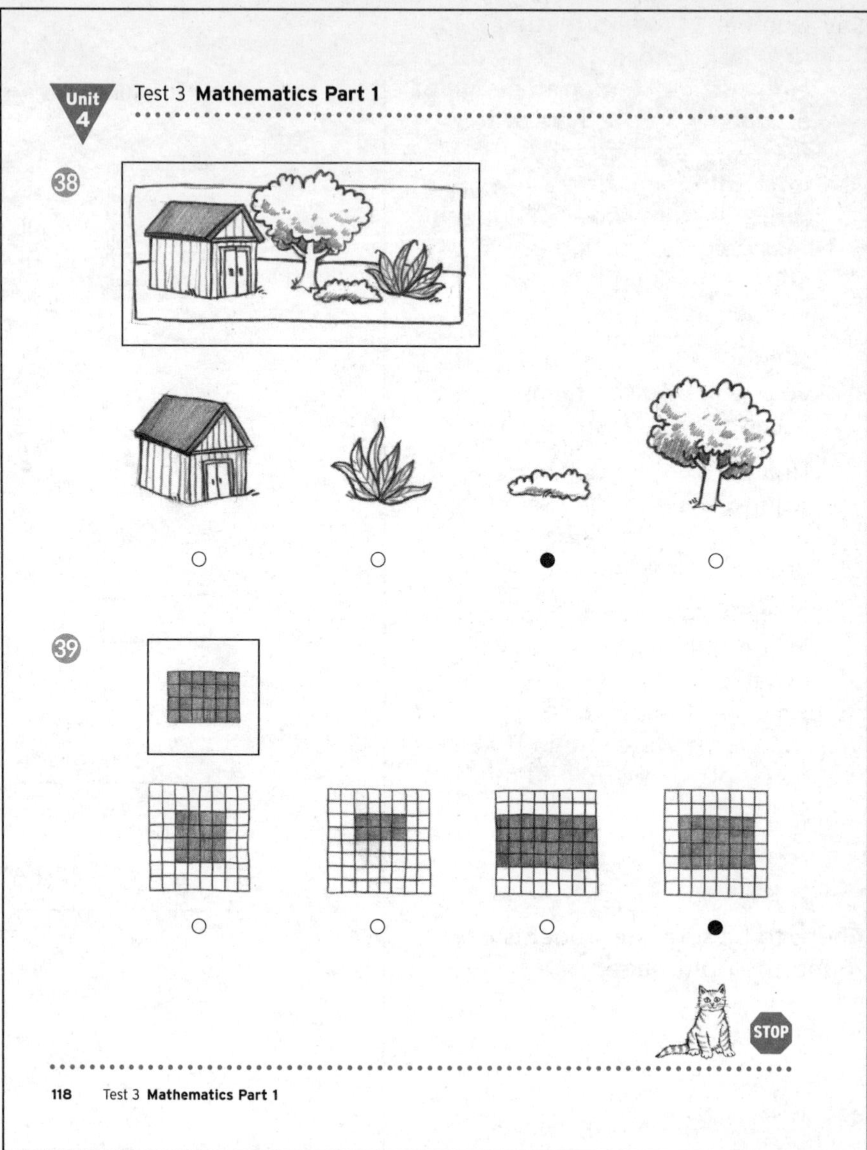